SHAKESPEARE'S QUEER ANALYTICS

THE ARDEN SHAKESPEARE STUDIES IN LANGUAGE AND
DIGITAL METHODOLOGIES SERIES

Series Editors: Jonathan Hope, Lynne Magnusson and
Michael Witmore

Arden Shakespeare Studies in Language and Digital
Methodologies seeks to identify, develop, and publish new
work on Shakespeare and his contemporaries with a focus on
language and/or digital methods.

Shakespeare's Common Language
Alysia Kolentsis
ISBN 978-1-350-00701-7

Shakespearean Character: Language in Performance
Jelena Marelj
ISBN 978-1-3500-0701-7

Reproducing English Renaissance Drama, 1711–2016
Brett Hirsch
ISBN 978-1-350-02186-0

Martin Droeshout, title page of *The arraignment of the whole creature
att the barre of religion, reason, and experience.* 1631. The British
Museum.

SHAKESPEARE'S QUEER ANALYTICS

DISTANT READING AND COLLABORATIVE INTIMACY IN *LOVE'S MARTYR*

Don Rodrigues

THE ARDEN SHAKESPEARE

LONDON • NEW YORK • OXFORD • NEW DELHI • SYDNEY

THE ARDEN SHAKESPEARE
Bloomsbury Publishing Plc
50 Bedford Square, London, WC1B 3DP, UK
1385 Broadway, New York, NY 10018, USA
29 Earlsfort Terrace, Dublin 2, Ireland

BLOOMSBURY, THE ARDEN SHAKESPEARE and the Arden Shakespeare logo are
trademarks of Bloomsbury Publishing Plc

First published in Great Britain 2022
Paperback edition published 2023

Copyright © Don Rodrigues, 2022, 2023

Don Rodrigues has asserted his right under the Copyright, Designs
and Patents Act, 1988, to be identified as the author of this work.

For legal purposes the Acknowledgements on pp. xiv–xv constitute
an extension of this copyright page.

Cover design: Series design by Louise Dugdale
Cover image: Vuur, Adriaen Collaert (1580–1584) (© Rijksmuseum, Amsterdam)

All rights reserved. No part of this publication may be reproduced or transmitted
in any form or by any means, electronic or mechanical, including photocopying,
recording, or any information storage or retrieval system, without prior
permission in writing from the publishers.

Bloomsbury Publishing Plc does not have any control over, or responsibility for,
any third-party websites referred to or in this book. All internet addresses given
in this book were correct at the time of going to press. The author and publisher
regret any inconvenience caused if addresses have changed or sites have
ceased to exist, but can accept no responsibility for any such changes.

A catalogue record for this book is available from the British Library.

Library of Congress Cataloging-in-Publication Data
Names: Rodrigues, Don, author.
Title: Shakespeare's queer analytics: distant reading and collaborative
intimacy in 'love's martyr' / Don Rodrigues.
Description: London; New York: The Arden Shakespeare, 2022. |
Series: Arden Shakespeare studies in language and digital methodologies |
Includes bibliographical references and index.
Identifiers: LCCN 2021033262 (print) | LCCN 2021033263 (ebook) |
ISBN 9781350178823 (hardback) | ISBN 9781350178847 (ebook) |
ISBN 9781350178830 (epub)
Subjects: LCSH: Shakespeare, William, 1564-1616. Phoenix and the turtle. |
Chester, Robert, active 1600. Loves martyr. | Queer theory. |
LCGFT: Literary criticism.
Classification: LCC PR2849.R63 2022 (print) |
LCC PR2849 (ebook) | DDC 822.3/3–dc23
LC record available at https://lccn.loc.gov/2021033262
LC ebook record available at https://lccn.loc.gov/2021033263

ISBN: HB: 978-1-3501-7882-3
PB: 978-1-3502-8869-0
ePDF: 978-1-3501-7884-7
eBook: 978-1-3501-7883-0

Arden Shakespeare Studies in Language and Digital Methodologies

Typeset by Integra Software Services Pvt. Ltd.

To find out more about our authors and books visit www.bloomsbury.com
and sign up for our newsletters.

Shakespeare's Queer Analytics

and *Pericles*, are 'less compelling' than works such as *King Lear* and *Othello*, such a view overlooks the obvious collaborative dynamics of *Love's Martyr*, in which 'The Phoenix and Turtle' not only appeared alongside but in striking dialogue with thirteen other poems in a supplement called the 'Poetical Essays'. As numerous critics have pointed out, each of *Love's Martyr's* guest poets had certainly read at least some of Chester's draft before publication, as evidenced by the responses they make to each other and the fact that each ascribes to Chester's unique 'Phoenix-Turtle' conceit. As for the question of any 'aesthetic benefits' to working in isolation, Shakespeare's poem in *Love's Martyr* is widely regarded to be one of his most singular achievements – a work, in Ralph Waldo Emerson's words, that 'comes along only once a century, and only from a genius'.[5]

Given these details, one might still question whether this poem is actually evidence of 'collaboration' at all – it was almost certainly composed solely by Shakespeare, even if, like so many of Shakespeare's works, it bears the influence of outside sources and voices. This poem, however, is only part of the larger story *Love's Martyr* plays in Shakespeare's career. Throughout the critical history on 'Phoenix' and *Love's Martyr*, scholars have noted, in G. Wilson Knight's words, 'certain Shakespearean reminiscences' interspersed throughout the volume, well beyond the boundaries of Shakespeare's 67-line poem.[6] Prompted by Emerson himself, Alexander B. Grosart's 1878 study of *Love's Martyr* detected various Shakespearean overtones in Chester's verse: 'there is in my judgement some probability for thinking that these are not casual coincidences … I think I can detect in some of [Chester's] lines a reflex or remembrance of the rhythm of Shakespeare's lines'.[7] Nearly eighty years later, in *The Mutual Flame*, Knight took Grosart's view several steps further, arguing that certain sections of the book signed by Chester cannot have been written by Chester or Chester alone. He suggested provocatively that Shakespeare edited or 'doctored' significant portions of text signed by Chester. With stunning precision, Knight explores the homoerotic or, in his words, 'homosexual' suggestions in these and other parts of the book, noting thematic and stylistic connections to Shakespeare's sonnets and other works.

INTRODUCTION: *LOVE'S MARTYR* AND THE CASE FOR QUEER ANALYTICS

> [I]f there were no divagations from normality, we should have no Shakespeares.
>
> – G. Wilson Knight, *The Mutual Flame*[1]

This book joins a larger effort to unsettle the long-standing critical narrative that Shakespeare collaborated mainly at the beginning (before 1595) and end (after 1606) of his career by examining the extent of his participation in Robert Chester's multiauthor volume, *Love's Martyr* (1601). Known primarily for containing Shakespeare's cryptic lyric 'The Phoenix and Turtle', *Love's Martyr* also attracted 'the best and chiefest of our moderne writers', counting George Chapman, Ben Jonson, and John Marston among the esteemed coterie brought together for the occasion.[2] Even so, critics have generally overlooked *Love's Martyr* when assessing the nature of Shakespeare's authorial activity in the years between 1595 and 1606. In this period, the narrative goes, Shakespeare wrote his greatest works entirely alone; Shakespearean collaboration therefore occurs not just 'especially early and late in his career', as Stanley Wells put it, but rather, in Ed Pechter's words, 'exclusively early and late'.[3] Pechter develops the observation that Shakespeare collaborated only for practical reasons – for 'help wanted during apprenticeship at one end of his career and gradual withdrawal from playwriting at the other' – by suggesting a link between solitude and intellectual fertility: 'that Shakespeare did not write collaboratively during the dozen or so years that constitute the peak of his career suggests aesthetic benefits – for Shakespeare anyway – derive rather from solo authorship'.[4] While one can debate whether Shakespeare's known co-authored works, such as *Henry VIII*

To Graham and Rudi, my Phoenix and Turtle

Figure 0.1 Martin Droeshout, title page of *The arraignment of the whole creature att the barre of religion, reason, and experience*. 1631. The British Museum.

CONTENTS

List of Plates, Figures and Tables	viii
Series Editors' Preface	x
Preface	xi
Acknowledgements	xiv
Note on Text	xvi

Introduction: *Love's Martyr* **and the case for queer analytics**   1

Part I   Queering computation

1   Queerness at scale: The radical singularities of *Love's Martyr*   31

2   Competitive intimacies in the Poetical Essays   69

Part II   Computing Queerness

3   'Neither two nor one were called': Queer Logic and 'The Phoenix and Turtle'   101

Afterword   131

Appendix 1 Technical appendix	135
Appendix 2 *Love's Martyr*'s Poetical Essays	157
Appendix 3 *Love's Martyr*'s Dialogues and Cantos	171

Notes	226
Bibliography	254
Index	270

LIST OF PLATES, FIGURES AND TABLES

List of Plates

1   Title page of *Love's Martyr*. Folger Shakespeare Library
2   Pages one and two of 'The Phoenix and Turtle'. Folger Shakespeare Library
3   Final page of 'Phoenix' and John Marston's response. Folger Shakespeare Library
4   Portrait of Sir John Salusbury reproduced in Thomas Pennant's *A Tour of Wales*, 1778. Llyfrgell Genedlaethol Cymru (The National Library of Wales)
5   *A phoenix sat atop a tree*. Engraving after Raphael (Raffaello Sanzio or Santi), 1530–60. Metropolitan Museum of Art
6   Ramist diagram of 'Fowling' from *The Gentlemans Recreation* by Richard Blome (1686). Folger Shakespeare Library
7   Ribbon diagram of *Love's Martyr*
8   Dendrogram of *Love's Martyr* with Shakespeare's Sonnets
9   Rolling attribution graph of *Love's Martyr*
10   Network analysis of *Love's Martyr*'s poets and their works

List of Figures

0.1	Martin Droeshout, title page of *The arraignment of the whole creature att the barre of religion, reason, and experience*. 1631. The British Museum.	vi
0.2	Dendrogram of *Love's Martyr*	18
1.1	Generic dendrogram after Lexomics study	33
1.2	'The table of the first section' in John Guillim's *A display of heraldrie*	35
1.3	Dendrogram of *Love's Martyr*	46

List of Plates, Figures and Tables

1.4	Dendrogram of *Love's Martyr* and *Romeo and Juliet*	50
1.5	Dendrogram of *Love's Martyr* and Marston's poetry	52
1.6	Dendrogram of *Love's Martyr* and Jonson's poetry	53
1.7	Dendrogram of *Love's Martyr* with Shakespeare's sonnets	54
1.8	*Love's Martyr* and Chester's MS poems	57
1.9	*Love's Martyr* and Salusbury's MS poems	59
1.10	*Love's Martyr*, Salusbury's poems, and the sonnets	60
1.11	*Love's Martyr*, Salusbury's poems, and the sonnets	61
1.12	Rolling NSC with verse from Salusbury and all other poets in *Love's Martyr*	65
2.1	Title page of *Love's Martyr*'s Poetical Essays. The Folger Shakespeare Library	75
2.2	Bootstrap consensus featuring *Love's Martyr*'s 'Vatum Chorus'	85
3.1	Master MZ, *Aristotle and Phyllis* (~1500). The Art Institute of Chicago	105
A1.1	Dendrogram of *Love's Martyr* and *Venus and Adonis* and *Rape of Lucrece*	140
A1.2	'Pellican' snapshot	141
A1.3	Dendrogram of *Love's Martyr* and Chapman's poetry	142

List of Tables

1.1	Ribbon diagram of *Love's Martyr*	47
2.1	NSC and SVM classification of Poetical Essays	84
2.2	NSC and SVM tests on dedication to Salusbury	84
A1.1	'Pellican' and 'The Phoenix and Turtle' stylistic similarities	138
A1.2	Table of 'Arabian' in *Love's Martyr*	143
A1.3	G. Wilson Knight comparison table	144

SERIES EDITORS' PREFACE

Arden Shakespeare Studies in Language and Digital Methodologies seeks to identify, develop and publish new work on Shakespeare and his contemporaries which draws on linguistic and/or digital approaches. While the series is open to work on language which is not primarily digital, and to digital or quantitative work which is not primarily linguistic, we bring them together because they share objects of interest, methodologies and often practitioners, and because their intersection has opened exciting new paths in research. A characteristic of the series is close engagement between the general editors and authors: we offer hands-on editing and collaborative engagement with ideas and methodology. We believe that the shape of literary studies is changing, and we look forward to working with scholars making that change happen.

Series Editors: Jonathan Hope, Arizona State University, USA
Lynne Magnusson, University of Toronto, Canada
Michael Witmore, Folger Shakespeare Library, USA

PREFACE

This study joins in spirit the rising tide of academic and cultural critique aimed at denaturalizing seemingly innate relationships between computation and white male heterosexuality. At its core, computation (and related quantitative fields) is thought to denote not only a certain way of thinking but also a certain kind of person, with a range of predictable somatic and characterological features. Indeed, it is hard to disagree with Andrea Zeffiro's stance that '[a] hetero-normative logic inscribes contemporary data cultures … it is a logic that pervades society including the technosocial'.[1] Even so, popular works like *The Imitation Game* (2014), *Hidden Figures* (2016), and *Glitch Feminism* (2020) attest to a compelling counter-narrative about computation and with it, fertile ground for feminist, queer, and queer of colour critique. These works show that computation, in one sense, has already been queered and, in another, was already queer to begin with.

Shakespeare's Queer Analytics: Distant Reading and Collaborative Intimacy in Love's Martyr carries this conversation to the early modern period and to stylometric theory and practice, which have shaped how scholars conceive of authorship during Shakespeare's time. My subject – Shakespeare's role in the enigmatic collection of verse known as *Love's Martyr* – requires me to focus on a time and place in which computation did not exist in the sense we know it today, which is not to say that it did not exist at all. What we find, particularly in Shakespeare's poem 'The Phoenix and Turtle', is an epistemology of logic and number that subtends modern-day computational rationality as well as a queer response to this way of viewing the world. I see in Shakespeare's queer critique of reason the first significant exploration of non-binary love and identity written in English, and I spend the second part of this

Preface

book showing how its immense power is best understood in these seemingly anachronistic terms.

While I see vital relationships between the work of this book and the work of queer and BIPOC coders, multimedia artists, and others practicing or theorizing queerness in terms of AI, virtual reality, mathematics, and related fields, I focus in these pages on a specifically literary critical approach to computational queerness. I envision a not-too-distant future when the work of these kindred spirits, not all of whom are academics, may be read together to posit a more capacious notion of queer analytics – a term I conceived, in part, to account for potential expansion and revision in various theoretical, temporal, and disciplinary directions. In the broadest sense, queer analytics accounts for any critical or creative practice that examines symmetries between the queer and the computational. In this book, for example, I show how queer critical approaches productively animate the interpretive possibilities of stylometric data; at the same time, I consider computation to be 'always-already queer' in a number of ways, especially in its ability to highlight patterns that more conventional interpretive approaches overlook or ignore. Queerness is all about excavating below the surface, the obvious, and isolating those hidden signals that render something normative or naturalized. In ways that are strangely analogous, computation summons up interpretations of texts that we might not have seen ourselves, unaided. Working with both computational data and conventional argument can therefore be perilous: since data exists independent of our wills, it exists independent of our arguments, too, and sometimes it may even contradict what we want to say. Working with computation, then, prompts a certain scepticism over conventional argumentative practice just as it asks us to consider the ways in which contradictory information and viewpoints may be held together to produce new meaning. In the spirit of other queer and deconstructive approaches, queer analytics is, at its core, both fascinated by and sceptical of the logic of non-contradiction; it seeks out ways to subvert binaries of all shapes and forms even as it deploys binary logic to produce meaning. It is relentlessly invested in deconstructing binaries even as it creates new ones, using the master's tools to unearth new ways to dismantle the master's house.

xii

Preface

Indeed, this book considers the possibility that the master's tools, when blunted and reshaped by queer hands, might be able to produce liberatory new objects. I do not think computation needs, necessarily, to be dismantled, but if this is going to happen, it requires more than just queer critique–for computation to be fundamentally transformed, we need to try to understand, to work with and not just against, computation and computational ways of organizing the world. Queer analytics is therefore as invested in queering existing computational models (the work of my first two chapters) as it is in the idea of computing queerness (the work of my third chapter)–that is, considering how a poem like 'The Phoenix and Turtle' generates a form of queerness through its play with logical and numeric concepts. In this way, I hope to invite critics who do not use digital tools in their research to consider how computational thinking often complements the queer, even if obliquely. I see the queer and the computational feeding one another in an infinite recursive circuit that works both to preserve itself and to create an infinite number of ruptures, each of which, fractal-like, take on this queer circuitry. Thinking about computation as constituting a symbiotic relationship with the queer may or may not lead to a dismantling of the master's house, though with this book I want to suggest that it may lead to a situation in which both possibilities might be true at the same time.

I depart with one final example of queer analytics, or how thinking about queerness and computation together may produce disruptive or liberatory potential. While I have long identified as queer, through the writing of this book – especially, my study of early modern deployments of and resistances to binary logic – I realized that I am and have always been non-binary. I did not expect queer analytics to take on an existential character, but it did, and I suspect strongly that I am not the first person to have made this kind of realization while confronting the violence but also the wonder of computational thinking, its perils and its possibilities.

ACKNOWLEDGEMENTS

Given my focus in these pages on the limits of quantification, attempting to itemize each influence on this book feels especially cruel. I thank friends, colleagues, and mentors who read drafts of this book in part or in whole: Leah Marcus, Kathryn Schwarz, Jay Clayton, Jeffrey Schnapp, Lynn Enterline, Hortense Spillers, Scott Juengel, Stephen Guy-Bray, Shelby Johnson, Terrell Taylor, Stephanie Straub, Cristina Cervone, Meghan Andrews, Mary Cappello, Heather Hirschfeld, Travis Williams, Galen Johnson, Cheryl Foster, Jennifer Fay, David Glimp, Michael Drout, Helen Shin, Joshua Philips, Scott Newstok, Lauren Mitchell, Deann Armstrong, Shawn Keener, and Petal Samuel. To my fellow Fellows at the Marcus Orr Center for the Humanities (MOCH) at the University of Memphis – Derefe Chevannes, Robert Kelz, Dannie Smith, Terie Box, Melanie Conroy, and Akil Mensah – I could not have asked for a better crew with whom to write out this pandemic.

I thank the MOCH for connecting me to this community and for the time away from teaching necessary to complete this work. The College of Arts and Sciences and the Department of English at Memphis have offered generous support for this book in the form of research funds and dedicated research time. Thanks also to the Folger Institute, whose Early Modern Digital Agendas seminars, helmed by Jonathan Hope and Michael Witmore, offered expert training and helped bring the ideas in this book to life; the metaLAB at Harvard, where I workshopped and developed an early version of this project as a predoctoral fellow; the Vanderbilt Center for Digital Humanities, which provided time and vital funding for my research; and the Department of English at Vanderbilt, for the dissertation completion fellowship I received there and for recognizing the promise of this work in 2018.

Acknowledgements

Special thanks to my mentor-editor Jonathan Hope, who saw potential in this project long before it took its current form, and who encouraged and refined my thinking every step of the way. My research assistant Jonathan Hicks transformed this project with his attention to detail and insightful thinking; the appendixes of this book, especially, would not exist without him. Thanks to The Arden Shakespeare editors Mark Dudgeon and Lara Bateman for kindly guiding me through the process of writing a first book, and to Kristen Abbott-Bennett and the anonymous readers who offered feedback on my chapter in her *Conversational Exchanges in Early Modern England*; parts of this work appear here in modified form in Chapter 1.

Two people no longer with us made this book possible in their own ways. Barbara Lewalski offered feedback and encouragement on an early version of my chapter on 'The Phoenix and Turtle', which I workshopped in her seminar on authorship at the Folger Shakespeare Library. Karen Keller Johnson, who welcomed me with open arms, new furniture, and a cart full of fresh Southern food when I moved to Memphis, taught me more about humility and love in the brief time we were friends than nearly anyone else I have known.

To my circle of close friends – Heather Lifland, Martin Brown, Amanda Lehr, Henry Gorman, Chelsea Land, Sari Carter, and Katie Eldridge – you have helped me through this project more than you can ever know. Stephanie Straub, thank you for being both an amazing friend and a Word Wizard – your finishing touches on this document made all the difference. Shelby Jonson, a perfect friend and writing companion, offered wonderful feedback and words of wisdom throughout this process. To my family in Rhode Island and Glasgow, thank you all for checking in on me and believing in me. Special thanks to my mother, Janice Rodrigues, for her relentless support of me, and to my mother-in-law, Jinty Laing, for her cheerful encouragement and efforts in chaperoning me to libraries across Scotland. Finally, thanks to my fabulous partner Graham and my (canine) son Rudi for moving across the world to be with me just weeks after I received the contract for this book on Valentine's Day, 2020. Thank you for keeping me sane, putting up with me through too many late nights of writing, and loving me through this difficult year.

NOTE ON TEXT

Throughout this book I maintain original spellings of early modern works but for those by Shakespeare. The long 's' has been modernized in all cases. For Shakespeare's plays I use *The Arden Shakespeare: Complete Works*, eds. Ann Thompson, David Scott Kastan, and Richard Proudfoot (London: The Arden Shakespeare, 2011). For modernizations of 'The Phoenix and Turtle', I adopt from Katherine Duncan-Jones and H.R. Woudhuysen's *The Arden Shakespeare: Shakespeare's Poems* (Third Series. London: The Arden Shakespeare, 2007, 2020). When citing *Love's Martyr*, I use the volume's original page numbers whenever possible, largely because this is how G. Wilson Knight (whose work I refer to throughout) chose to do this.

Introduction

Shakespeare's Queer Analytics takes up and develops Knight's intuitions on both of these counts. Using techniques in computational stylistics, or stylometry, alongside queer theory, this book demonstrates that parts of *Love's Martyr* may indeed have been edited or 'doctored' by Shakespeare, thereby deepening the case for Shakespearean collaborative activity at the turn of the century. Written in the same creative cycle as works such as *Hamlet* and *Troilus and Cressida*, this material – located in two main areas of *Love's Martyr*, its 'Dialogues' and Cantos – bears striking stylometric similarity to Shakespeare's poetry, particularly his sonnets, and striking dissimilarity to work in manuscript by Robert Chester. Computational data, generated over a span of more than seven years using various statistical approaches, software packages, and curational methods, consistently support Knight's interpretations. Moreover, contemporary queer theoretical approaches – especially, those attuned to questions of male friendship and stylistic deviation – support the idea that areas of *Love's Martyr* noted by Knight as 'Shakespearean' are also those very areas saturated with queer-encoded symbolism. A work grounded in playful interactivity between some of the brightest English poets of the early seventeenth century, *Love's Martyr* has eluded queer theory for too long, a problem I hope to rectify with this book.

In a sense, this book is a digital reply to G. Wilson Knight's pre-digital study and its then-pioneering methods. Decades before the arrival of either queer theory or digital humanities, Knight's work strikingly elucidates both queer and 'computational' readings of *Love's Martyr*. His work shows how attention to style is always, to some degree, attention to encoded or sublimated modes of expression. Knight presents a proto-computational stylometric methodology that goads us to think about style not in terms of distance but in terms of intimacy, of a meticulous examination of words, collocations, and patterns of language. Such an approach is computational in that it involves counting these entities and drawing conclusions from the data; I present Knight's data alongside my own in Chapter 1. His approach turns queer, or rather becomes attuned to the queer, as he begins counting the many instances of homoerotic insinuations, puns, and supposed 'errors' throughout the volume. Knight essentially

3

Shakespeare's Queer Analytics

excavates the text to expose its queer-encoded meaning, concluding that *Love's Martyr's* 'sexual and other confusions are throughout so closely inwoven that they appear to be part of the plan'.[8] Though Knight had neither computers nor queer theory at his disposal, his readings show that attention to authorial style is far from a 'distant' concern; rather, such attention highlights *Love's Martyr's* most intimate collaborative dimensions, and further envisions a place for queer intimacy in stylometric theory and practice.

Building on Knight, *Shakespeare's Queer Analytics* demonstrates the surprising fungibility of fields that, on the surface, might seem to have nothing to do with one another. It posits that computation and queerness share a number of noteworthy similarities, particularly with regard to reading strategies more conventional methods may overlook or ignore. Focused on counting entities at scales beyond the ken of normal human perception, computation is like queer theory in that it nudges below the surface of a text to unearth patterns invisible to typical or 'normative' forms of comprehension. In early modern queer theory especially, we find an abiding interest in textual irruptions, puns, narrative gaps, pronominal confusions, aberrations and outliers of all sorts – what one might call 'queer data'. Such data informs various subfields in queer theory, from Jeffrey Masten's queer philology (which examines the sexual qua textual dimensions of etymology) to Stephen Guy-Bray's queer representations (which describe textual moments that resist or defy narrativizing impulses).[9] Thinking about this information as data places us on course to establishing an epistemological bridge between queerness and computation – a way towards a possible methodological synthesis of these apparently opposed but surprisingly interconnected fields.

While arguing that queer and computational methods not only intersect in practice but share similar epistemological strategies, this book examines *Love's Martyr* as a test case for what I call queer analytics: an approach to computational study attuned to queer encoded forms of expression and an approach to queerness attuned to computational ways of ordering the world. Queer analytics yields the insight that *Love's Martyr's* most stylistically outlying or 'aberrant' sections – those that depart, in ways that may be rendered

4

Introduction

computationally, from the larger narrative organized by Chester – are those very areas where we witness collaborative play, where multiple authorial voices overlap and intersect. These areas, moreover, turn out to contain queer representations of various types – material that queer theory would designate as very queer indeed.

In each chapter of this book, I present and respond to aspects of Knight's theories, which arise from a form of comparative analysis that presciently anticipates current stylometric methods. In what remains of this chapter, I focus first on certain foundational aspects of *Love's Martyr*, including its publication history. Following this, I clarify what is meant by and at stake in 'queering' computational analysis whatsoever. What, indeed, might a queer computational study look like? Why should we – as queer theorists, as computational critics, as scholars of early modern literature – care about either computation or computational ways of ordering reality?

Strange love and *Love's Martyr*

To say the least, *Love's Martyr* is an unusual book. Four copies are known to exist; three of these are dated 1601, and one is a reissue made in 1611.[10] It was printed by Richard Field, who also printed Shakespeare's *Venus and Adonis* and The *Rape of Lucrece*, and published by Edward Blount, best known for his work on the First Folio. The 1601 Folger copy, a sleek volume bound in citron goatskin, presents little evidence of having been read but for creases and smudges appearing on the corner pages of its most noteworthy inclusion, Shakespeare's untitled poem known today as 'The Phoenix and Turtle' (Plates 2–3). Its physical condition attests, perhaps, to the obscurity of its principal author and editor, to whom only this volume of published work has been attributed, and it may reflect the curious fact that the title page (Plate 1) does not contain the names of its famous guest contributors. The title page focuses instead on Chester's invention, which brings renewed attention to the myth of the phoenix by way of Chester's unprecedented decision to hand it a mate. Chester's phoenix story appears, in fact, to be entirely *sui generis*; in no previously known

5

Shakespeare's Queer Analytics

iteration was the self-sufficient phoenix tasked to seek out an opposite-sex lover for procreative purposes. His startling reinvigoration of the phoenix myth likely provided these poets with a certain fertility and attraction to the vehicle, perhaps even a competitive catalyst to improve upon the allegorical conversation initiated by Chester.

While scholars tend to chastise Chester for his uneven and often-rambling farrago, there is much to be admired in this work. *Love's Martyr* is at turns strikingly beautiful, technically masterful, and intellectually ambitious, which is precisely why scholars like Knight and Grosart have speculated over its wild inconsistency. Given its strange content and organization, it is hard to describe *Love's Martyr* in strictly narrative terms; to my mind, it is indeed what Guy-Bray would call a queer representation in that it routinely frustrates the reader seeking narrative cohesion and momentum. It tells the tale of a disconsolate Phoenix who has lost her self-fecundating powers as a result of some mysterious depletion of energies in her native Arabia, where the fabled bird traditionally resides. Upon being alerted to this crisis, Nature urges the Phoenix to travel with her by chariot to the island of Paphos, whose verdant climate will restore the Phoenix's generative capacities and enable her to reproduce with the assistance of the Turtledove residing there. Though both birds are sometimes described as actual birds, with 'feathers' and 'plumage', they are also clearly intended to represent someone or something else. Indeed, the allegorical valences and political circumstances of the volume, printed after the Earl of Essex's 1601 rebellion and subsequent execution, incite endless speculation. Was the volume published to honour Salisbury's recent knighthood, bestowed upon him for his opposition to and suppression of the rebellion? Does the Phoenix of Chester's poem represent the Queen, on the verge of death herself in 1601? Might the Turtledove, then, stand in for the fallen Essex? If so, how do we read Shakespeare's radical reappraisal of Chester's allegory in his own work, in which the unitive love between the Phoenix and Turtle defies reason and yields not a new bird but rather an 'eternitie' of death?[11]

Questions such as these dominate the history of scholarship surrounding both Chester's long allegorical poem and the collection of shorter works that follow his and conclude the volume.[12] This

Introduction

study joins a critical history that acknowledges these metaphoric possibilities while resisting the tendency to assign potentially reductive analogies to figures that appear outside of the book. Given the Queen's association with the phoenix in portraiture, the Phoenix of Chester's poem might plausibly represent Elizabeth, but a number of other possible candidates have been raised. These include Urslua Salusbury, John Salusbury's wife, rendering the new knight the Turtledove. Law professors John Finnis and Patrick H. Martin join Clare Asquith in suggesting that the poem is about Jesuit martyrs. For Asquith, the poem commemorates Robert Southwell and Henry Walpole; for Finnis and Martin, the phoenix is Anne Line, a Catholic executed in 1601, and the turtle, her exiled husband, Roger Line.[13] Theories such as these are, to my mind, all more or less equally fascinating, but probably impossible to prove given our historical distance from the time of *Love's Martyr's* publication. The meanings, of course, may be multiple, and I see no reason for discounting allegorical multivalence as an interpretive possibility. My stance towards this variety of scholarship on both *Love's Martyr* and 'Phoenix' is best summarized by mid-century critic Ronald Bates: '[T]he occasion of the work and the actual persons symbolized by Phoenix and Turtle have so taken up scholarly interest as to leave the poem itself a relative mystery.' Thomas P. Harrison puts it baldly, arguing that 'any effort to read Shakespeare's "The Phoenix and Turtle" in terms of Elizabeth and Essex or of any other such couple does violence to this great poem' and, by extension, to the book in which it is contained.[14] I am not sure about violence, but I agree that *Love's Martyr* risks descending into an inescapable interpretive abyss when approached in this reductive fashion.

What is not in question is the basic purpose of *Love's Martyr*, which was, by all credible critical accounts, to celebrate the knighthood of John Salusbury of Lleweni (see Plate 4). The Salusburys were a wealthy family that had long occupied Denbighshire, in northeast Wales. Sir John was a lawyer and patron whose other notable projects included Robert Parry's *Sinetes Passions* (1597) and a book of Welsh grammar, *Egluryn Ffraethineb* (1595) written by Henry Perry.[15] Salusbury was also an occasional poet, whose contested verse prompted William

7

Shakespeare's Queer Analytics

Empson to argue that Salusbury is the author of *Love's Martyr's* Cantos – a point to which I will return in Chapter 1.[16] Less is known about Robert Chester, whose *Love's Martyr* is the only volume of verse known to have been published by him. Like Salusbury, he was certainly Welsh, and also intimate with Salusbury, as evidenced by his fawning poetry. Grosart argued that Chester was an equal of Salusbury's, identifying him with a certain Robert Chester, Esq., of London, who would have been Salusbury's peer; however, as Carleton Brown first argued, Chester's deferential tone to Salusbury in his dedication to *Love's Martyr* and in poems discovered in the Christ Church 184 manuscript strongly suggest that Chester was a subordinate, possibly a secretary or family chaplain.[17] To be sure, Chester was neither an aristocrat nor a reputable poet, either before or after the publication of *Love's Martyr*, and this book might never have been published had Salusbury not needed an occasion to show off his recent good fortune.

The question is, then, how did Salusbury recruit the likes of Chapman, Jonson, Marston, and Shakespeare to this vanity project? Katherine Duncan-Jones speculates that Marston – like Salusbury, a member of the Middle Temple – brought them together,[18] while others argue for Jonson; given the discovery of Jonson's poetry in the Christ Church manuscript together with the verse of Chester and Salusbury, it is likely that Jonson and Salusbury were on personal terms.[19] However it was organized, one must imagine that these 'best and chiefest' poets were not drawn primarily or only to the project due to the quality of Chester's verse. As Peter Ackroyd and James Bednarz have argued, the draw for these poets, and Shakespeare in particular, was likely political.[20] The evening before the Essex uprising against the Queen on February 8, 1601, a group of Essex supporters paid the Lord Chamberlain's Men to put on *Richard II*, including its infamous deposition scene, at the Globe. This, of course, was an exceedingly bold move; the parallels between the former king and the aging Elizabeth would not have been lost on anyone. The following day, Essex mounted a failed coup and was promptly arrested, tried, and shortly thereafter beheaded. Without question, these events would have placed the author of *Richard II* in a vulnerable position. So, it would have been expedient for Shakespeare to distance himself

Introduction

from both Essex and his former patron, the Earl of Southampton, who helped organize the coup; Southampton, we recall, was the man to whom Shakespeare dedicated both *Venus and Adonis* and *The Rape of Lucrece,* and he may very well have been the 'fair youth' of his sonnets. Shakespeare then had every reason to forge an alliance with Salusbury, a sworn enemy of Essex and a staunch supporter of the Queen. He obviously did this by contributing his 'Phoenix' poem to the book.

Given Shakespeare's precarious political situation, he may very well have been persuaded to do more than submit this short poem to Chester's collection. In line with Knight's theory of Shakespearean doctoring, Shakespeare had every reason to lean deeply into Chester's project, and, by extension, the sanctuary afforded by Salusbury's rising fortune. It is also likely that Shakespeare and his confreres were handsomely paid, and I can imagine, too, that these poets would have been genuinely intrigued and inspired by the erotic potentialities ushered in by Chester's vehicle, with his surprise casting of a mortal, male turtledove to unite with a female phoenix.

Queering computation/computing queerness

This book's most controversial claim – that Shakespeare likely edited text originally authored by Robert Chester – is probably more conservative than it sounds. Shakespeare partook in a literary tradition marked by collaboration. Given what we now know about early modern work-sharing practices, there is no reason to be shocked that Shakespeare would edit the work of a friend or associate without seeking credit, and, of course, he is known to have collaborated widely.[21] Emphatically, I am not here arguing for new Shakespearean material, a project steeped in generally unqueer attitudes about authorship and textuality. Rather, I want to consider new ways of talking about something like a 'Shakespearean presence' in a text without defaulting to traditional, and sometimes inaccurate, notions of the author.

In posing these questions, this project engages several fields, particularly queer theory and attribution studies. I should say more about these fields at large. I begin with attribution studies because an

Shakespeare's Queer Analytics

overview of the field demonstrates opportunities for queer critique and intervention of the kind that I perform in this book. What, indeed, is at work when one attempts to graft an authorial 'hand' onto data, whether tabulated by persons or produced by computers? Long before computer-assisted stylometrics, generations of scholars turned to stylistic and terminological patterns in the attributed and contested works of Shakespeare to address the so-called 'authorship question'. The first to do so was likely one Richard Roderick, whose 1758 'Remarks on Shakespeare' called into question the authorship of *Henry VIII* by observing metrical, stylistic, and tonal inconsistencies.[22] Recent studies have drawn attention to the various factors at play when one seeks to map authorial presence in contested early modern works.[23] John Jowett's watershed Arden edition of *Sir Thomas More,* which synthesizes traditional and stylometric methods to establish Shakespearean authorship for Hand D, serves as a representative approach for contemporary scholarship in attribution studies. Jowett summons R.W. Chambers to argue that 'verbal associations' and 'turns of phrase' in Hand D are so 'distinctively Shakespearean' that, in Chambers' words, it 'becomes absurd to speak of fortuitous combinations'.[24] Jowett notes the importance of thematic context as well as attitude, or the author's approach towards 'doctrinal issues' when assessing the status of Hand D.[25] Jowett's conclusions rest, in large, on the strength of terminological associations between Hand D and other works by Shakespeare. Such an approach has gained broad acceptance in attribution studies. This book advances its arguments and methods from the increasingly uncontroversial presumption that there is a bridge between the stylistic and terminological decisions authors make and authors themselves.

It would be disingenuous, then, to claim that my approach is not concerned with attribution. In order to discuss the ways in which collaboration or 'doctoring' might occur in a text like *Love's Martyr*, one must first locate stylistically coherent sites within the text and, using more traditional investigative approaches, map these patterns onto authors, of whom we can then speak as collaborators or editors. This process is essentially what stylometric analysis provides to scholars interested in using quantitative methods, ideally in conjunction with

Introduction

textual, archival, and other forms of data, to make holistic conclusions about the stylistic and collaborative contours of a text.

Despite my confidence in the accuracy and utility of these methods – in fact, because of this confidence – I believe that they can and should be subjected to critique and interpretation using both traditional and computational approaches. Many scholars question the literary critical value of computational data, which too often presents itself as epistemologically impenetrable or self-evidently irrefutable.[26] Concerns such as these were raised, most notably, in Nan Z. Da's widely discussed 2019 *Critical Inquiry* piece, 'The Computational Case against Computational Literary Studies'.[27] Da disputes the value and purpose of computational approaches to literature, claiming that computational tools attempt to measure something beyond the ken of those tools; there is a fundamental and fatal mismatch between the method and the object of study. Da argues that these tools yield nothing new, or nothing that could not be first and more intuitively explained using traditional close reading. In her companion piece in *The Chronicle of Higher Education*, she writes, 'Literary studies has always offered large explanatory paradigms for moving from local observations to global ones; computationally assisted distant reading has no inherent claim on scale'.[28] In one sense, Da is exactly right: earlier 'exploratory paradigms' concerned with scale do indeed resemble computational methods. This is particularly true when one examines computation with a queer eye: with a focus on the aberration, the glitch, the error, or what manifests as 'the queer art of failure', as Jack Halberstam describes it.[29] I am especially drawn to Halberstam's injunction that '[as] a practice, failure recognizes that alternatives are embedded already in the dominant and that power is never total or consistent'.[30] Referring to Shakespeare's sonnets, Richard Halpern similarly likens the queer to the 'sodomitical discourse' that is not 'expelled' but rather 'relegated to a nonspace within the poems. That is to say, it abides in the half-light of wordplay, implication, and insinuation. Sodomy subsists as the speaking of the unspeakable, as the *topos* of the inexpressible or unnamable'.[31] To adopt Halberstam's terms, Shakespearean sodomitical discourse is an '[alternative]' that becomes 'embedded' within a 'dominant' discourse, in this case,

Shakespeare's Queer Analytics

romantic heteronormativity. Errant gestures, such as the numerous pronominal and sexual confusions found in *Love's Martyr*, give way to an errant undercode: an erotic counter-narrative summoned into being through queer-encoded textual irruptions. These tears essentially become nodes in a broader interpretive network. This is how queerness becomes, to use Knight's term, 'inwoven' in *Love's Martyr*: granular-level flirtations coordinate to transform the heteronormative or obvious reading *in toto*.

Queer readings, then, are like computational readings in that they highlight patterns that more traditional readings may fail to account for. These patterns might be statistical outliers, but they might also be core patterns that traditional reading considers too frequent to be significant (e.g. frequencies of common words). For this reason, I see not opposition between queer and computational methods but continuity, that is, a direct if not entirely straight line from close reading to computation, with a particular place for queer close reading practices. In fact, this project's 'distant' readings of *Love's Martyr* attest to forms of collaborative intimacy that queer theory and close reading alone could not identify. In particular, these stylistic outliers – which I discuss in detail in Chapter 1 – point consistently to areas of text very likely to have been written collaboratively. Could it be that the queerest parts of *Love Martyr* are also the parts most likely to have been collaboratively composed – certainly by Chester and Shakespeare but then also, perhaps, Chester and Chapman, Marston and Jonson?

Normativity and anti-normativity

At this juncture I should address how I am using the term 'queer', which can mean many things. Perhaps, some have argued, too many things: A number of queer scholars have raised the alarm, I think justifiably, at the overuse or misuse of the term, which, of course, carries distinctly political and identitarian overtones. On the one hand, this project joins Valerie Traub, Will Stockton, and others who militate against a desexualized, dematerialized, and ahistorical notion of the queer that would see queerness in anything that 'goes against the

Introduction

norm', a shifting category that comes to impose a negatively defined conception of queerness right back onto the resisting or hypothetically queer entity. This deconstruction-centred tradition in queer theory held near absolute dominance over the field for two decades, resulting in an unintentional calcification of queerness as anything one might construe in terms of aberration.[32] Joining Traub and Stockton, I take up an embodied consideration of the queer in my chapter on 'The Phoenix and Turtle', a poem all about the ways in which queer bodies risk annihilation as a result of their inability to conform to dominant conceptions of desire, identity, and sociality. At the same time, I do think there is something critically important and valuable to an anti-normative conception of the queer, particularly when one applies the term to consider nonhuman entities. When thinking especially about something like a computational queerness, I believe that it makes sense to consider the queer as, in David Halperin's words, 'by definition whatever is *at odds* with the normal, the legitimate, the dominant', or in terms of Lee Edelman's claim that the queer 'can never define an identity; it can only ever disturb one'.[33] These notions of the queer productively enable an understanding of computational queerness as comprising statistically outlying or aberrant data – data that may be useful, potentially, insofar as it may reveal traces of a counter-narrative. Of course, aberrant data is often useless. In many of the computational graphs we produced for this study, for example, certain segments of text had to be 'muted' in order for us to observe meaningful relationships between the larger, and more interesting, data segments; otherwise, these small or unusual bits of data (such as a book's title page) can create either the mere illusion of difference or a difference that is not interesting or meaningful. To call a title page 'queer' simply because it does not look or behave like the rest of the book of which it is a part is not, emphatically, how I adopt the term in this book.[34]

The question is, can this general approach to determining what one might call 'good working data' apply to queernesses that exist or may be discovered outside of computation? To my mind, queer theorists engage processes such as this all of the time, whether or not they are conscious of doing so. For example, on the grounds that the queer is

Shakespeare's Queer Analytics

'whatever is *at odds* with the normal', one might reasonably conclude that QAnon supporters are 'queer', being about as 'anti-normative' as one might get in the year 2021. A queer theorist, however, will note that QAnon only appears, on its surface, to go against normativity, and that the far-right politics that subtend the conspiracy point to a radicalization of rather than resistance to the normal. In other words, as queer theorists and as computational scholars, we must examine each instantiation of aberration on a case-by-case basis and ground our interpretations within larger epistemic contexts. More often, we may simply dismiss the aberration outright because intuition tells us that it does not lead in a generative direction.

I mean, then, for the queer to signify in multiple ways throughout this book. This does not mean that I am after something ineffable, something that cannot be known or isolated whatsoever – if that were true, computation would indeed have no place in queer theory. Like Halberstam and Masten, I see substantial room for queer critical intervention in examining the spurious, the out of synch and the fallacious: that which resists rather than abides by positivist conceptions of data and identity.

It is at precisely this juncture that queer analytics intervenes in traditional approaches to computational literary study. Holding traditional critical and computational methods together, using each to inform the other, queer analytics builds on emerging integrative approaches in computational literary studies – approaches that attempt to synthesize quantitative and qualitative methods. I see strong potential for queer critique, for example, in what Hoyt Long and Richard Jean So call 'literary pattern recognition', an approach to analysing literature that 'synthesizes humanistic and computational approaches'.[35] In their study of the modernist English haiku, Long and So deploy three approaches to textual analysis – close reading, sociohistorical analysis, and a machine-learning framework – to show that 'each of these modes harbours its own ontology of the text, and that each reveals an understanding of literary pattern and stylistic influence tied to this ontology'.[36] *Shakespeare's Queer Analytics* also examines facets of a common object from multiple perspectives, with a key difference. My focus is not on textual ontologies per se.

14

Introduction

I use stylometric tools to capture the style of Shakespeare and his colleagues, but I do not ascribe to this data anything resembling 'essence', in terms of either authorship or queerness. While Long and Ho make a compelling case for an ontology of the haiku, patterns in themselves do not necessarily indicate ontologies; in fact, much of queer theory has been concerned with the decentring of ontology, or more specifically the 'deconstruction of social ontology', as queer sociologist Adam Isaiah Green puts it.[37] Patterns may sometimes hint at ontologies, but queerness will always be concerned with strategizing to undermine and overturn these products of essentialist intellectual histories.

Departing from an ontological theoretical paradigm, I seek to demonstrate patterns of meaning-making that emerge through forms of analysis attuned to stylistic deviation. I am interested not in the purported essence of a thing but rather the fissures that render it always, on some level, imperfect and unsettled: those very aspects of a thing that undermine its ontology. By sidestepping the notion that some kind of literary 'essence' may be revealed through one interpretive method or another, queer analytics focuses not on essences but on glitches – errant clues and hints that, when taken together, reveal meanings that subvert dominant or hetero/normativizing reading practices. I seek, in short, not an ontology but an epistemology, not an essence but a process; what Halberstam, David L. Eng, and José Esteban Muñoz claim to be the 'continuous deconstruction of the tenets of positivism at the heart of identity politics'.[38]

If queerness denies the text its ontological purity, then queer analytics denies the computational reading its unencumbered positivist aura. In attempting to grasp the meaning-making potentiality of minute but interconnected textual disruptions alongside large-scale computational data, it views computational methods as one of several that may be useful when seeking to examine textual deviance.[39] But it is crucial to speak of computation, insofar as is possible, as not only capable of being queered but as queer in itself, of producing data that we can recognize as queer.

Several theories of computation already practiced regularly in digital humanities settings address this issue, albeit indirectly. Machine

15

learning is one computational approach that may be described as queer, built as it is upon logical foundations that are multivalued or 'fuzzy' in nature as opposed to binary, Boolean, or Aristotelian. I explore the history and character of this 'deviant reason' in my chapter on Shakespeare's 'The Phoenix and Turtle'; here I show that multivalued conceptions of reason pervaded early modern discourses on logic, and that these discourses were eroticized in early modern poetry. For now, I want to emphasize that machine learning espouses an epistemology that resists simplistic, binaristic (and therefore unqueer) conceptions of quantification. Ted Underwood and others have shown machine learning techniques to be eminently capable of returning subtle and specified results with an array of variables. Underwood explains:

> A theory of modeling that reflects explicitly on the value of imperfection (the technical term is 'bias') has built a new kind of bridge between quantitative and qualitative description. Instead of reducing a poem to two or three variables, we can now multiply variables as needed to reflect the complexity of the evidence, while acknowledging the necessary imperfection of our model.[40]

While Underwood does not focus on queerness or sexuality, he describes a queer or 'transverse, oblique, crosswise' approach to thinking about computational textuality, with both multivalence and 'the value imperfection' at its foundation.[41] Such a theory of modelling asks us to question long-standing assumptions about the epistemological foundations of computational literary study, as it is currently understood and being performed by many scholars. In important respects, traditional literary critical practices and computational analysis share a great deal in common – a fact that queer analytics acknowledges and acts upon.

A computational method used extensively in this book establishes not 'a new kind of bridge' between literary study and computation, but rather demonstrates how these fields have always been implicitly connected. The approach, known as hierarchical agglomerative clustering (HAC), reveals direct connections between philology

Introduction

and stylometric computation. Seth Lerer was among the first to show that bodily and biological metaphors pervade philological literature; according to Lerer, '[c]omparative philology … reads like an investigation into family relationships'.[42] The same may be said of HAC, called 'cladistic' or 'lexomic' analysis by some. Michael Drout, co-developer of the *Lexos* suite that I use in this study, notes that statistical analysis of large literary data is modelled on methodological approaches derived from bioinformatics and population genetics. These methods in turn have roots in philology; genomics and bioinformatics drew upon philology to form 'textual' readings of DNA sequences:

> Bioinformaticists analyze patterns of bases in DNA and by treating bases as an alphabet and genomes as texts, they have reinvented a number of techniques originally developed by philologists. But the sheer size of genomic texts has also forced bioinformatics to move beyond traditional philological methods and to use information processing and statistical techniques to analyze patterns that are otherwise too large or too subtle to be noted by the unaided eye.[43]

The essential goal of lexomic analysis is to represent varying levels of 'familiarity' (or familial similarity) among groups of data that can be classified as distinct from one another – different texts or portions of them, cut into pre-defined segments by the user.[44] This is done by counting the n-grams or words in a text and ordering them from most to least frequently used. One may choose various distance metrics when generating these images; the most commonly used are Delta and Euclidian, though we mainly use Delta.[45] The method yields a series of plots which may be visualized as dendrograms, or branching diagrams, to show distances as well as hierarchical relationships between the data segments. Consider, for example, this dendrogram of *Love's Martyr* (Figure 0.2) spliced into segments based on natural textual boundaries.[46]

In Chapter 1, I focus considerable time on this image; for now, I want to draw attention to its basic structure and the kinds of questions and problems it introduces. Preparing *Love's Martyr* for analysis

17

Shakespeare's Queer Analytics

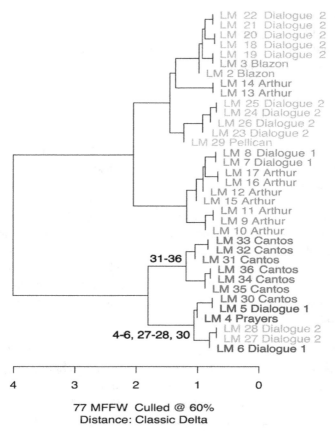

Figure 0.2 Dendrogram of *Love's Martyr*[47]

created 43 segments of text based on natural boundaries that appear in the book. To compare these segments to one another meaningfully, smaller segments (such as poems by individual authors) were omitted; these smaller segments require more specific and focused analysis. The most obvious feature of the dendrogram is the 'bifolious' or two-leaved clade structure, which separates the poem into A) one smaller clade (the bottom one) containing segments 4–6, 27–28, and 30–36, and B) the other, larger clade containing all the rest of the book. In terms of computational aberration, the most striking data points are

18

Introduction

segments 4–6, which one would expect to cluster with other segments containing Dialogue 1, yet segments 4–6 group with segments 27–28 and 30 – the end of the main narrative proper and beginning of the Cantos, respectively. Less striking, but noteworthy, is segment 29, which groups with the middle segments of Dialogue 2. One might be curious as to why segments 4–6, 27–28, and 30–36 seem so unrelated to the rest of the book – cladistic segmentation indicates that these segments are utterly dissimilar to the rest of the text in terms of the presence and frequency of function words. Without even having read *Love's Martyr*, we know from this graph that these stylistically disruptive areas are behaving queerly.

Observing this image, one might claim that if 'computationally assisted distant reading has no inherent claim on scale', then non-computationally assisted close reading has no inherent claim on intimacy. I argue that cluster analysis produces outcomes that indeed record a kind of intimacy, in the sense 'close in acquaintance or association; closely connected by friendship or personal knowledge; characterized by familiarity (with a person or thing); very familiar'.[48] But what, if anything, would make these relationships queer? What might these relationships of familial intimacy have to say about queerness, as well as hetero/normativity, on a computational scale?

Of course, these relationships are not necessarily queer, focused as they are on familial and therefore reproductive metaphors of textuality – precisely those aspects of philology Masten sets out to critique using queer theory. I must therefore attend to how one might go about queering this computational approach, as well as why such a task is worthwhile.

Dis/stance

If we are to believe what some critics have to say about 'distant' forms of reading, then computation stands inherently at odds with intimacy. Quantitative tools have no place in evaluating or estimating fundamentally humanist things like personality, will, desire, and, of course, queerness. In this sense, computation should

Shakespeare's Queer Analytics

have nothing to do with queer theory, if only to serve as a potential object of critique. Such critique is of course necessary, perhaps more now than ever; computational literary studies is a growing yet still largely white, male, and heterosexual field. I therefore intend this study to be, in part, an instance of queer critique, even as I theorize methodological harmonies between seemingly disparate approaches to literary and cultural analysis. In this I join Jacob Gaboury, who argues that to compute queerness, 'we must begin by acknowledging what queerness offers to a critique of computation', even as he seeks out ways 'to make queer theory speak to technology on its own terms', as through alternative programming languages like INTERCAL and bodyfuck.[49] My focus in this book, similarly, is to both examine computation as queer in itself and something deeply in need of being queered. I should explain, then, how I am using certain key terms, especially distance and intimacy, and how these terms bear upon the computational approaches I take in this book.

When I use 'distant' or 'distance' to refer to computational practice, I generally place the word in quotation marks because it is not and has never been quite the right word for the kinds of interventions made possible when using computational tools. 'Distant' comes from the Latin *distānt-em*, meaning 'standing apart, separate, distant, different'. Franco Moretti's term suggests that there is not just 'space' but a functional separation between the method of analysis and the object of study; a belief shared by those critical of computational literary studies as a field. Consider how the term is used in 'The Phoenix and Turtle':

> Heart remote, yet not asunder;
> Distance, and no space was seen
> 'Twixt this Turtle and his *Queen*;
> But in them, it were a wonder.

(29–32)

'Distance' would appear to collapse in the intersubjective bond forged between the Phoenix and Turtle; between them 'no space' is seen because they have merged as one in love. But '[d]istance' is deployed

Introduction

by Shakespeare with etymological precision. Described as having been 'seen', distance signifies here exactingly to indicate 'standing apart, separate', thus highlighting the tension and intensity of a merger in which 'no space' exists between the two lovers. The turtle and his '*Queen*' engage, in Bednarz's words, 'a radical formulation of ideal love as an experience in which the self and other merge while remaining distinct in a state that guarantees community and independence'.[50] If being 'distant' means to be recognizably 'apart' or 'different' from something, then it is does indeed describe a subset of computational scholarship, the kind that views computational data as a substitute for rather than representation of literary meaning and character. But for many, 'distance' is the wrong word to describe the vantage taken by the computational scholar with regard to his/her/their material. That is, when applying computational methods to literary works, one may come at or engage this material from a perspective of positivist aloofness or from a place of intimacy and familiality, where 'Distance, and no space [is] seen' between the literary critical method applied and the object of study. In this sense, a queer computational reading is in fact a 'distant' reading: it is drawn to that which 'stands apart' from the ontology of the text, those normative (and often, too, heteronormative) literary signals that essentialize the text in this way or that. It shows us where the corpus splinters at the level of style, revealing 'distance" to be, somewhat strangely, the correct term after all for a queer reading of computational data.

As for intimacy, one might consider the possibility of computational intimacy in one of at least two ways. Most superficially, one could imagine it in terms of deep textual examination, or reading at the atomic level – indeed, this is the sensibility adopted by the lexomics group.[51] After all, what could be a 'closer' reading than a reading which accounts, with mathematical precision, for every character, word, and turn of phrase to be counted in a text or corpus? But this sense of intimacy is misleading, since it is this very form of 'intimacy' that enables Moretti's 'distant' analysis; through computation, such intimacy merely cedes to distance. Literal, practical, and measurable,

Shakespeare's Queer Analytics

this version of intimacy essentially translates as ontological proximity, established through the measurement of vectors that compute degrees of similarity or difference between units isolated by the script.[52]

Queer analytics queers computation by examining the cracks in these ontologies of propinquity and by proposing alternative possibilities for analysis. It does so by questioning the impulse towards ontological outcomes in many digital humanities projects; these projects may include claims for autonomous authorship, gender-detection software, and to a lesser (and far less problematic) degree, studies that use quantitative information to capture the 'essence' of literary genres or qualities such as 'tragedy' or 'haiku-ness'. Queer analytics asks, what else might these computational patterns tell us? Where, indeed, might they lead us, other than in some ontological or teleological direction?

In addition to providing constructive critique, queer analytics proposes alternative ways of imagining what one might do with quantitative data. Crucially, it envisions critique as part and parcel of its productive capacities; in this sense, it is ideologically aligned with Masten's injunction that '[philology] be read and practiced in a way that will highlight its own normativizing categories and elisions'.[53] At the level of praxis, queer analytics asks us to think not (or not only) in terms of textual essences, but in terms of imperfect and unstable things like textual processes – for example, authorial practices as opposed to entities such as 'authors' that may be said to reside virtually within a text. In this way, it disrupts computation qua philology's focus on the logic of the corpus, its obsession with familial origins, the 'roots' and 'stems' that give way to a thing's true / 'tree' nature. In short – and for example – computational forensic data may reveal as much about authorship as it does about early modern text-making practices, which require us to think about authorship in collaborative terms, particularly in the years before copyright law.

To choose a more specific and pressing example, how might one queer or read 'crosswise' the dendrogram of *Love's Martyr* I earlier produced? To begin with, we must ask: is the dendrogram inherently unqueer in some way, erected as it is upon foundations of quantitative specificity and hierarchical organization? Can one speak of queer data at all if the model is itself unqueer? I think the answers must be yes, and yes. While dendrograms and other visualizations yield to unmistakably hetero/normative notions of hierarchical and binaristic reasoning, these structures are imperfect; they contain noise; they are in places promiscuous. Even unqueer objects such as these contain traces of queerness that, like the language of 'sodometry' in the sonnets, is not 'expelled' but 'relegated to a nonspace within'. It is in precisely those areas of the graph that meaningfully break with the larger pattern – segments 4–6, 27–28, and 30–36 – that we detect various epistemic, rhetorical, and authorial subversions. I therefore spend a significant amount of time in this book examining these and other oddly behaving data segments to see what they may reveal on closer inspection – that is, with the coordinating tools and vantages of queer theory.

In other words, this book brings the queer and computational together not merely to pull off some theoretical stunt – though, as Gaboury argues, such a task may be worth pursuing in itself – but rather because doing so grants us unique insight into the undoubtedly strange textual universe that is *Love's Martyr*. My concerns are theoretical but also bear particularly upon certain material circumstances in early modern England, namely the collaborative, interactive, and erotic dimensions of textual production between men. These concerns ask me in turn to consider the organizational and political circumstances of such collaborative activity. As Brian Vickers has claimed:

> To understand the situation of the Elizabethan dramatist we need to project ourselves back in to the Renaissance, when a very different mode of artistic production was recognized … Against the Romantic notion of individual inspiration, free of any financial considerations, we need to conceive of an artifact produced by a work-sharing process, in which certain elements of the composition are delegated to other hands under the supervision of the master craftsman.[54]

This study aims to isolate and theorize the 'work sharing process' that culminated in *Love's Martyr*. Commissioned by Sir John

Shakespeare's Queer Analytics

Salusbury, himself a poet of minor stature; printed by Richard Field for Edward Blount, perhaps the most esteemed publisher of his day; and 'supplemented' with cryptic yet often stunning poems by the most prominent literary figures of the early seventeenth century, *Love's Martyr* is, on more levels than can be treated in this book, a thoroughly collaborative work teeming with fascinating intersections and contradictions. Scholars have long speculated why and under what terms the literary stars Salusbury or Chester enlisted could justify appending their names and contributions to Chester's often ineptly handled poem. Following statistical analysis of the text, I have a hypothesis as to how this might have happened; the theory is precisely in line with speculations raised by Knight over sixty years ago. In Chester's dedication to Salusbury, he addresses him, 'Honorable Sir, hauing according to the directions of some of my best-minded friends, finished my long expected labour … I am emboldened to put my infant wit to the eye of the world vnder your protectiõ, knowing that if Absurdutie like a Theefe haue crept into any part of these Poems, your well-graced name will ouer-shadow these defaults.'[55] Knight believes Shakespeare to have been one of Chester's 'best-minded friends' to offer such 'directions'; 'or, if not', he opines, 'the necessity of revision may have been so obvious to the various poets lending their names to the publication that Shakespeare was asked to do some final polishing, and, once started, he might not have known where to stop.'[56]

Stylometric analyses of *Love's Martyr* lend quantitative support to Knight's claims, and they may aid us in solving a related matter. Might the undeniably 'Shakespearean reminiscences' in the text be one cause for the excision of Robert Chester's name from *Love's Martyr's* title page, and so too his dedication to John Salusbury, when the book was reissued ten years later?[57] While the nature of the work-sharing processes between Chester and his collaborators may remain a mystery, the findings of this study suggest that these processes occurred, and that they resulted in outcomes we can now measure with degrees of healthy scepticism.

Building on G. Wilson Knight's insights in *The Mutual Flame*, my first chapter focuses on Shakespeare's possible role in editing or 'doctoring' *Love's Martyr's* Cantos. Evidence will be shown to indicate

Introduction

that imitation of Shakespeare by Chester would not be likely, given the stylistic properties of Chester's other work. Rather, the Cantos, written in acrostic form, greatly resemble verse written by the volume's patron, Sir John Salusbury. Tests focusing on function words strongly suggest that Chester did not write this verse alone, and that his most likely collaborator was Shakespeare. I will turn to stylistic evidence provided by Knight, showing how queer and computational methods complement one another both epistemologically and in terms of the conclusions derived. Shakespeare emerges from this chapter as collaborator who works with his peers while subtly subverting their material, playing with pronominal logic and the idea of intentional error to create a queer-encoded network for understanding the love between the Phoenix and Turtle. At the beginning of this chapter, I draw upon Fred Moten and Machiavelli to develop a theory of collaborative authorship to account for Shakespeare's presence in *Love's Martyr*, which I read not in terms of 'authorship' per se but rather as a kind of authorial spectre, a Chester-becoming-Shakespeare, that may be visualized computationally using various tools.

The second chapter focuses on *Love's Martyr's* Poetical Essays, setting up my later reading of 'The Phoenix and Turtle' as one of fourteen poems in a collection about the phoenix myth composed directly in response to Chester's novel Phoenix-Turtle romantic motif. I treat Shakespeare's poem, in which the Phoenix and Turtle die and do not reproduce, as a challenge to Chester that prompts an impassioned response by Marston, who rejects Shakespeare's claim by resurrecting the dead Phoenix within the stanzas of his poem. Chapman and Jonson respond in turn, taking up a stoic attitude about desire that stands in stark contrast with the earlier material. It is important, then, that the Poetical Essays of *Love's Martyr* be treated as a single work with a quasi-narrative structure that concludes with copious verse by Jonson, who leaves open the possibility that the dead Phoenix is still alive. Computational data in this chapter reveals stylistic relationships in the Poetical Essays and concludes with the claim that Jonson most likely wrote some of its anonymously composed sections (namely, the dedication to Salusbury): a counterintuitive conclusion given Jonson's affiliation

25

Shakespeare's Queer Analytics

with possessive and proprietary notions of authorship. In all, *Love's Martyr's* Poetical Essays emerge as a thoroughly collaborative effort, one that shows each of these star poets responding in erotic verse to a common theme.

My final proper chapter, a reading of 'The Phoenix and Turtle', brings together the queer and computational strands of this project by arguing that its achievement lies in its devastating critique of binary logic, even as the poem acts as a recursive mini-computer unto itself. Read against Chester's narrative, as I think it must, Shakespeare's poem denies the Phoenix the regenerative power it has travelled the world to secure from the Turtledove. Instead, the Phoenix and Turtle merge in a profound synthesis that defies the laws of logic, thereby prompting personified Property and Reason to decree that the birds must not 'remain' within the realm of the physical. At the conclusion of the poem, Reason mourns their deaths, yet it is Reason's judgement that leads to this problem in the first place. At the same time, in the very first stanza of the poem, an unidentified Arabian 'bird of loudest lay' – coded to be the Phoenix – heralds a troupe of birds to mourn the deaths of the Phoenix and Turtle. By situating this poem in its intellectual history, I read the poem's ambiguity and paradox in terms of its critique and rejection of binary or Aristotelian logic, leaving open the possibility that the birds might survive despite having been crushed by artificial societal dictates. In other words, this poem grants access to a utopic potentiality buried within the mythos of the Phoenix itself by considering the possibility that logic might yield something other than what Reason says should be the case. This alternate reality in which the Phoenix and Turtle might live on suggests not the end of futurity but the opening of an entirely new order that requires the very destruction of reason itself.

This book concludes with three appendixes: (1) a gathering of additional computational graphs and findings; (2) a textual reproduction of the Poetical Essays; and (3) a reproduction of extended verse from *Love's Martyr* – its Dialogues and Cantos – for the first time in a modern edition. The reader may wish to consult supplements 2 and 3 and work backwards, or at least glance at these areas before reading the book proper; virtually all the material

26

Introduction

I analyse appears here roughly as it did in 1601. Though I have reproduced only a small portion of *Love's Martyr* in this book, my hope is that these appendixes will aid students and scholars of early modern poetry interested in learning more about it. What you will find here is only the tip of the oddly formed iceberg that is *Love's Martyr*, though you may access the entire work and additional resources in high resolution through the Folger Library's LUNA database.

I want to conclude the introduction to this book by returning to an earlier claim, that computational studies often needlessly replicate the work of earlier, non-digital studies. In a sense, this study is a paradigmatic example of this tendency: It lends computational support to claims earlier established using traditional critical methods. Such an approach is 'uninteresting', according to some, because it contributes nothing new to ongoing scholarly conversations. However, in many critical and theoretical fields, 'new' scholarship is often the product of the meticulous retreading of earlier critical claims. One might turn to Fred Moten's readings of Frantz Fanon or Judith Butler's readings of Hegel for evidence of this tendency in the non-computational humanities. In fact, rereading and then re-establishing the relevance of earlier critical claims is a hoary practice with a history as old as criticism itself. One might ask, then: Why is this approach to argument-testing revered in the traditional humanities but deemed evidence of either intellectual sophism or lack of originality in computational literary studies? Herein lies a questionable assumption that undergirds a significant amount of criticism levelled against the digital humanities at large: that computational criticism is synonymous with the data it produces; that its very 'arguments' take on the form of data, or visualizations thereof. If this were strictly true, then this book would begin and end with a claim for new Shakespearean material: '*Love's Martyr's* stylometric tests indicate Shakespearean authorship for Chester's Cantos, case closed. This is not my conclusion, in part, because queer theory enjoins me to consider *Love's Martyr's* authorial structures in relation to its collaborative network as well as its encoded homoeroticism, producing an argument not for Shakespearean authorship but for something more far more subtle, and indeed interesting: the possibility of collaborative editorial activity occurring

Shakespeare's Queer Analytics

in the most erotically charged as well as statistically aberrant sections of the book. Such an argument would be difficult to make using either traditional or computational methods alone, and this is one reason I bring these seemingly disparate approaches together in this book.

PART I
QUEERING COMPUTATION

CHAPTER 1
QUEERNESS AT SCALE: THE RADICAL SINGULARITIES OF *LOVE'S MARTYR*

Mutare dominum non potest liber notus.
– Martial, *Epigrams* (1.66)

The cryptic Latin inscription on *Love's Martyr*'s title page – 'a famous book is not able to change its author' or 'a famous book is not able to change its master' – hints that this book will be as much about authorship as about legendary birds.[1] But just what notion of the author does it announce, and are the numerous voices convened by its occasion united in their theorizations and deployments?

In this chapter, I lay out *Love's Martyr*'s authorial terrain at a certain scale so that we can begin to address these questions with any precision. I turn first to Fred Moten, a master of yoking together disparate entities, to develop a theory of authorship grounded in both queer theory and computation. In an essay-interview with Adam Fitzgerald, Moten ruminates on Shakespearean authorship and collaboration through a concept that he calls 'the radicalization of singularity'.[2] For Moten, collaboration is 'not about being in the same place at the same time but it is about a kind of presence shared in and as displacement': a state or zone in which multiple voices come together to inaugurate a form of virtual transport vis-à-vis the utterances of a single body. Moten sees collaboration occurring not just '*in real time in common*',[3] as in a jazz ensemble, but in the kind of state we might imagine *Love's Martyr*'s poets to have inhabited in the act of writing their individual-yet-collective works – what he calls

> that illusorily solitary practice of remixing and reorganizing, which is, you know, a different modality of sociality that occurs remotely and in ways that are based on a certain kind, or a certain sense, of space-time separation. So like I'm sitting in my room writing something and I'm in conversation with Donne and Shakespeare and Baraka and Mama and my grandfather and, you know, Louis Armstrong and Charlie Patton. And all these people, they're in my head and they're in my body, you know, they're sort of animating my flesh, disrupting the body I guess I thought was mine, but there's another kind of sociality that's given in the close quarters of the living, I guess you could say, that I would like to try, that I would like to do, to fade into.[4]

Moten's vision of a becoming-singularity that is, in effect, both plural and 'social', addresses cognitive processes that bear primarily upon creating, not reading or interpreting, written work. But his flesh-animating, many-valued author recalls early modern theories of authorial interactivity that speak to the interpretive implications of such a model. In a letter to a friend, Machiavelli famously claims that, upon retiring to his study at night and donning his 'regal and curial robes', he '[enters] into the ancient courts of ancient men and [is] welcomed by them kindly … I am not ashamed to speak to them, to ask them the reasons for their actions; and they, in their humanity, answer me'.[5] He adds, crucially, 'I become completely a part of them'; like Moten, he has been transformed by an encounter with a virtual presence that emerges again in the thoughts and writing he will go on to produce.[6] Moten's 'close quarters of the living' is like Machiavelli's 'ancient courts of ancient men', a magical circle of authorial sociality and interactivity erected by transhistorical discourse between and among kindred spirits. One implication of the Motenian-Machiavellian view of authorial interactivity is that multiple bodies and voices may be present in any act of written expression, prompting a critic perhaps to wonder: who are these folks, who or what comprises this company? Who other than the person we know or assume to be the author is present in a given work?

My focus in this chapter on *Love's Martyr* – a text known to contain multiple authors – grants me the occasion to consider

Queerness at Scale

Moten-Machiavelli's ghostly assemblage in a more pragmatic sense, that is, in terms of the network of figures involved in its production. While there are many ways to put Moten's theory of radical authorial singularity into practice, computational stylistics offers a unique way to demarcate and visualize the multiple authorial presences in a text. Queer analytics, which may be understood as an ad hoc or nonce methodology blending quantitative and queer methods, is especially suited to the task in that it demands and thereby enunciates queer critique of the computational in its very articulation of any ostensible authorial ontology.[7] That is, it allows us to see the multiple in the singular without altogether eliminating ontological boundaries – such as the authorial style of author X over that of author Y – that are indeed useful to us as critics and make criticism of authors per se possible. When we have excellent plausibility that two or more authors might be working together on a project, we can imagine and even visualize these authorial shadows. They may be rendered in what is called a 'dendrogram', or branching diagram, similar in function and appearance to Ramist logic trees. Consider the structure of a Ramist diagram of 'Fowling' (Plate 6) alongside a generic dendrogram (Figure 1.1).

In both Ramism and 'dendrogrammatology', to use Michael Drout's turn of phrase, information is arrayed hierarchically and with a logic

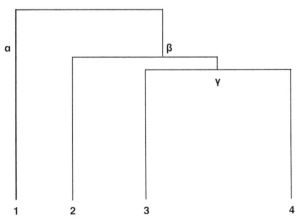

Figure 1.1 Generic dendrogram after Lexomics study

Shakespeare's Queer Analytics

that proceeds from the most general to the most particular.[8] In the 'Fowling' diagram, Blome's taxonomy of fowl begins on the left with a binary splitting-off between 'water fowle' (anseriformes) and 'land fowle' (galliformes), with further subdivisions into (respectively) birds 'on the water' or 'of the water' and 'Great' or 'Small' birds, and so on, on down until the master-concept 'fowle' cannot be meaningfully further subdivided or specified. As Walter Ong pointed out, these diagrams bear more than a superficial similarity to modern computational graphs, and indeed to modern computation itself: '[p]erhaps nothing shows more strikingly the subterranean connections between much that was going on the sixteenth-century consciousness and what is going on in the modern world'.[9] With their binary organization and heuristic function, Ramist charts not only look but act like computer programs. While in Blome's diagram hierarchical tiers correspond to ever more-specific avian attributes, in a dendrogram, clusters or groupings of most-similar data may correspond to concepts such as author, genre, or style; it is the critic, ultimately, who assigns such meaning. For a more conventional-looking Ramist diagram, see the 'Table' of John Guillim's *A display of heraldrie* (Figure 1.2);[10] note the hierarchical structure and topical subdivisions.

I begin with an examination of dendrograms not only because of their naked resemblance to early modern ways of organizing data, but because of all the methods used in this study, they are perhaps the easiest to read and reproduce. Put simply, hierarchical cluster analysis – the name for the math behind the graph – provides scholars with a visual representation of word frequency in a text or set of texts.[11] These frequencies, largely invisible through normal comprehension, can be used to analyse relationships between texts and their authors, sources, and other texts. At first rendered as a series of points on a two-dimensional graph, a hierarchical agglomerative clustering of these points, which demonstrate distances between points, is the raw data used to construct a dendrogram.[12] Producing one involves computing the relative frequencies of each word in a text by dividing the number of times it appears in a pre-defined segment by the total number of words in that segment. With those frequencies calculated, the analyst

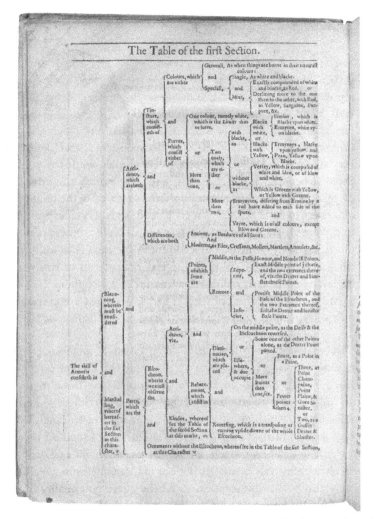

Figure 1.2 'The table of the first section' in John Guillim's *A display of heraldrie*

can apply statistical methods to compare the segments. Downey, Drout, Kahn, and Leblanc, the creators of the Lexomics cluster analysis software package, present a cogent summary of how to interpret a

Shakespeare's Queer Analytics

generic dendrogram.[13] Figure 1.1 reproduces their generic graph, and I quote their analysis of it in full:

> The dissimilarity between clades[14] is represented by the vertical length of the line connecting the clades. This graphical representation of the distances indicates, in our sample figure, that texts 3 and 4 are most similar; text 2 is closer to the clade, β, that contains both 3 and 4, and text 1 is least like the other texts. In this example, the vertical distance between text 2 and clade β is very small, indicating that they are very similar, while the vertical distance between 1 and clade β is much larger, indicating that 1 is quite different from the remaining texts. Any level of the branching diagram can be identified as a clade, and we label clades from left to right using Greek letters, first labeling all clades at the same level of the hierarchy and then descending to the next level and again labeling left to right. Thus ... the text is made up of two major clades, α and β. Clade α contains text 1; clade β contains 2, 3, and 4; and clade γ contains only texts 3 and 4. Because clade α contains only one text, it is said to be single leafed or *simplicifolious*.[15]

The Lexomics group notes that these statistical methods emerge from population genetics, and, as discussed in the introduction, similar methods have been used to sequence DNA. These methods were, in turn, derived from techniques in philology, thereby establishing an epistemic framework for using cluster analysis in literary study. What, though, is queer about such a method or way of organizing data? Not much on the surface, we might say, since we are likely to intuitively dissociate notions of hierarchy from queerness; we may also be equally sceptical about the queer potentiality of any method derived from 'phallology', to use Carla Frecerro's brilliant pun.[16] Moten's theory of radical singularity can help us, I believe, see the queer resonances in an object like a dendrogram when he claims, 'the authority that we tend to want to invest in authorship is always-already broken and disrupted and incomplete, so that in a weird way to say that authorship is collaborative is to say that it doesn't exist at all. Now, how do we come up with a more precise way of talking

36

Queerness at Scale

about what does exist, what is?'[17] Moten asks us to consider that while authorship is always collaborative on some level and perhaps inherently messy, this does not mean that we are obliged as critics to capitulate to confusion or a position of interpretive scepticism when thinking about questions of authorship, co-authorship, or collaboration. Instead of reading authorial collaboration in terms of the prevailing author/collaborator dyad, we might very well look with greater precision at what is actually there in the text, the 'what is' – that very 'quiddity', to use an early modern term, of Moten's 'always-already broken' authorial singularity.[18] Importantly, again, it is the analyst, not the machine, who grafts the value of 'author' onto a piece of data; we may very well imagine and argue for adjacent assignments, including editor or co-author, as computational critics have already plausibly demonstrated.[19] Queering computation, for the purposes of this project, therefore means thinking about authorship in multivalent terms that yield greater, not lesser, precision – a way into mapping and sorting out, with a degree of quantitative specificity, the very terrain of the 'close quarters of the living' in a given textual body or corpus.

I direct such attention in this chapter mainly to those areas of *Love's Martyr* identified by G. Wilson Knight as bearing a certain Shakespearean imprint: three distinct sections of verse that come close to the end of the book and an isolated section of text, a Dialogue between the Phoenix and personified Nature, that occurs towards the beginning. At 11,873 words of text in a volume of 38,453, this material accounts for a significant share (30.88 per cent) of the overall book. More important than quantity, or even quality, is rhetorical strategy. These locations, to my mind, are far from arbitrary; it makes sense that if an editor were hired to do, in Knight's words, some 'final polishing' of the text, these prominent areas are exactly where we might expect such attention.[20] I believe that the volume's patron, Sir John Salusbury – at his height of wealth, fame, and reputation following his knighthood in the summer of 1601 – hired Shakespeare and possibly others to establish his reputation as a new Maecenas. With *Love's Martyr*, Salusbury crowns himself, more so even than Chester, as herald of a poetic order shrouded in secrecy and profound sexual ambiguity. A text remembered mainly because it includes 'The

Shakespeare's Queer Analytics

Phoenix and Turtle', *Love's Martyr* is unlikely to have lived up to its lofty expectations, but it bequeaths to us today a singularly outstanding chronicle of Shakespeare's collaborative poetic activity in 1601 – one that casts more than a shade of doubt at the idea that he was working in conditions of solitude at the turn of the century.

Sensing style: Knight's queer connoisseurship

Knight was not the first scholar to notice 'Shakespearean reminiscences' in *Love's Martyr*.[21] He had some precedent for his views in A.B. Grosart, whose 1878 edition of *Love's Martyr*, organized at the behest of Ralph Waldo Emerson, remains the only edition of the book beyond the 1601 original and its 1611 reprint.[22] Noting similarities between parts of *Love's Martyr* and *The Rape of Lucrece* and *Venus and Adonis*, Grosart cagily opines, '[T]here is in my judgement some probability for thinking that these are not casual coincidences ... I think I can detect in some of [Chester's] lines a reflex or remembrance of the rhythm of Shakespeare's lines.'[23] At the same time, Grosart is quick to characterize Chester's verse as generally 'poor'.[24] Setting the tone for modern criticism of *Love's Martyr*, he finds 'almost innumerable instances of lines and phrases inserted, more to complete the rhythm and rhyme, than for reason's sake'.[25] While Knight rejected Grosart's claim that the Phoenix and Turtle represent Queen Elizabeth and the Earl of Essex, he shared – even expanded upon – Grosart's pejorative view of Chester's verse, which forms the basis for his claim that Shakespeare 'may, indeed, have written, or doctored' its Cantos and other parts of the book.[26]

Knight's observations on *Love's Martyr*'s style and authorship arise from a much longer discussion on tendencies he identifies in Shakespeare's sonnets towards a 'higher' or 'bisexual integration' that occurs through the poet's reconciliation of conflicting desires for the "Fair Youth" and "Dark Lady" – a tension Knight reads in terms of the Nietzschean distinction between Apollonian (sun, poetry, male) and Dionysian (moon, music, female) principles.[27] Predating by decades theories of early modern male friendship as being inextricable from

Queerness at Scale

same-sex love and eroticism, Knight claims that during Shakespeare's time 'there was romance in friendship; and by "romance" I mean something that expresses itself naturally in such poetic idealisation as Shakespeare devotes to it'.[28] He is blunt in his use of terms that, in 1955, would have been both subversive and scandalous; in 1952, we might recall, Alan Turing, also a British intellectual and homosexual, was arrested and later punished with chemical castration for the crime of 'gross indecency'. Nonetheless Knight describes Shakespeare's work, beyond the sonnets and in many plays, as indulging in an erotics of idealized homosexuality. We can easily imagine a pearl-clutching mid-century critic happening upon the following assessment: '"Homosexual," as I use the term, is not intended to signify physical intercourse. But it does involve, and I think Shakespeare's sonnets do also, physical and sexual attraction … "Sex" is not only within it, but a large and valuable part of it'.[29] As for the gender dynamics in the sonnets, he writes, using now-outmoded language, 'When Shakespeare as lover of the Fair Youth shows jealousy of the Dark Lady he is, in this regard, functioning as a female partner; we can say that the female aspect of his personality is engaged'.[30] We may be willing to forgive Knight for collapsing homosexuality with masculine gender nonconformity when we encounter Fred Moten's claim, made exactly 60 years after the publication of *The Mutual Flame*, on Shakespearean interiority:

> I don't know that Shakespeare invents [interiority], but I think that Shakespeare—and by Shakespeare I mean this intense and absolutely emphatic radicalization of singularity that now we know under the name of Shakespeare—announces it, which is to say announces as an insistent irruption that he also enacts. By *he* I mean something much more like *they*; like the gendered personal pronoun is totally inappropriate for Shakespeare and for all the folks we've been talking about, it seems to me.[31]

I find it particularly telling that Moten's topic at hand is not gender or gender identity. It is in his attempt to address this notion of a Shakespearean singularity, a collective force culminating in the

Shakespeare's Queer Analytics

singular entity that is 'Shakespeare', that Moten stumbles into the problem of pronominal assessment. Knight did not quite have the singular 'they' at his disposal for expressing such a concept, but he considers the idea that Shakespeare the person, as reflected in his body of work, comes to us as seraphic, double-sexed, Tiresias-like.[32] Joining Wyndham Lewis's gnomic assessment that Shakespeare was 'a sort of feminine genius' who had 'turned into a female at an early age',[33] Knight details how works such as *Venus and Adonis* show him eminently capable of articulating 'a heterosexual passion from the woman's view'.[34] For Knight, as for many critics and audiences, Shakespearean love is indeed most authentic, personal, and convincing when it comes out of the mouths of his women characters; '[w]here love poetry is concerned', he uncontroversially claims, 'we look for it in women'.[35] Citing *Antony and Cleopatra, Troilus and Cressida, All's Well, Romeo and Juliet*, and more, Knight lays out the theory that 'Shakespeare is always "within" his women, as lovers; the men are, as lovers, presented objectively and critically'.[36] Moreover, it is in his androgynes – Rosalind, Portia, Viola, Adonis, and of course the Fair Youth – that erotic desire is often most concentrated.

What, though, does such an epicene poetic schema have to do with *Love's Martyr* or with the claim that Shakespeare doctored or edited parts of it? Knight establishes the connection through time-honoured connoisseurship, using his vast knowledge base to detect Shakespearean singularities in parts of book that express the kind of impassioned, alert, and deeply eroticized feminine agency we see in *Venus and Adonis* and elsewhere. He also uses more traditional methods of textual comparison to establish the connection. Below is one extended excerpt from *The Mutual Flame* representative of his attunement to thematic patterns, collocations, and idioms in the Shakespearean canon; a comparison chart of these and other observations by Knight may be found in Appendix 1. They show, overwhelmingly, that Knight's segments correspond almost exactly with those identified as computationally distinct from the rest of *Love's Martyr*.

With 'map of sorrow' (125 / 133) and 'great map of beauty' (136 / 144), both applied to a person's outward appearance, compare

40

Queerness at Scale

'Thus is his cheek the map of days outworn' in Sonnet 68, and 'thou map of honour' at *Richard II*, V, i, 12; with 'Fall thou a tear' (125 / 133) compare Antony's 'Fall not a tear' at *Antony and Cleopatra*, III, ix, 69. Phoenix' breasts as 'two crystal orbs of whitest white' (4 / 12) recall the 'ivory globes' of *The Rape of Lucrece*, 407. 'Thoughts are his heralds, flying to my breast' (151 / 159) recalls Juliet's 'Love's heralds should be thoughts', and 'Shame is ashamed to see thee obstinate' (139 / 147) recalls her line 'Upon his brow shame is ashamed to sit', at *Romeo and Juliet*, II, v, 4 and III, ii, 92. 'Quite captivate and prisoner at thy call' (138 / 146) parallels 'Leading him prisoner in a red-rose chain' at *Venus and Adonis*, 110, and the 'liquid prisoner pent in walls of glass' of Sonnet 5 ... With 'my love-lays in my love's praise always written' (143 / 151) compare Sonnet 76, especially 'you and love are still my argument'; also Sonnet 108 … 'To thy sweet self' (139 / 147) reminds us of 'sweet self' in Sonnet 144 and 'as thy sweet self grow'st' in Sonnet 126.[37]

Such comparisons continue for pages. Here and elsewhere, references to the sonnets and Shakespearean tragedies dominate discussion. Knight discerns not only terminological, stylistic, and metrical similarities between parts of *Love's Martyr* and these works but also critical thematic similarities. As he points out, themes that course through the sonnets appear interspersed throughout *Love's Martyr*; the poet's preoccupation with the youth's transient beauty, his reputation, and the attention he receives from competitors is recalled, often vividly, in *Love's Martyr*'s dialogues between the Phoenix and personified Nature and the Phoenix and Turtle. One representative example, cited and modernized by Knight, appears in an early section of the second Cantos:

My care to have my blooming rose not wither,
Self-loving envy shall it not deny,
And that base weed thy growth doth seek to hinder,
Mine hands shall pull him up immediately.
Are they not envious monsters in thine eye,
      Always with vain occasions to enclose
      Thine ever-growing beauty, like the rose? (145–46)[38]

Shakespeare's Queer Analytics

As Knight postulates, 'the thoughts and impressions', throughout the Cantos and elsewhere, 'continually suggest the theme of Shakespeare's Sonnets'.[39] He provides further evidence: 'Phrases such as "the fresh bloom'd rose within her pride" (137 / 145) and "singing thy pride of beauty in her height" (139 / 147), recalling the "youth's proud livery so gaz'd on now" of Sonnet 2, are more obviously applicable to a youth whose charm is evanescent than to a lady whose beauty might be supposed to grow from strength to strength.'[40]

In this very section of the dialogue, Knight observes: "'Look, Phoenix, to thyself do not decay' (137 / 145); Phoenix is a rose which, if not gathered at the time of 'chiefest beauty', will be thereafter neglected."[41] It is difficult to disagree that the style and sensibility is thoroughly Shakespearean.

In these very areas of *Love's Martyr*, Knight detects an emphasis on 'masked' language that could suggest homosexual desire. He discovers, for example, 'one piece of direct evidence that the Phoenix' feminine attributes are part of a mask': 'I being forc'd to carry Venus' shield / Had rather bear a Phoenix for my crest', since 'we are told "her beauty is the best"'.[42] The suggestion is that a greater or truer love exists or is possible than what is 'forced' upon the Turtle. Moreover, he claims, throughout 'we find suggestion of secrecy, as in "me may you count your unknown Turtle-Dove"' and 'Other sweet motions now I will conceal; / Grace these rude lines that my heart's thoughts reveal'.[43] These moments, of course, need not pertain to a homosexual love but could signify an illicit heterosexual love, such as the possible love affair between Sir John Salusbury and his sister-in-law, Dorothy Halsall.[44] In fact, in the Christ Church 184 manuscript at Oxford, containing Chester's poems as well as personal documents related to the Salusbury circle, Brown came upon a series of acrostics in praise of Halsall.[45] In form and style, these resemble the cryptic verse of the Cantos, which contain both tantalizing sexual tension and moments of genuine uncertainty over who is speaking and to whom. The following acrostic, part of the later Cantos, includes a pronominal glitch in the seventh line that Knight believes may be intentional:

> *Ah quoth she, but where is true Loue?*
> *Where quoth he? where you and I loue.*

Queerness at Scale

> *I quoth she, were thine like my loue.*
> *Why quoth he, as you loue I loue.*

Ah	Ah thou imperious high commaunding Lord,
quoth	(Quoth he) to *Cupid* gentle god of Loue,
[s] *he*	**He that I honor most will not accord,**
but	But striues against thy Iustice from aboue,
where	Where I haue promist faith, my plighted word
is	Is quite refused with a base reproue :
true	True louing honour this I onely will thee,
loue?	Loue thy true loue, or else false loue will kill me.[46]

Knight argued that A.B Grosart's emendation – from *he* to [s] *he* – was a distortion of the text rather than a 'correction' of what easily could have been regarded as a printer's error.[47] The problem, Knight claims, is that 'he' is repeated twice, suggesting that if the mistranslation of pronouns were a printer's error, the printer had made two sequential mistakes. According to the logic of the acrostic, Grosart and defenders of his editorial decision are technically correct; moreover, his decision maintains that a description of heterosexual love between the at-times female Phoenix and the at-times male Turtledove is taking place in these lines. However, as I examine more closely in my next chapter, Chester's 'Pellican' verse makes same-sex erotic attraction rather explicit with the announcement that the Phoenix, suddenly gendered male, would unite ideally with a '*second he*, / A perfect form of love and amitie'.[48] Towards the end of Chester's Dialogue between the birds, we find the following stanza spoken by the Turtle, who laments the loss of an unknown previous love:

> My teares are for my *Turtle* that is dead,
> My sorrow springs from **her** want that is gone,
> My heauy note sounds for the soule that's fled,
> And I will dye for **him** left all alone:
> > I am liuing, though I seeme to go,
> > Already buried in the graue of wo.[49]

So, is the Turtle's former lover male or female? We cannot merely suppose that this, too, is but a printer's error: the gender confusion

Shakespeare's Queer Analytics

here is not the result of a misplaced letter in an acrostic but an emphatic development of a single concept (mourning 'the soule that's fled') using two genders. While William Matchett, ridiculing Knight's study in thinly veiled homophobia, denounces his views as 'perversions' of the text, the confusions Knight unearths are right there to be examined.[50] To ignore or correct them so as to make our lovers conform to a heterosexual reading is, to my mind, both unnecessary and irresponsible. To the mind of queer theorists and textual scholars, homoerotic desire is quite often enough hiding in plain sight.

It would seem, then, that all of this confusion is indeed 'part of the plan' – an articulation of same-sex sexual desire implemented through encoded and submerged language.[51] It is also possible that the inconsistencies are the result of a work-sharing process, of two voices working together but, perhaps, not in perfect harmony. Either way, confusion and disruption permeate the text in critical moments so as to throw the rest of the book into a kind of chaos over the gender of the allegorized lovers – a pattern that, I believe, spills over into the appended verse in the Poetical Essays.

While Knight reads these confusions agonistically, calling his experience of trying to sort them out 'a positive torment', I find that the book's mistake-making practices ask us instead to consider how gender ambiguity and indeterminacy create new possibilities for reading and comprehending the otherwise conventional Petrarchan love poetry we encounter in this book.[52] These textual irruptions – fodder for contemporary queer theory if ever any existed – ask us to consider the epistemological status of the mistake, which becomes, in turn, a question of both destabilized identity and aberrant erotic desire, even if potentially of the heterosexual kind.

The question is, do these segments in question merely betray a vaguely Shakespearean quality, one that might have been made in imitation of his well-known style, or do they indicate a possible role for Shakespeare as co-author or editor? Whether or not Shakespeare had a larger role in *Love's Martyr*'s production – and I believe that he did – we encounter in it something very much like a Shakespearean singularity: his very lines and phrases, possibly lifted from other sources, materialize in the text like a series of loose gems mounted

44

Queerness at Scale

in new settings. We should therefore consider how these results align with computational data, which aid us in making more specific claims regarding Shakespeare's presence in the book.

Visualizing *Love's Martyr*

To test Knight's theories, we gathered word frequency data which we visualized into a series of dendrograms and other computational forms; I include here only those most pertinent to my claims, though others can be found in Appendix 1.[53] Completing the dendrogram of *Love's Martyr* alone (Figure 1.3) involved three steps. The first involved 'scrubbing' the text of all formatting and punctuation and replacing all capital letters with lower-case letters, noting potential confusions that may occur in this translation process. The scrubbed text was then partitioned into segments at natural textual boundaries within the book – i.e. between distinct sections of it large enough for stylometric analysis at this scale.[54] The scrubbed, partitioned text was then processed to count word frequency, visualized here as dendrograms. While I situate my theoretical approach to computation in methods used by the Lexomics group, our results here were generated primarily using the high-powered stylometry suite in R called *stylo*, which allows somewhat greater flexibility in presentation.[55] Numerical markings on the dendrogram indicate areas of interest that will be further discussed.

The dendrogram reveals several pieces of data about the text's macro-level structures. To understand the graph, notice how it splits on the left into two main branches, then into further subdivisions, until hierarchical relationships between each discrete element in the graph – in this case, each numbered segment of *Love's Martyr* – have been established. The branches split the text into stylistically similar groups based on the frequency of each segment's function words as compared with the rest of the segments. The graph tells us, most prominently, that *Love's Martyr* contains two main stylistic components: One branching network on the bottom of the graph consisting of segments 4–6, 27–28, and 30–36, and another at the top

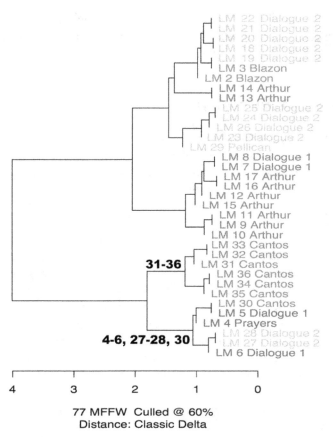

Figure 1.3 Dendrogram of *Love's Martyr*[56]

consisting of all the other material. In the ribbon diagram (Table 1.1), which is also enlarged and colourized in Plate 7, notice comparisons between segments appearing in the dendrogram and *Love's Martyr*'s natural boundaries. The bolded, labeled segments denote areas of particular interest.

The segments of *Love's Martyr* correspond to its narrative as follows. The book opens with miscellaneous prefatory matter, including a dedication to Salusbury, followed by an elaborate blazon that details the features of the Phoenix in highly sensual language. Segment 4

Queerness at Scale

Table 1.1 Ribbon diagram of *Love's Martyr*

Segment	Contents
1	Prefatory matter, dedications
2	Blazon of the Phoenix begins
3	Blazon ends
4	**Prayers**
5	**'A Dialogue' between Nature and the Phoenix begins**
6	**'A Dialogue' between Nature and the Phoenix continues**
7	Dialogue turns to historical detail; annotations begin to populate the margins
8	Dialogue turns to monologue; Nature instructs the Phoenix on world history
9	The 'Birth, Life, and Death of Honourable Arthur King of Brittaine' begins
10	'Arthur' continues
11	'Arthur' continues
12	'Arthur' continues
13	'Arthur' continues
14	'Arthur' continues
15	'Arthur' continues
16	'Arthur' continues
17	'Arthur' ends
18	'A Dialogue' between Nature and Phoenix begins; flowers, herbs discussed
19	'A Dialogue' continues; herbs, 'balmes', vegetables considered
20	'A Dialogue' continues; herbs, 'balmes', vegetables considered continues
21	'A Dialogue' continues; plants, 'rootes', trees, fruit
22	'A Dialogue' continues; fish, gemstones, ores, spices
23	'A Dialogue' continues; fish, gemstones, ores, spices continues
24	'A Dialogue' continues; mammals, monsters, mythical beasts
25	'A Dialogue' continues; insects, reptiles, birds

Shakespeare's Queer Analytics

26	'A Dialogue' continues; insects, reptiles, birds continues
27	Nature departs; Phoenix meets Turtle; their 'Dialogue' begins
28	'Dialogue' continues; the sacrifice is done
29	'Pellican' and Chester lament
30	'Cantos, Alphabet-wise' begin and end
31	'Cantos Verbally written' begin
32	'Cantos Verbally written' continue
33	'Cantos Verbally written' continue
34	'Cantos Verbally written' continue
35	'Cantos Verbally written' continue
36	'Cantos Verbally written' end; Chester signs off
37	'Poetical Essays' begin
38	Unattributed poems signed Vatum Chorus
39	Unattributed poems signed Ignoto
40	William Shakespeare's poem
41	John Marston's poems
42	George Chapman's poem
43	Ben Jonson's poems

includes several prayers that precede the first eighteen stanzas of 'A Dialogue' between Nature and the Phoenix (segment 5), in which the despondent bird laments her 'Beauty' as a 'vading Flower' (p. 17), opines, 'What is my Beautie but a painted wal' (p. 16), and asks, 'What is my Vertue but a Tablitorie: / Which if I did bestow would more increase? / What is my Wit but an inhumane glorie: / That to my kind deare friends would proffer peace?' (p. 17). In response to these complaints, Nature wonders who 'blots thy Beauty with foule *Enuies* crime, / And locks thee vp in fond *Suspitions* cage?' (p. 18), then threatens to 'chaine foule *Enuy* to a brazen Gate' so that the Phoenix may 'catch the hot *Sunne* with thy steeled glasse' (p. 18) and join her in the chariot to Paphos to greet the Turtle. Notably, segment 5 is the first named Dialogue that appears in the text. It continues, albeit

Queerness at Scale

in greatly modified form, as the two board the chariot and observe the features of Britain over which they pass. The remainder of this dialogue comprises segments 7 and 8; it is here that a series of textual glosses intrude upon the text, instructing the reader in a whimsical synthesis of British folklore and history.

Following the first Dialogue, Chester's multi-genre narrative of the 'Birth, Life, and Death of Honourable Arthur King of Brittaine' (p. 34) commences and proceeds for a significant portion of the volume (p. 77); it occupies fully segments 9 through 17. Following this is a second Dialogue between the Phoenix and Nature that contains a compendium of early modern artistic and literary symbology. This continues at length until, at long last, the Phoenix is united with the Turtledove at Paphos, the Dialogue turns impassioned (p. 123), and the birds prepare for and enter the sacrificial fire (p. 131). The event is followed by commentary by the Pelican, observing the spectacle in a nearby bush, and then by Chester himself, offering his own signed commentary (pp. 131–134). The 'Cantos, Alphabet-wise', contained wholly in segment 30 of the dendrogram, then begin; following these are the 'Cantos Verbally written' (p. 141), which appear in segments 31–36. These riddling love lyrics and acrostics continue through the conclusion of the Chester's signed narrative (pp. 141–167), whereupon we encounter the collaboratively signed Poetical Essays (pp. 170–187) that close the project.[57]

In brief, then, the areas of *Love's Martyr* of particular interest are the prayers (segment 4), the first Dialogue (5–6), the end of Chester's second dialogue (27–28), and the two Cantos (30, 31–36). We have reproduced this poetry in its original form in Appendix 3 with notes from some of *Love's Martyr*'s most famous commentators.

These intratextual relationships established, the next step towards making meaningful use of the data required testing *Love's Martyr* against representative works by authors known to have contributed to the volume – that is, those most likely to have engaged in the kind of editing or doctoring Knight theorizes.[58] This step was taken to account for what attributionists call 'the negative check', a process of comparative exclusion to ensure that results are based on more than mere 'verbal parallel', which, Brian Vickers claims, are often 'seized

49

on without any reflection on their potentially deceptive nature'.[59] Dendrograms demonstrating levels of similarity and difference between *Love's Martyr* and the collected poems and plays of Chapman, Marston, Jonson, and Shakespeare were produced; comparisons were also made between the poetry of Chester and Salusbury, himself a

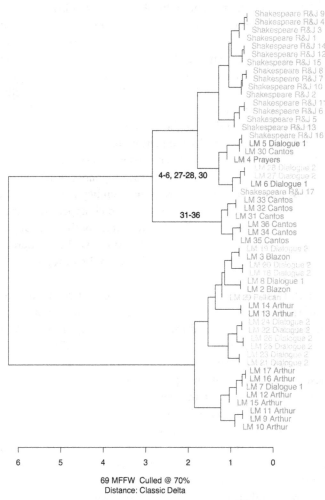

Figure 1.4 Dendrogram of *Love's Martyr* and *Romeo and Juliet*

Queerness at Scale

minor poet, in manuscript and (where available) print.[60] In all but the Shakespearean examples, data yielded remarkably similar hierarchical structures, as typified by the dendrogram containing *Love's Martyr* and Marston's work (Figure 1.5). Both *Romeo and Juliet* (Figure 1.4) and the sonnets (Figure 1.7) produced results that may support Knight's theory regarding Shakespearean editing or doctoring in the two Cantos (segments 30 and 31–36), in and around the first Dialogue (segments 5–6), and at the tail end of Chester's narrative, prior to the 'Pellican' stanzas (segment 27–28).

In Figure 1.4, segments 4–6, 27–28, and 30–36 fall into the same large clade with the known Shakespearean text, therefore signifying as more similar to this work than to the bulk of work signed by Chester. The clade containing segments 4–6, 27–28, and 30, which returns conjoined in most of our tests, appears even closer in kind to *Romeo and Juliet* than it does to the material that appears in segments 31–36 of *Love's Martyr*. Strikingly, segments 16–17 of the play – corresponding to Act 5, scene 2, line 5 through the end of the play – is 'more similar' to this material than it is to rest of the play.[61] In terms of vocabulary frequency and style, then, these outlying segments of *Love's Martyr* are more similar to *Romeo and Juliet* than they are to the rest of *Love's Martyr*. A similar pattern may be observed in dendrograms comparing *Love's Martyr* with *The Rape of Lucrece* and *Venus and Adonis* (see Appendix 1). The dendrogram comparing *Love's Martyr* with known poetic works by Marston indicates that the clustering pattern in Figure 1.4 is not mere coincidence (see Figure 1.5).

But for the inclusion of Marston's poetry, which hangs together loosely within the same large clade, the dendrogram's presentation of *Love's Martyr*'s cladistic structures is remarkably similar to what we see in the *Love's Martyr*-only graph. Consecutive segments 31–36 still cluster together in a single clade, as do segments 4–6 and 30. This basic pattern recurs in dendrograms performed on Chapman's and Jonson's poetry (see Figure 1.6).

In this graph, *Love's Martyr*'s cladistic structures shift in place but the leaves remain stubbornly attached to patterns that appear in the original, *Love's Martyr*-only dendrogram; clades containing consecutive segments 7–26 (the bulk of the book) and 31–36 remain in place, as

51

Shakespeare's Queer Analytics

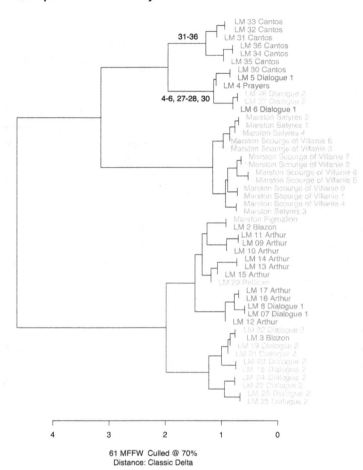

Figure 1.5 Dendrogram of *Love's Martyr* and Marston's poetry

do segments and 4–6, 27–28, and 30.[62] Again, this basic pattern holds for all works tested but for Shakespeare's poetry and most of his plays, which we elected to test in order to check against the possibility that we are merely observing a pattern foisted by genre – strong similarity to theatrical as well as poetic works in the most frequent function words used suggests a general authorial style in common rather than (merely or only) a generic connection. *Romeo and Juliet*, as shown, introduces a

Queerness at Scale

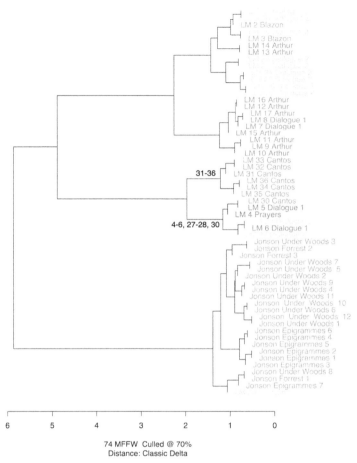

Figure 1.6 Dendrogram of *Love's Martyr* and Jonson's poetry

subtle but significant shift in hierarchical arrangement; the dendrogram of *Love's Martyr* and the sonnets (see Figure 1.7; see also Plate 8) demonstrates a similarly striking pattern.

Plate 8, to our mind, is the most important and compelling dendrogram in this book. As discussed earlier, tests using various statistical approaches, software packages, chunking methods, and curational practices – operated by two human analysts working

Shakespeare's Queer Analytics

Figure 1.7 Dendrogram of *Love's Martyr* with Shakespeare's sonnets

separately – have, over several years, returned nearly identical results. In this dendrogram, segments 31–36 and segments 4–6 fall into the same large clade with the known Shakespearean text, therefore signifying as more similar to this work than to the bulk of work signed by Chester. Moreover, the clade containing segments 5–6 and 30, which returns conjoined in every test, appears even closer in kind to the material of the sonnets than it does to the material that

Queerness at Scale

appears in segments 31–36 of *Love's Martyr*. The similarity between *Love's Martyr*'s speculated segments – critically, those identified by Knight without recourse to these tools – is well outside the realm of coincidence.

The results suggest, above all, either that someone other than Chapman, Martson, Jonson, or Shakespeare wrote the majority of *Love's Martyr*, or that a collection of persons did. To be sure, data reveals that the poem known as 'Love's Martyr' simply cannot be the work of a single stylistic – and hence, perhaps, authorial – presence. Data indicates that segments 4–6, 27–28, and 30–36 – a significant portion of material for a volume of this size – distinguish themselves completely and consistently from everything else in this book. To bring Moten's terms into play with the vocabulary of stylometry, we detect multiple authorial singularities, each hailing a distinct 'bank' of words and phrases, where we expect only one. We can say that no contributor to *Love's Martyr* other than Shakespeare likely had a significant hand in writing or editing material that appears in these segments. Remarkably, specific portions of *Love's Martyr* suggest greater stylistic consistency with Shakespeare's poetry and drama than with other segments of text in the volume signed by Chester.

To test the accuracy of these results, we turned also to the Lexomics stylometry suite, which uses math identical to that used in the *stylo* package but produces slight variations in terms of visual output; we also explored alternative visualization methods, from PCA (principal component analysis) to bootstrap consensus trees, which effectively take iterative snapshots of multiple dendrogrammatic images and blend them into a single object, thereby reducing error. Some of these graphs, which reinforce the readings above, may be accessed in Appendix 1. Collectively, they prompt the obvious question: What is distinctive about the text contained in those outlying segments – 4–6, 27–28, and 30–36 – and how might one account for stylistic similarities between those segments and the Shakespearean texts? Also, why does segment 29, the 'Pellican' verse, consistently drift away from its neighbours (27–28 and 30–36)?

55

Shakespeare's Queer Analytics

The higher integration

Stylometric and textual data suggest several possibilities. First, it is conceivable, as Knight argued, that Shakespeare edited or altogether composed certain parts of *Love's Martyr's* Cantos and Dialogues. Thus, a collaborative or conversational authorial dimension may be mapped on to the selected segments, which, as mentioned, are formally structured as conversations between Nature and the Phoenix and between two impassioned lovers.

At this juncture, it is worth taking a look at Chester's verse outside of *Love's Martyr* as well as the work of John Salusbury, whose verse does indeed resemble parts of the Cantos.[63] Arguably, data may indicate that Chester or Salusbury might have learned a few rare words or Shakespearean turns of phrase and made editorial changes reflecting this knowledge. First, consider the dendrogram containing Chester's verse (Figure 1.8) discovered by Carleton Brown in the Christ Church manuscript 184.

The dendrogram suggests a strong affiliation between this verse (labelled 'Chester Poems') and the beginning segments of Dialogue 2 of *Love's Martyr*. Chester's 'King Arthur' narrative (segments 9–17) appears in a separate clade structure from the material in question (segments 4–6, 27–28, and 30–36). Below is one such poem written to Salusbury, modernized by Knight:

> I charm the coldness to forsake my hand,
> I conjure up my spirits at this time.
> Good-meaning tells me he my friend will stand,
> To under-prop my tottering rotten rhyme;
> And I being arm'd with a presumptuous love,
> From my goodwill disdainfulness will shove:
> Therefore to thee, sole patron of my good,
> I proffer up the proffer of my heart,
> My underserved favours understood
> To thee and none but thee I will impart.
> O grace them with thy gratious gracing look
> That in pure kindness much have undertook.[64]

Queerness at Scale

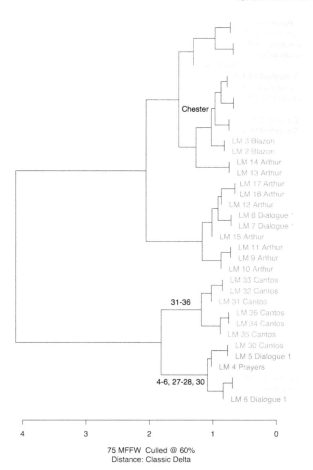

Figure 1.8 *Love's Martyr* and Chester's MS poems

Dwelling upon these lines, Knight inquires, 'How does the writer's paucity of vocabulary compare with the technical virtuosity of our Cantos? A note to "kindness" tells us that it is crossed out in the manuscript; and so might more have been. Peter Quince could have done as well.'[65] Despite my generally greater appreciation for Chester's work than may be found in the scholarship on *Love's Martyr* – and the fact that dedicatory verse often takes on a distinct tone – I agree with

Shakespeare's Queer Analytics

Knight's appraisal that Chester's poems 'do little to associate him with any of the best pieces of *Love's Martyr*', though not with his assessment that Chester's verse is 'far weaker than Sir John Salusbury's'.[66] This view, I believe, is largely the result of persistent anti-Chesterian bias in scholarship on this book.

What, then, of this verse by Salusbury? Salusbury's poems, collected here from Carleton Brown's study, presents a similar set of concerns. His verse bears little stylistic similarity to the speculated material (Figure 1.9). The results are similar to those obtained when we compared Chester's work with *Love's Martyr*. Interestingly, the Salusbury verse falls into a clade containing verse from the second Dialogue (18–26) minus the tail end, segments 27–28, which consistently link up with Shakespeare. Data seems to suggest that Salusbury may be lurking in this part of the book. This result prompted us to complete several additional tests comparing Salusbury's verse to other Shakespearean material, yielding (among others) Figure 1.10, containing the sonnets.

With Shakespeare's sonnets in the mix, Salusbury's verse moves from the larger clade containing the second Dialogue (segments 18–26) to a clade containing Shakespeare's sonnets, showing close similarity to segment 9 (or sonnets 105–118) of the sequence. Similar tests with the Salusbury verse and Shakespearean verse return similar results: Salusbury suddenly sounds more like Shakespeare's sonnets than even the Cantos or Dialogues of *Love's Martyr*. However, other tests of most frequent function words, performed at differing culling rates, show Salusbury's poems behaving erratically. In Figure 1.11, his verse migrates from the grouping with Shakespeare's sonnets to the clade containing the Cantos and other 'hot' material.

The easiest explanation for the alignment of Salusbury's verse with the sonnets is that he styled his verse – all of it passionate love poetry – after the style of Shakespeare, whose *Venus and Adonis* had been widely read and appreciated, and whose sonnets had been circulated in manuscript. Such imitation, of course, was not uncommon. The second possible explanation is related to the first: in a dendrogrammatic scheme, all data entered for comparison must land somewhere, and

58

Queerness at Scale

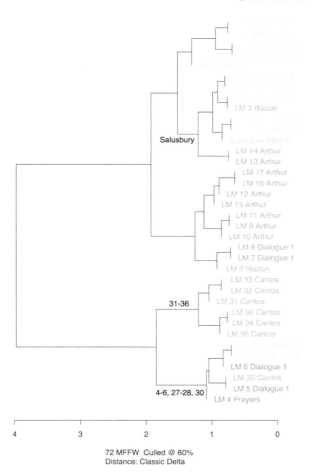

Figure 1.9 *Love's Martyr* and Salusbury's MS poems

Salusbury's verse is simply 'most similar' to Shakespeare's sonnets, at least in some of these tests of most frequent function words.[67]

The Salusbury verse adds a complicating factor to the picture when considering the issue of who might have edited or doctored segments 4–6, 27–28, and 30–36 of *Love's Martyr*. We have established that Chester very likely did not write this verse alone. Could Salusbury, then, have been his collaborator? Indeed, if Salusbury was skilled

Shakespeare's Queer Analytics

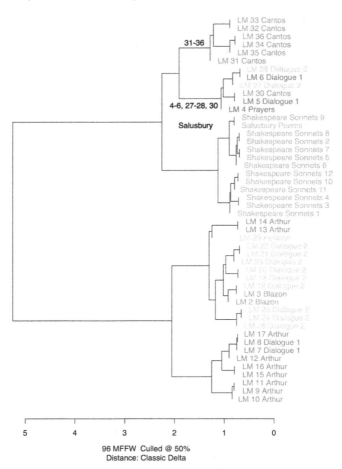

Figure 1.10 *Love's Martyr*, Salusbury's poems, and the sonnets

enough at imitating Shakespeare that his known verse appears close in kind to the core grouping of sonnets, then he very well might have been up to the job of editing or doctoring the segments in question. However, there are at least two problems with this possible assessment. As Brown first pointed out, Chester and Salusbury were not social equals – far from it. Chester's verse, as in the example included above from the Christ Church 184 manuscript, is universally deferential

Queerness at Scale

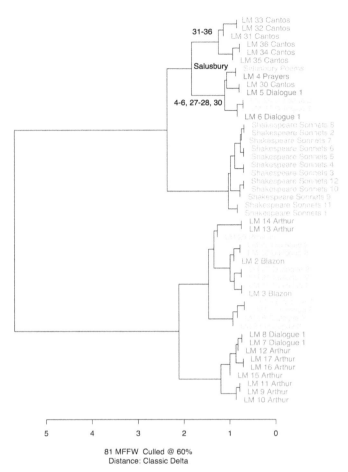

Figure 1.11 *Love's Martyr*, Salusbury's poems, and the sonnets

to Salusbury, indicating that the two shared an intimate relationship but not one of equality. Given Salusbury's station, it is unlikely that he would endeavour to improve upon the poetry of a subordinate working in his household. It is much more likely that Salusbury, a man on the rise in 1601, would simply hire someone else to take care of the problem. The second reason is that Salusbury's verse, while bearing some superficial, structural similarities to the segments in question,

Shakespeare's Queer Analytics

tells quite a different story about romantic love and desire than does the material of the Dialogues or the Cantos. Here is part of one of his poems in praise of Dorothy Halsall:

> Her naked necke as white as silver swanne
> As silver swanne or rarest lilie flowre
> Let silver byrd or lily flower wax wan
> Such white is hers as ever shall endure
> Appelles payntinge venus face and breaste
> Lefte the other partes impolisd without arte
> Lord all the world canot expresse the rest
> of this sweete wighte sole solace of my harte.[68]

In this stanza, Salusbury repeats the word 'silver' three times in the first three lines; conventionally describes his mistress as being exceedingly 'white' twice; uses the phrase 'as silver swanne' twice, consecutively, in the second instance to fulfil the requirement of the acrostic; and describes the woman as 'lilie' or 'lily' twice in succession. Such repetitions may be found throughout Salusbury's verse which, to my mind, is not significantly stronger or more varied than Chester's. It is difficult to imagine that the writer who composed the above lines also composed these below without assistance; they appear in segment 36, closely associated cladistically with the sonnets.

> Yet my soules life to my deare lifes concluding,
> Nere let Absurditie that villaine, theefe,
> The monster of our time, mens praise deriding,
> Lesse in perseuerance, of small knowledge chiefe,
> Keep the base Gate to things that are excelling,
> Thou by faire vertues praise maist yeeld reliefe,
> > My lines are thine, then tell Absurditie,
> > Hart of my deare, shall blot his villainie.[69]

Here, as in the lines excerpted earlier from segment 5, Knight observes 'a quality in the use of abstraction and personification that I would call deeply Shakespearean. The firm statement, so vividly recalling sonnet 121, finds exact place in the poetic argument'.[70] I detect a stronger rhetorical resemblance, not noted by Knight, between sonnet 152 and

62

Queerness at Scale

the following verse in segment 5 of the dendrogram. I excerpt from sonnet 152 for comparison.

> Oh how thou feed'st me with thy Beauties praising!
> Oh how thy Praise sounds like a golden Toung!
> Oh how thy Toung my Vertues would be raising!
> And raising me though dost corrupt thy song:
> Thou seest not Honie and Poison mixt among;
> Though not'st my Beautie with a jealous look,
> But dost not see how I do bayte my hooke.
>
> (17)

> …   I am perjured most,
> For all my vows are oaths but to misuse thee,
> And all my honest faith in thee is lost:
> For I have sworn deep oaths of thy deep kindness,
> Oaths of thy love, thy truth, thy constancy,
> And to enlighten thee gave eyes to blindness,
> Or made them swear against the thing they see:
>   For I have sworn thee fair: more perjured eye,
>   To swear against the truth so foul a lie!
>
> (6–14)

The sentiment in the couplet of sonnet 152 and the line, 'And to enlighten thee gave eyes to blindness', compares exactly, albeit inversely, with the line, 'And raising me though dost corrupt thy song': in both cases, an act of encomium is revealed by the speaker to befoul the person speaking the praise because it comes from a place of questionable authenticity. Joel Fineman, among others, locates in sonnet 152 a kind of distillation of the Shakespearean thesis on interiority.[71] In the corresponding verse in *Love's Martyr*, we witness virtually the same idea except that here, the emphasis is on exteriority: using sound instead of vision to communicate the problem of other minds, the Phoenix reveals not that she is self-deceived by artifice and a desire 'to misuse thee', but that she herself has deceived her interlocutor with those very qualities. The Phoenix sounds like she is addressing a lover, but she will wait a long time before she meets her Turtle; here, very early in the book, she is in

Shakespeare's Queer Analytics

dialogue with dame Nature, who is perhaps notably personified female. It is possible, then, to read this dialogue, which frames and thematically underscores the vast majority of Chester's narrative, in terms of female homoeroticism – all the more tempting to do when we see a possible implicit connection, noted by Knight, between the disposition of Phoenix of these lines and the Dark Lady. What we see here is a kind of inverted triangulation of Eve Sedgwick's theory of male homosocial desire: instead of two men mediating their desires in and through a fetishized female object, we witness two (allegorized) women doing basically the same thing, with the male Turtle the distant object on the horizon.[72]

Connections like this – and many more might be made – are impossible to ignore as one reads through *Love's Martyr* with the sonnets, *Venus*, *Lucrece*, and other such works in mind. Instead of pointing out every instance, I recommend the reader to Appendix 3, where parts of the Dialogues and Cantos have been excerpted for further study.

I should point out one additional test result, this one derived from a technique called 'rolling attribution' or 'rolling stylometry'. The technique, which combines supervised machine-learning classification with sequential analysis, was designed by Maciej Eder to deal specifically with the problem of 'mixed authorship' or stylometric fuzziness. The tests corroborate the findings of the other computational results. Specifically, they indicate that in those very areas of *Love's Martyr* marked by Knight as stylistically anomalous, we witness a rupture in the pattern of Chesterian authorship seen throughout most of the book. I have included a colorized image in Plate 9 and one here in greyscale (Figure 1.12).[73]

More than any other technique we use, rolling attribution visually approximates the notion of textual and authorial multiplicity suggested by Moten. The graph charts a chronological development of *Love's Martyr* – from left to right, the image corresponds exactly with how the book unfolds. On the far left, the machine guesses that the training set of Chester's verse (in green) corresponds most with segments 1–3; next, Shakespeare (in pink) is the most-likely candidate for segments 4–6, the first Dialogue. The Chesterian signal resumes at

Queerness at Scale

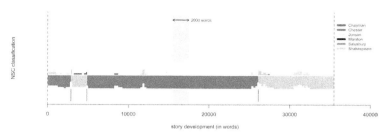

Figure 1.12 Rolling NSC with verse from Salusbury and all other poets in *Love's Martyr*

the beginning of segment 7 and continues, with minor interruptions, through the Cantos, which the algorithm hands to Shakespeare. We may also observe the machine attempting guesses at who the 'second most likely' candidates for the verse might be; the beginning of the book seems to exude a certain Chapmanian style, indicated by the bump on the top stripe on the far left, while in the middle of the Cantos, we see the suggestion of Salusbury, marked in yellow. Above all, the image shows that, even when compared with Salusbury's poetry, the Shakespearean training set is 'most similar' to the Dialogues and Cantos of *Love's Martyr*. The thicker the band, the stronger the result: The machine is quite confident in its predication that segments 4–6, 27–28, and 30–36 harbour a Shakespearean singularity.

In short, *Love's Martyr's* Cantos (30, 31–36) and parts of its Dialogues (segments 4–6, 27–28) demonstrate both consistent dissimilarity with the rest of the book and consistent similarity with Shakespearean works of drama and poetry. Joining Knight, then, one might reasonably conclude that Shakespeare collaborated with Chester in editing or revising these segments of the book, or that someone masterfully doctored only those sections of it using strikingly Shakespearean language, style, thematic concerns, and metrical patterns. Again, given the quality of Chester's general work, it is doubtful that he could have been up to the job alone, and to my mind, it is equally doubtful that Salusbury would have been his collaborator. Since we are looking in this chapter at frequencies of function words, and not words that may be easily transplanted or imitated, the likelihood of sole Chesterian authorship is even lower. Held in tandem, computational, textual, and cultural data strongly suggest that the collaborative or conversational contract between Shakespeare and Chester, or between Shakespeare and Salusbury, extended far beyond the 67-line poem signed by Shakespeare at the very end of the volume.

The following now bears emphasizing: like the other poets, Shakespeare certainly had read at least some of Chester's 'Love's Martyr' before composing his contribution, since in it he carefully adopts aspects of Chester's unique Phoenix-Turtle conceit. So, even if he did not write or edit portions of the Cantos, Shakespeare likely would have noticed that the language in those sections was both utterly dissimilar to language appearing in Chester's main narrative and quite similar to his own – sometimes with virtual word-for-word transpositions from his other works. In subsequently contributing his work and signing it, he gave his consent to the doctoring, lifting, or transplanting of words and ideas that took place. Shakespeare therefore either made these edits himself, or he noticed that someone other than him doctored text to resemble his. Thus, it is next to implausible to excuse his approbation, if not direct intervention and supervision, of the segments in question. Far more likely, he was paid handsomely for the work by Salusbury, who, we can speculate, might have been goaded to do so by his friend Ben Jonson; certainly, Jonson would not have withheld his criticisms of Chester's weaker verse.[74] Again, from what we know about Salusbury, he could have afforded to hire Shakespeare for such a purpose in 1601. As for Shakespeare, appeasing the newly knighted Salusbury would have been both lucrative and politically expedient. Given Shakespeare's association with the Earl of Southampton, an Essex collaborator, allying with Salusbury would have been a judicious way to distance himself from his former patron, in print if not in reality. For a moment, not to last long, Salusbury held the Queen's favour and the power to assemble together England's brightest wits. Shakespeare would have been reasonable to go along for the ride, including by taking on the role, in Chester's words, as 'one of [his] best minded friends' who offered him support in his 'long expected labour'.[75]

Queerness at Scale

These findings may prompt one reasonably to inquire why I have not altogether attributed at least some of this verse – again, specifically segments 4–6, 27–28, and 30–36 – to Shakespeare, as Knight seems inclined to do. First, as discussed in my introduction, I have little interest in participating in the generally unqueer project of 'discovering new Shakespeare'. Less defensively, and more to the point, I see no reason to argue that Chester was wholly uninvolved in the composition of these segments, which are after all signed by him, and that we are indeed witnessing a collaboration between Chester and Shakespeare and possibly between Chester, Shakespeare, and Salusbury. As Moten might have it, what we see in *Love's Martyr* is not a question of Chesterian, Salusburian, or Shakespearean authorship, but a gathering of these voices that renders the very concept of 'author' here somewhat beside the point. While I do think it is useful to know that Shakespeare collaborated on this verse – something computation has aided us in making clearer – this data does not show that Shakespeare, any more than Chester, was the 'author' of this verse. Rather, the notion of the 'author', as we know and use it, simply fails to assist us in illuminating these collaborative dynamics. We encounter instead something akin to the Machiavelli-Moten spectre, a mystical yet somehow-calculable dimension of textual style and personality.[76] Derived from a queered conception of authorial ontology, Moten's radical singularity highlights what Michel Foucault calls a 'second self' that arises from textual practice, a construct 'whose similarity to the author is never fixed and undergoes considerable alteration within the course of a single book'.[77] Computational methods give us another way of testing out, indeed quantifying, Foucault's poststructuralist intuitions: the very marks that appear in computational pictographs reveal neither authors not 'authorships' per se but rather linguistically constituted textualities that emerge 'out of [the] scission' between biological writer and fictional narrator – 'in the division and distance of the two'.[78] In short, I want to suggest that one approach these 'graphs, maps, and trees' not as immutable statements of fact but rather with considered openness to forms of intimacy, aberration, and multivalence that may emerge. From here, we may be able to

Shakespeare's Queer Analytics

defend against the strangely nostalgic position that quantitative and qualitative methods need not and should not mix.

The goal of this chapter has been to highlight Shakespeare's collaborative activity by examining *Love's Martyr* at some distance. Before turning with specificity to Shakespeare's 'The Phoenix and Turtle' – the purpose of my final chapter – I examine the authorial and cultural contexts of this collection by focusing on the book's concluding Poetical Essays. Using, again, a mixture of queer and computational methods, I consider how computational data helps illuminate questions of authorship in the Poetical Essays, where one encounters strikingly differentiated theories of the author. Queer of colour critique goads us, too, to observe in *Love's Martyr* a pattern of masculine competitiveness with surprising contemporary resonances.

CHAPTER 2
COMPETITIVE INTIMACIES IN THE POETICAL ESSAYS

Shade

What do the playwrights of 1590s England have in common with the competitive drag queens of 1980s New York? Beyond sharing a general flair for the dramatic, both were expert at the art of 'throwing shade', an idea without a name until the documentary *Paris is Burning* (1990), where the queen Dorian Corey described it this way:

> [W]hen you are all of the same thing, then you have to go to the fine point. In other words, if I'm a black queen and you're a black queen, we can't call each other 'black queens' because we're both black queens. That's not a read – that's just a fact. So then we talk about your ridiculous shape, your saggy face, your tacky clothes. Then reading became a developed form, where it became shade. Shade is, I don't tell you you're ugly, but I don't have to tell you, because you *know* you're ugly. And that's shade.[1]

Corey's definition of shade, as a development of the more literal 'read', speaks to an attitude regarding the bounds of acceptable and effective behaviour when competing with peers – 'when you are all of the same thing', and it becomes necessary to express 'the fine point'.[2] Notably, shade is not intended to be overtly malicious; it works precisely because it emerges from a feeling of camaraderie, a sense that one is working with – and against – one's equals.

We witness a brilliant deployment of shade in the duelling prologues of Ben Jonson's *Poetaster* (1601) and Shakespeare's *Troilus and Cressida* (1602). Jonson's prologue opens with a lengthy complaint

Shakespeare's Queer Analytics

by the character Envy, who makes an abortive effort to skuttle the production by infecting it with her venomous snakes. She is supplanted by a warrior Prologue, who champions the author's cause like a knight errant:

> I salute the stage,
> An armed Prologue; know, 'tis a dangerous age:
> Wherein who writes, had need present his scenes
> Forty-fold proof against the conjuring means
> Of base detractors, and illiterate apes,
> That fill up rooms in fair and formal shapes.
>
> (Prologue, 5–10)

In response to this militant pro-authorial stance – and possibly its insinuation that Shakespeare or his friends might be one of those 'illiterate apes' – Shakespeare's prologue addresses the question of why an author must 'arm' himself at all:

> And hither am I come
> A Prologue arm'd, but not in confidence
> Of author's pen or actor's voice, but suited
> In like conditions as our argument ...
> Like or find fault; do as your pleasures are:
> Now good or bad, 'tis but the chance of war.
>
> (1.1.22-25; 30–31)

The 'war' to which Shakespeare's prologue refers is almost certainly twinned: It alludes to the war within the world of the play, between 'Trojan and Greek', and to the larger literary conflict of which *Troilus* was a part, the so-called 'poets' war' or 'war of the theaters' that grew noisily out of the 1599 ban on printed satire.[3] Beginning that year with Thomas Dekker's *Histriomastix* – a play that brutally satirizes Jonson – the poets' war includes responses by Jonson, Thomas Middleton, John Marston, and Shakespeare, who also briefly references the conflict in *Hamlet*. At the crest of the fray, Shakespeare's reply to Jonson in *Troilus* deftly rejects the very terms of dialectical agon that gave rise to it in the first place, initiating a dialogue buttressed not by Jonson's 'well erected confidence' but by radically contingent 'like conditions as our

Competitive Intimacies in the Poetical Essays

argument'. That is, Shakespeare replies to Jonson by not quite replying to him at all – by effectively stating that he has costumed his prologue in armour only because his play, about war, would be inappropriate without it. Jonson's investment in scurrilous banter, embodied by the figure of Envy, is not worth Shakespeare's time; 'Like or find fault; do as your pleasures are', he claims, and then moves on with his purpose, which emphatically does not involve or require Jonson's continued presence.

In terms of how the poets' conflict played out, the literary scene of late Elizabethan England resembles the world of competitive drag more than one might think. Like the 1980s urban drag scene, characterized by cut-throat competition born out of intimate homosocial proximities, the group of poets and playwrights that emerged in the 1590s were deeply similar in terms of social class and creative disposition; they even had different 'houses', representing one theatre troupe or another at any given time. As one critic reflecting on the feud between Jonson and Marston put it, 'men who are identical to one another fight in order to establish the differences that can serve as the basis of a new social order'.[4] The poets who contributed to the poets' war demonstrate notable artistic and intellectual differences, yet it is the very fact of their similarity that made competition possible in the first place. These men, all seeking literary patronage in one form or another, needed to find increasingly creative ways to differentiate themselves, a fact that the Bishop's ban seems to have exacerbated. Without recourse to printed satire to express such differences, these poets found other ways to make their mark and to mark their enemies, throwing shade at one another with varying levels of effectiveness.

Love's Martyr's Poetical Essays supplement is an especially fascinating object in this context. In a literary culture full of 'the common back-biting enemies of good spirits', to quote from Robert Chester's dedication in the book, we find an ambiguously congenial and fraternal network of relationships: a collection of fourteen poems all dedicated '*to the loue and merite of the true-noble Knight, Sir Iohn Salisburie*', all featuring verse focused on the intellectual and erotic potentialities of Chester's novel Phoenix-Turtle conceit. Three of the supplement's poets – Jonson, Shakespeare, and Marston

Shakespeare's Queer Analytics

– contributed directly to the fracas, and all of them worked with each other collaboratively outside of this book. Yet, the notion that friendship yokes these poems together has not gained significant traction in studies of the Poetical Essays, and no study of them has engaged the methods of queer theory.[5] To be sure, there is ample reason to read the collection in terms of competition, which has been done by numerous critics.[6] These readings often capitalize on the fact that the poets' feud spilled dramatically outside the bounds of the theatre; apparently, Jonson beat and robbed Marson, and he later bragged about the incident to a friend.[7] Thanks to his reputation for being brutish and confrontational, Jonson's pugilism looms large over perceptions of the poets' conflict, and his barbs have undoubtedly set the tone for modern-day scholarly commentary. These overtly combative dimensions of the feud, reflected in the plays themselves, are no doubt highly entertaining, but this critical focus runs the risk of underplaying the intimate and coterie dynamics of the poems in *Love's Martyr*, even where Jonson himself is concerned. To be sure, it risks ignoring the degrees of shade thrown about in and beyond this collection, which establishes a clique of self-others by way of expressing differences obliquely and indirectly. The collection shows that one need not exclude competition as a motivating factor in order to highlight intimacy or cooperative interplay: Anyone who has seen an episode of *RuPaul's Drag Race* will tell you that competition can be extremely queer, especially when it gets coloured by intimate, and potentially erotic, relationships between men.

More to the point, queering competition in the context of early modern male friendship asks one to place pressure on the collaboration/competition dyad itself. When trying to assess what brought *Love's Martyr's* poets together, one might reasonably read this competition as a collective effort to address and reconcile the paradoxes of love – including deviant or aberrant love – using Chester's new Phoenix-Turtle archetype and Salusbury's elite patronage as afflatus, enabling an extraordinary fusion of intellectual, erotic, and political interests. I therefore focus in this chapter on the fraternal network established in these poems and argue that *Love's Martyr* afforded these combatants a unique opportunity, through the prestige of print, to engage seminal

Competitive Intimacies in the Poetical Essays

intellectual questions with a degree of intimate respect that befits both their talents and their exalted subject matter. It is not exactly my goal here to queer the *Poetomachia*, but I hope to initiate a critical turn in this direction by examining the Poetical Essays as a site of queer collaboration and conversational exchange.

As in Shakespeare's response to Jonson's prologue, we detect in the Poetical Essays collection an ambivalent stance towards the macho-man theatrics that defined the poets' conflict, and so too the paradigm of authorial mastery and possessiveness espoused by Jonson's armed and armoured prologue. We witness, that is, resistance to an authorial paradigm of literary possessiveness, where early modern authors engage in increasingly proprietary relationships to their written material. Using stylometric methods noted for their effectiveness in analysing small samples,[8] such as those that comprise the Poetical Essays, we are in a position to perform credible analyses on the unattributed verse in the Poetical Essays grouping – particularly, those paired poems signed 'Vatum Chorus' – yielding results that both uphold and challenge the possessive thesis. Jonson, the writer most insistent elsewhere on making firm declarations of what he did or did not compose, is the likely author of the unattributed dedication to Salusbury, revealing an unexpectedly promiscuous attitude towards authorship. Such an interpretation is supported by analysis of Marston's play *What You Will* (1601), which inserts this verse in the mouth of a character meant to lampoon Jonson. An unexpected chiasmus emerges: Jonson appears to shirk the very protocol of authorial control with which he is correctly associated outside of *Love's Martyr*, only to be put back in his place by a rival not generally associated with such an ascriptive authorial mode.

If the telos of this collection gestures towards the war outside its walls, then, it does so in a most shrewd way. The Poetical Essays stoked competitive flames and yet, formally, each poem pollinates the one following it in an elegant game of call-and-response. This intellectual volley even extends backwards chronologically: Chester's poem 'Pellican' and the brief conclusion to his book-length poem were almost certainly written with a draft of his collaborators' work before him.[9] The organizing theme we observe in the Poetical Essays is not

Shakespeare's Queer Analytics

competition per se but unity by way of competition, and indeed unitive desire: a theme we see embedded in the content and also made apparent in the overall design of the appended works. Ordered as a two-part dialogue with Shakespeare and Marston one on side of the dialectic, Chapman and Jonson on the other, the Poetical Essays ask us to unpack and explore the structuring dynamics of early modern collaborative authorship between men.[10] The verse exemplifies the principle that competition begets intimacy through dialectical intercourse, a process of carefully calibrated tension and release that structures the Poetical Essays as a unified work unto itself, one that formally exceeds itself through its retro-development in Chester's verse.

To say that I see queerness as the defining feature of *Love's Martyr*'s Poetical Essays is also to say that I see more ambivalence, more amity, more camaraderie, and less hostility than has been traditionally observed, but it is not to say that I detect a lack of competitive energy. What we ultimately witness in these love lyrics is a fanciful game-test that affords each of these poets a rare occasion to strut his intellectual stuff – to work the room, as it were – while making bold declarations about the relationship between reason and desire. In engaging this conversation, these star poets imbue Chester's Phoenix-Turtle conceit with a keen imaginative force that is fundamentally collaborative in nature, even as each poet develops his own unique take on the implicit challenge posed by Chester.

Love's Martyr's collaborative network

The Poetical Essays constitute a rare site of reflective and sensuous interaction among a group of men who, in other spheres of their lives, were often indeed at each other's throats. The internal title page of the Poetical Essays (Figure 2.1) immediately establishes a tone of amity and community.[11] We are told that the following fourteen poems, *'never before extant'*, have been 'consecrated by them all generally, *to the love and merit of the true-noble Knight, Sir Iohn Salusburie'*, whose knighthood had been conferred in the summer of 1601.[12] The first poem or 'essay', titled 'Invocatio' and

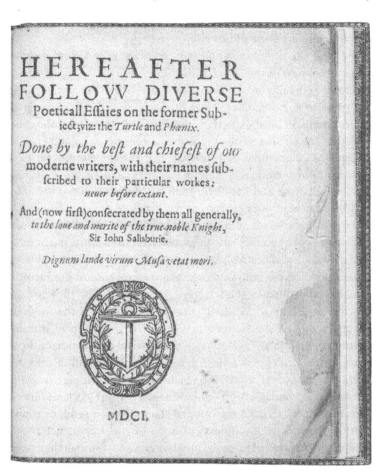

Figure 2.1 Title page of *Love's Martyr*'s Poetical Essays, Sig. Z1ʳ

signed by 'Vatum Chorus', describes a fraternal ceremony in which these poets 'sustend / Our mutuall palmes'[13] and take a sip from a 'Castalian boule', then pass it along to the next.[14] The striking image of these poets extending their 'palmes' to one another firmly establishes, at the outset of a collection 'consecrated' and signed by all, a circuit of consensus and ritualistic inspiration. What then to make of the aggression that seems to pervade the atmosphere of the

Shakespeare's Queer Analytics

time in which these poets came together to produce the celebratory and often moving verse of this collection?

There is an enormous body of scholarship attesting to the competitive spirit of the age in which *Love's Martyr* was produced. I detect two general critical trajectories in this work. The first, focused on aggression and difference, generally locates the conflict in material and economic circumstances; it may be summarized by James Shapiro's claim that 'the writing of plays remained a commercial and therefore inescapably competitive enterprise'.[15] The second strand, focused on intimacy and sameness, examines discursive institutions such as courtly interaction and friendship, and has therefore been critical to the development of early modern queer theory. In *Textual Intercourse*, Jeffrey Masten offered up a now-canonical way of thinking about Renaissance collaboration among men as a queer activity. Examining early modern collaborative plays and gentleman's conduct manuals, he used philological analysis to unearth an aesthetics of homoerotic sameness embedded in the language. He showed how these works 'inscribe an erotics of similarity that goes far beyond the modern conception of mere sameness of sex. Gentleman friends are identically constituted, as both the rhetoric and the material production of these texts in print suggest'.[16] For Masten, this erotics of similitude informs the entire apparatus of discourse on male friendship, helping to explain how intimate bonds between men, including overt declarations of love, aided in calcifying a man's social status. To be a gentleman was to prioritize one's relationships with men of equal or higher social standing, whereas male-female bonds espoused through marriage speak to a 'lower' kind of love, as we see in Shakespeare's 'Dark Lady' sonnets and in Montaigne's essays. In 'Of Friendship', for example, Montaigne declares, 'Vnder this chiefe amitie [friendship], these fading affections [desire for women] have sometimes found place in me ... So are these two passions entred into mee in knowledge one of another, but in comparison never'.[17] Friendship is a 'chief amitie' consisting of possible attraction to both men and women, though these 'passions' are not to be compared because, in the misogynist discourse of early modern male friendship, relations between men and women are socially subordinate to those between men.[18]

Competitive Intimacies in the Poetical Essays

Despite his reputation for brutishness, Ben Jonson has become a paradigmatic figure in this second critical strand. Numerous critics have shown that Jonson was insistently preoccupied with a notion of literary virility that requires both the expulsion of feminine ornament and the implied expression of certain truths – implied but not directly expressed, because the 'manly' poet tends toward insinuation and silence.[19] Indeed, as Jonson told his friend Drummond, many contemporary epigrams were 'ill' because they 'expressed … what should have been understood'.[20] This tacit mode of expression bears particularly on Jonson's deployment of allusion, through which he envisions and constructs an ideal, all-male literary coterie. As Lorna Hutson brilliantly argues, 'Jonson's use of allusion … constitutes the interlocutor or reader as ideally virile to the extent that he understands the application of allusion in question and understands why it remains unexpressed'.[21] She shows how the 'unexpressed' in Jonson often alludes to homosexual discourses and images, as we see in Jonson's translations of Martial, which pointedly elide certain well-known sexual images so as to draw critical attention right back to them, that is, to the select few who would understand the critical move.[22] This masculine practice of verbal subtlety works to establish a literary community predicated upon suppressed homoerotic and homosexual images that nonetheless figure centrally in its construction and operation. This practice in turn reifies a conception of masculine poetic intimacy: 'The tacitly understood sexual allusion [in Jonson] unites both interlocutors, or the author and the reader, in an intimacy of shared literacy and sexual knowledge and pleasure, and makes that intimacy (which is itself characterized as virile) depend on the unspeakable quality of that knowledge and pleasure'.[23] Though Hutson refers here to *Everyman in His Humour*, this attitude towards secrecy and allusion informs Jonson's literary production throughout his career, and it may even assist in contextualizing the 'sons of Ben' coterie that was erected in response to Jonson's rising fame.[24]

With these two theoretical trajectories – one characterized by difference and aggressiveness, the other by intimacy and sameness – before us, we may ask to what extent they constitute a joint critical ideology within the culture of the early modern gentleman. Such a

Shakespeare's Queer Analytics

synthesis occurs most evidently, I believe, the closer one homes in on the literary scene of late Elizabethan England, where we find *Love's Martyr's* guest poets looking remarkably similar while also straining to distinguish themselves, effectively breaking the discursive mould while operating within it. In his biography of Jonson, David Riggs speaks of Jonson and Marston thus: 'A contemporary [Elizabethan] observer would … have surmised that two men who resembled one another so closely were bound to quarrel. The Elizabethan theory of social order rested on the assumption that two individuals will behave peacefully if – and only if – they can assign each other to a graduated social hierarchy'.[25] Rivalry, resemblance; errancy, similitude; competition, collaboration: We witness in the work and play of these figures a queer dialogic relationship between seemingly opposed categories that, in practice, literally co-operate, yielding a formula whereby difference emerges through sameness. Elizabethan critic Francis Meres saw the poetic jousts that characterized late Elizabethan literary culture in a positive light because they brought about intellectual balance while unburdening audiences of possible 'infection' by proximity:

> As that ship is endangered, where all lean to one side, but is in safety, one leaning one way, and another another way; so the dissension of Poets among themselves, doth make them, that they less infect their readers. And for this purpose our Satirists, Hall, [and] *the Author of … Certain Satires* [Marston] … are very profitable.[26]

Fuelled by both order and disorder, a striving towards balance deriving from 'dissension', the poets' conflict effectively feeds on its own tail, establishing a ludic hermeticism characterized by the coexistence of difference and sameness required of effective sport. In the spirit of Dorian Corey's thesis on shade, Wayne Koestenbaum captures, *mutatis mutandis*, the spirit of queer rivalry I detect in early modern collaborative love poetry written by and between men: 'Gays are not always nice to each other, and opera queens rarely are. Anger (among its many uses) is a form of flirtation. Opera queens hold their heads high as divas concerned about a draft's effect on the voice: tension at Tower Records because there are three opera queens in line, three of

Competitive Intimacies in the Poetical Essays

us, too many, density in the air as if before a cat-fight or mating. We have too much in common and therefore proximity is painful.'[27]

The analogy is anachronistic but, as Michelle O'Callaghan has shown, speaks precisely to habits of 'learned play' put on at the Inns of Court, which 'incorporated ritualized forms of aggression' – especially, the practice of flyting, a premodern form of 'reading'[28] – that 'helped to constitute the social space of the convivial society, the arena in which social competence is produced and cultural value attributed'.[29] Through sameness, difference and through difference, sameness: The tension between similitude and difference not only animates and makes possible the kind of literary conflict we see in late Elizabethan England, but also asks one to reframe this conflict in an erotic cum intellectual discursive space stationed both within and outside traditional notions of masculine competitiveness.

The operative rational mode of this discourse is contradiction, an insistence on the possibility of two opposing entities residing in the same space. A queer analytical approach holds that contradictory views can be held together simultaneously – it prioritizes the non-binary logic of contradiction over that of Aristotelian non-contradiction, which I examine more closely in my next chapter. The logic of contradiction is precisely what fascinates Shakespeare in 'The Phoenix and Turtle', and it also forms the basis for a queer methodological intervention in computational analysis. Indeed, stylometric analysis of unattributed verse in the Poetical Essays indicates several seemingly incompatible but actually complementary conclusions, though we must attend carefully to the methodological paradigms involved and how these may be said to fructify one another.

Computing anonymity

Two theories of early modern authorship connected loosely to the critical trajectories I have described loom large over late Elizabethan literary culture in general, and the Poetical Essays grouping in particular. We have already seen how a theory of collaborative textuality, like Masten's textual intercourse, informs early modern

Shakespeare's Queer Analytics

attitudes toward authorship, yielding a view of the Renaissance writer that precedes 'post-Enlightenment paradigms of individuality, authorship, and textual property'.[30] On the other hand, a possessive attitude towards authorship is often claimed to have influenced literary production through the seventeenth century. In *Ben Jonson and Possessive Authorship*, Joseph Lowenstein suggests the gradual development of an increasingly proprietary approach to authorship, where authors seek further control and 'authority' over their works: 'In the Early Modern period', he argues, 'the proper-ness of books is shaped, even determined, by the ways in which quasi-proprietary claims were asserted by the possessors of manuscript copies, by printers, by publishers, and by authors. And although individual authors might experience this connectedness idiosyncratically, we may speak of the cumulative effect of such experiences, which was to transform authorship into a form of public agency increasingly distinguished by possessiveness'.[31]

How does such a theory of authorship fit into or complicate the discourse of early modern male friendship I have articulated, and how does it hold up upon examination of the Poetical Essays?

We might begin, again, at the beginning, with the very first poems of the Poetical Essays grouping, those signed 'Vatum Chorus' and 'Ignoto'. Two poems are signed 'Vatum Chorus', or 'Chorus of Poets': the first, a two-stanza poem titled 'Invocatio', the second an untitled dedication to Salusbury. Following these, we find two single stanza-length poems – the first titled, oddly, 'The First', the other titled 'The Burning' – signed 'Ignoto' or 'unknown'. The question of who authored these poems, which immediately precede Shakespeare's 'Phoenix', is one of the most persistent among scholars of both *Love's Martyr* and the Poets' War.[32] Following a close study of these poems alongside various dramatic works by Jonson and Marston, Charles Cathcart concludes that the 'various features of the "Vatum Chorus" poems, of the "Essays" themselves, and of independent writings by Jonson and of Marston, consistently implicate the two poems in the pair's rivalry'.[33] At the same time, 'each item of evidence' to which he draws attention 'potentially admits of the theory that either one of

Competitive Intimacies in the Poetical Essays

the poets was responsible for their composition'; that is, 'the same items of evidence seem jointly to indicate two possible conclusions'.[34] The evidence 'hardly [supports] the possibility that the collective designation' was 'consecrated "by them all generally"', as is advertised in the title page of the Poetical Essays. In other words, in this view, one and only one author, whoever he was, likely composed those poems. Given the totality of data and other forms of evidence that can be extracted from the final pages of *Love's Martyr* – as well as the queer theoretical intuition that seemingly opposed entities can be held up together to produce new meaning – I would suggest another possible conclusion. Data shows that Robert Chester, quite surprisingly, may be involved in the composition of 'Invocatio', yet Jonson appears most likely among this troupe to have written the dedication. Moreover, compelling evidence implies a collaborative aspect to these poems that would unsettle any theory of 'straight up' attribution, asking us to consider alternate interpretive possibilities when confronted with the positivist allure of data.

The most critical information for understanding who might have written the dedication to Salusbury is found outside of *Love's Martyr*, in Marston's *What You Will* (1601). Verse from the dedication appears as a collocation in the play, where it is inserted into the mouth of Lampatho Doria, a clear caricature of Jonson.[35] In Act Four, Lampatho performs a series of overwrought lines before a group of bystanders; while performing, Quadratus comments upon the quality of his verse and draws particular attention to the line, 'if thou canst taste the purer juice of love'. Here Quadratus interrupts Lampatho and proceeds to humiliate him:

Quadratus:	'If thou canst taste the purer juice'; good still, good still. I do relish it, it tastes sweet.
Lampatho:	Is not the metaphor good, is't not well followed?
Quadratus:	Passing good, very pleasing.
Lampatho:	Is't not sweet?
Quadratus:	Let me see't. I'll make it sweet: I'll soak it in the juice of Helicon. [Thrusts the sonnet into his wine.] (1539–45)

Shakespeare's Queer Analytics

The line is a collocation taken from the dedication to Salusbury, which is reproduced in full in Appendix 1:

> Noblest of minds, here do the Muses bring
> Unto your safer judgments taste,
> Pure juice that flow'd from the Pierian springs[36]

The lines confirm, in Cathcart's words, 'that Marston opens the poem to a public reproof within his comedy'.[37] Following the exchange, Lampatho claims, 'I'll be reveng'd'; Quadratus responds, 'How prithee? in a play?' (1555). At first glance, the logic here seems to point to a clear end: Marston, mocking Jonson in these lines, seems also to be mocking lines Jonson is likely to have composed, perhaps even wishing to 'expose' him as the author of the bombastic verse that opens the appended collection. In making this move, Marston may be distancing himself from *Love's Martyr's* collaborative dimensions and from the vehicle itself, thereby implicitly drawing attention to his role as sole author of four specific poems in the volume. If one follows this line, Jonson is, of the two, the likely author of the unattributed poems. The second stanza of the poem contains further possible evidence; the words 'envy' and 'merit' are used together, a Jonsonian tick seen in *Poetaster*, where the two words are yoked together three times.[38] Another possibility, imaginatively advanced by MacDonald P. Jackson and Michael Neil, neither precludes Marston's involvement nor casts Lampatho as a mere stand in for Jonson; rather, it posits Lampatho as a 'teasing anamophmic double-portrait'.[39] One might concede that in *What You Will*, Marston mocks himself and perhaps, too, the entire poet's conflict.

Despite this evidence, there is reason to think Jonson would not have been involved in the composition of the dedication to Salusbury. His first signed contribution to the Poetical Essays, his 'Praeludium', begins with an extended invocation that contradicts the rhetoric appearing in the first of the unattributed poems.[40] 'Invocatio' opens by expressly invoking 'Good Fate, faire *Thespian Dieties*', and its title implicitly entreats the assistance of Apollo; the full title of the poem is 'Invocatio, *Ad Apollonem & Pierdes*'. But in 'Praeludium', Jonson enters the collective by categorically rejecting the assistance of the

Competitive Intimacies in the Poetical Essays

muses – Hercules, Phoebus (or Apollo), Dionysus ('Lord of the Vine'), Pallas ('Mankind Maide'), 'light Venus', Hermes, and so on – finally exclaiming, 'No, we bring / Our owne true Fire; Now our Thought takes wing / And now an Epode to deep eares we sing'.[41] Why, the reasoning goes, would Jonson have written two opposing invocations, one ecstatically drawing upon the muses and the other firmly rejecting them? The clash, according to Cathcart, may suggest Jonson's 'wish to dissociate himself from an "Invocatio" in the composition of which he had no part, which he deplored, and with the demerits of which he was unwillingly implicated through the claim that the poem was a collective one'.[42] Cathcart amasses a wealth of terminological, technical, and personal details, including extensive evidence from *Poetaster* and other works, that variously favour Jonsonian or Marstonian authorship.[43] Oddly, though, he argues against the notion that the poems might have been written collaboratively, a claim that does not, in my estimation, follow necessarily from the wealth of impressive evidence he gathers.[44]

Computational analysis of the two 'Vatum Chorus' verses suggests that each poem carries a stylometric signal connected primarily to one author, but it does not preclude the possibility of joint authorship. Tests that count variations in word frequencies, largely invisible to human comprehension, indicate close similarity between Jonson's collected verse and the dedication to Salusbury containing the collocation found in *What You Will*. Table 2.1 displays results from a machine learning classification technique called Nearest Shrunken Centroids (NSC) – especially effective in analyses of small data samples, as Matthew Jockers and Daniela Witten have shown in a benchmark study – and Support Vector Machine (SVM).[45]

Even with the tiny sample sizes found in the Poetical Essays, the two classifiers, trained on random samples of poetry from Chester, Shakespeare, Marston, Chapman, and Jonson, consistently attributed each signed poem in the Poetical Essays to the correct author using most frequent words, though less successfully when using most frequent function words only (see Appendix 1).[46] Table 2.2 contains additional results on the dedication using NSC and SVM at different frequencies using different training data and most frequent word counts.

Shakespeare's Queer Analytics

Table 2.1 NSC and SVM classification of Poetical Essays

Text	NSC 69MFW @ 80%	SVM 69MFW @ 80%
LM 38: Salusbury dedication	Chester	Jonson
LM 40: Shakespeare	Shakespeare	Shakespeare
LM 41: Marston	Marston	Marston
LM 42: Chapman	Chapman	Chapman
LM 43: Jonson	Jonson	Jonson

Table 2.2 NSC and SVM tests on dedication to Salusbury

Parameters	89 MFW @ 80%	100 MFW @ 0–60%	200 MFW @ 0–40%	300 MFW @ 0–20%
NSC @ 2000 words	Jonson	Jonson	Jonson	Jonson
SVM @ 2000 words	Jonson	Chester	Jonson	Jonson
NSC @ single texts	Jonson	Jonson	Jonson	Jonson
SVM @ single texts	Jonson	Jonson	Jonson	Jonson

Results suggest the possibility that the dedication to Salusbury – which is after all signed 'by them all' – may have been written collaboratively, but between Jonson and Chester. These results were generated using Chester's verse in manuscript and segments within *Love's Martyr* that do not, per the results of my previous chapter, indicate authorial meddling, so we can weigh them with some degree of healthy scepticism. Again, these tests return reliable results on the known, signed works of the other poets in the collective; Chester only appears to rear his head in the Poetical Essays in the unattributed sections of verse, including the 'Invocatio' that precedes the dedication.

Tests using a bootstrap consensus tree (BCT) – which essentially takes repeated snapshots of dendrogrammatic data on most frequent function words and arrays the averages of these results arounds a central point – show Chester aligned closely with 'Invocatio' while seemingly excluding either Marston, Jonson, or Shakespeare. Figure 2.2 visualizes the affiliation between 'Invocatio' and Chester's

Competitive Intimacies in the Poetical Essays

known verse as well as its stylistic relationship to known works by the other collaborators.

The graph resembles a colour wheel, and in fact may be read as such.[47] Observe in the upper-right quadrant the segment titled 'LM 38' (representing 'Invocatio'), placing the segment firmly within the tree of data containing other branches of material signed by Chester. It suggests that of these writers, Chester's work is closest in kind to 'Invocatio'; it also seems to exclude Jonson's, Shakespeare's, or Marston's involvement, as these authors sit on the opposite side of the

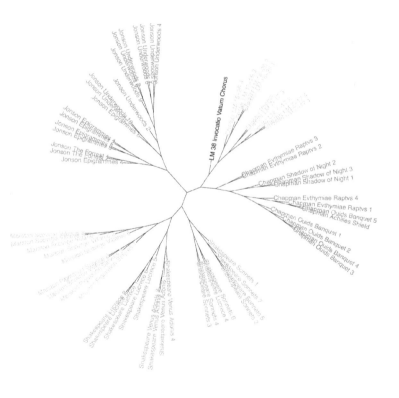

Figure 2.2 Bootstrap consensus featuring *Love's Martyr*'s 'Vatum Chorus'.

Shakespeare's Queer Analytics

wheel, indicating strong dissimilarity. However, the BCT data hints at similarities with Chapman's known verse – both Chapman's and Chester's work fall within the same larger tree of data – though not, to my mind, strong enough to make a case for authorship.

These findings present at least two significant interpretive problems. Most pressing is that Jonson seems likely to have either authored or co-authored the dedication, thereby lending credence to the long-held view that he was involved in the composition of this verse while also suggesting that he did not do this entirely by himself. Using a cluster analysis of most frequent words, I first posited this theory several years ago, but this new data is significantly more compelling.[48] Whether or not Jonson collaborated with others in composing this verse, it betrays enough of a Jonsonian signal to call it, using Fred Moten's term, a Jonsonian singularity – a segment of verse that carries the sub-stylistic personality and features of Jonson's other writings. If this is correct, then this finding troubles the notion that Jonson always sought ultimate control over works signed in his name or that he cared to sign his name to all of the things he wrote. In the 1605 quarto of *Sejanus*, in his epistle 'To the Readers', Jonson ostentatiously declares that he felt compelled to rewrite his unnamed co-authors' scenes: 'Lastly I would informe you, that this Booke, in all numbers, is not the same with that which was acted on the publicke Stage, wherein a second Pen had good share: in place of which I haue rather chosen, to put weaker (and no doubt lesse pleasing) of mine own, then to defraud so happy a Genius of his right, by my loathed vsurpation.'[49] This is Jonsonian shade of the highest degree – a subtle and indirect attack, unlike the 'reads' of his more pointed *Poetomachia* transgressions. Jonson, then, appears in the Poetical Essays to shirk the very authorial paradigm with which he is correctly associated outside of *Love's Martyr*.

We find an adjacent attitude toward authorship in Jonson's other verse in the Poetical Essays. When Jonson claims in 'Praeludium', 'No, we bring / Our owne true Fire; Now our Thought takes wing / And now an Epode to deep eares we sing', he appears to acknowledge that the verse is part of a collective effort. But the argument has been made that Jonson adopts the *pluralis majestatis* or 'royal we', thereby

Competitive Intimacies in the Poetical Essays

further distancing himself from his peers by taking on a regal authorial perspective.[50] This interpretation makes sense given what we know about Jonson's attitude towards authorial possessiveness, but it becomes harder to accept when we examine the full scope of his involvement in *Love's Martyr*. We see Jonson likely sharing authorial control in the composition of the dedication, composed by '*our retentiue braine*', and we have reason to think that he maintains this friendly disposition in his signed contributions.[51] In an earlier draft of this poem, circulated in manuscript and partially published in Robert Allott's miscellany *England's Parnassus* (1600),[52] Jonson speaks using first-person pronouns; in both 'Praeludium' and the following 'Epos', his pronouns shift from 'I' to 'we' throughout.[53] Here, I believe, we see Jonson behaving rather unusually, and cordially, to his friends, effectively welcoming them into his verbal universe as he concludes the collection on behalf of them all. This does not mean that I dismiss the suggestion of regal authority, which can and should be held in mind with the notion of collective cooperation: The pronominal shift introduces an ambivalent stance, an 'anamorphic double pronoun' if you will, that gives Jonson the best of both authorial worlds, both the duck and the rabbit. Such a move would be typical of Jonson's interest in tacit, multivalent meanings and is also characteristic of his literary expansiveness. As Hugh Craig has shown in his study of Jonsonian stylistics, Jonson makes frequent use of the binary 'or' not to individualize and separate but rather to expand and extend, using the conjunction as a 'particular kind of *copia*'[54] that allows for 'minute adjustments and supplements' as a character speaks.[55] Another of Craig's findings is particularly telling in this light: his study shows that Jonson makes far less use of possessive pronouns 'me' or 'my' than his contemporaries, including all of his peer poets featured in *Love's Martyr*'s poetic supplement. To an attuned early modern spectator, Craig surmises, the dialogue in Jonson's plays 'would be remarkable for its projection of an isolated, freewheeling self; for the scarcity of fustian drama; for the lack of specificity in motions to and from individuals; and for *the absence of possessiveness*, and thus of a focus on the extended self in his characters'.[56] Jonson, then, is eminently capable of acting 'freewheeling' and even non-possessive, and this, I believe, is the Jonson we find in *Love's Martyr*.

Shakespeare's Queer Analytics

If my view is right, then Jonson rather brilliantly both begins and ends the Poetical Essays while masking his identity through the notion of collective designation. That is, he maintains authorial control in a sense by producing or co-producing this verse, yet disavows the notion of absolute, uncontested 'possession' by signing his first contribution 'Vatum Chorus' and metaphorically weaving the voices of his peers into his 'Praeludium'. There is another good reason to think that Jonson adopts a genial and fraternal tone in his signed poems. In 1601, Jonson was just twenty-nine years old, while Chapman and Shakespeare were already established literary heavyweights. The elder gentlemen in this collection would have commanded respect and authority, even from someone like Jonson, who at this relatively early date in his career had not yet changed his last name from less Latinate 'Johnson'. Jonson's authorial attitude in this collection, at this very time, is quite literally in transition. Perhaps in deference to Salusbury or the poetic vehicle itself, he decided or was cajoled to express a politeness, civility, and feeling of intimate respect that may sometimes be difficult to locate in his private life and public conduct.[57] I believe that he is effectively reined in by a tacit rule set embedded in the very coterie dynamics of *Love's Martyr*. That is, he seems to behave queerly in this text if not in works like *Poetaster* and *Sejanus,* where he is indeed preoccupied with developing a muscular conception of masculine authorship.

Authoring 'Invocatio'

The second issue raised by our computational tests, that of Chester's possible presence in the Poetical Essays, may be more controversial. Results consistently show stylistic similarities between Chester's known verse and the opening poem in the Poetical Essays collection, 'Invocatio' – it is more similar to works by Chester than by any other figure known or speculated to have contributed verse to *Love's Martyr*, including Salusbury.[58] To my knowledge, I am the first person to suggest that Chester may have contributed anything to the Poetical Essays grouping; scholarly consensus is that Chester produced only

88

Competitive Intimacies in the Poetical Essays

his book-length epic poem, to which 'the best and chiefest poets' then respond in their individual 'essays'. What can we make of this most unlikely of outcomes given what we know about Chester, who is not credited with having contributed any verse to the Poetical Essays supplement, whose name was struck altogether from the 1611 reissue, and who was emphatically not one of 'the best and chiefest poets' of his time, as the title page alleges?

These are genuine questions, and they require us to consider additional evidence, since there is little in the poem itself to indicate that it must be Chester's. If anything, the poem reads like a fabulous four-headed beast, with hints of Chester, Jonson, Chapman, and Marston strewn throughout. The first stanza contains an elaborate extended metaphor that borders on euphuism:

> GOod Fate, faire *Thespian Deities*,
>   And thou bright God, whose golden Eies,
>   Serue as a Mirrour to the siluer Morne,
>   When (in the height of Grace) she doth adorne
> Her Chrystall presence, and inuites
>   The euer-youthfull *Bromius* to delights,
> Sprinckling his sute of *Vort* with Pearle,
> And (like a loose enamour'd Girle)
>   Ingles his cheeke; which (waxing red with shame)
>   Instincts the senslesse Grapes to do the same,
> Till by his sweete reflection fed,
>   They gather spirit, and grow discoloured.[59]

The verse is distinguished by its repeated parenthetical interjections; in twelve lines, we find three of them. These embellishments strike me as Marstonian; Marston's response to Shakespeare, his 'Narration and Description', also contains three such parenthetical statements. The orchidaceous imagery could be Marson's, and it certainly does not sound like Chapman or Jonson; to my mind it recalls verse from Chester's 'Pellican', where we stumble upon the strained image, 'Lovers are like the leaves with Winter shoken, / Brittle like glasse, that with one fall is broken'.[60] Moreover, it contains the unusual spelling of crystal with a 'y', a Chesterian habit.[61]

Shakespeare's Queer Analytics

The second stanza, much of which I have already excerpted, reads indeed as if it were written by a different person, and it contains 'illustrate' as an adjective, a Jonsonian tick. William Matchett suggested that Chapman might be involved here or in the 'Ignoto' verse by pointing out that the poets who contributed to the volume loosely followed a pattern of submitting paired poems, one that serves as an invocation of sorts, the other constituting the poetic 'main event'. For example, with Jonson, his first poem introduces and effectively clears the way for what follows in his 'Epos'. According to Matchett's criteria, Chapman alone does not abide by the rules of the assignment, unless we entertain the possibility that he composed or co-authored either or both the 'Ignoto' and 'Vatum Chorus' poems. In a buried note, Grosart refers to the 'Ignoto' verse – too small for accurate statistical sampling of the kind we perform in this study – as 'like Chapman at his worst'.[62] In fact, a number of Chapmanian quirks may be identified in 'Invocatio', including a reference to the 'juice' brimming over 'Castalian bowles' in *The Shadow of Night* (1594):

> Presume not then ye flesh confounded soules,
> That cannot beare the full Castalian bowles,
> VVhich seuer mounting spirits from the sences,
> To looke in this deepe fount for thy pretenses:
> The iuice more cleare then day, yet shadows night,
> VVhere humor challengeth no drop of right[63]

(162–7)

This sounds quite similar to what we see in the collection's opening verse: our intuition does not require computational assistance. Then again, Shakespeare also refers to the above image, which may be attributed back to Marlow's translation of Ovid's *Amores*, in his epigraph to *Venus and Adonis*: 'Vilia miretur vulgus; mihi flavus Apollo / Pocula Castalia plena ministret aqua' ('Let the common herd be amazed by worthiless things; but for me let golden Apollo provide cups full of the water of the Castalian springs'). The reference, then, may be said to implicate Ovid by way of Marlowe, not Chapman, and certainly not Shakespeare.

90

Competitive Intimacies in the Poetical Essays

In short, there is no current way to 'prove' Chapman contributed to the anonymously written poems, but the strongest computational data we currently have cannot exclude him from this possibility. This ambiguity may be disconcerting from a positivist view that would ask for or expect a neat and clean return from data that is indeed 'clean' and well-curated. At this juncture, queer analytics assists in accounting for contradictions in our data without excluding these contradictions, as Aristotelian or binary logic requires that we do. Instead of throwing out such data because, held together, it misbehaves or behaves erratically, we should consider the possible directions to which these contradictions point. To return to my earlier inquiry, the data does **and** does not support a preoccupation with proprietary authorship among the authors of the Poetical Essays insofar as (1) Jonson seems likely to have assisted in the composition of unattributed verse; (2) Chester may have authored or co-authored some of Invocatio, potentially in consultation with others; and (3) Marston, sometimes associated with a promiscuous or non-proprietary attitude towards authorship, may be acting more 'possessive' here than expected insofar as he directs attention, in *What You Will*, to the authorship of a competitor's work who has denied his role in its composition.

Love's Martyr would not be the only place where Marston raises such questions. In his *Satires*, we see him thinking intently about authorial possession. Discussing a succession of famous Roman patricians, Marston asks hypothetically:

Shall *Matho* raise his fame
By printing pamphlets in anothers name,
And in them praise himselfe, his wit, his might,
All to be deem'd his Countries Lanthorne light?
Whilst my tongue's ty'de with bonds of blushing shame
For fear of broching my concealed name?

(127–32)[64]

One can never be too certain regarding intent when considering this group of authors, particularly Marston, and particularly when he is being expressly satirical. But we can at the very least detect a certain anxiety around questions of authorship and ownership, between

Shakespeare's Queer Analytics

'pamphlets in anothers name' and those written, perhaps, in one's own 'concealed name'. All of this asks us to question if a theory of literary possessiveness, as well as the forms of competition engendered by such a theory, is adopted in any consistent way by the authors of the Poetical Essays. We seem instead to see these poets behaving queerly, which is to say both oddly and unexpectedly, in these rarefied pages.

Shade and interactivity

Beyond his citation of the Poetical Essays in *What You Will,* Marston offers keen insight into his methods – and to the collaborative and competitive dynamics of the Poetical Essays as a whole – by way of his reply to Shakespeare within the book. His response establishes that it had to have been written with a draft of Shakespeare's poem before him; it is the clearest evidence we have that the poems of the Poetical Essays are interactive in nature. The critical tendency is to assume that Shakespeare hands his 'Phoenix' poem off to Marston (or Marston by way of the publisher, Edward Blount), who then responds with a tone of defiance.[65] But, as Katherine Duncan-Jones has argued, it is unlikely that Marston would do this without consulting Shakespeare, a man he imitated and idolized; correctly I think, she calls Marston a member of Shakespeare's 'fan club'.[66] Far more likely, Marston sought permission and perhaps even worked with Shakespeare to construct his lyric reply. Facing the third page of 'Phoenix' (see Plate 3), Marston's poem establishes both a development of and dialectical turn against Shakespeare's declaration that the phoenix is dead:

A narration of and description of a
most exact wondrous creature, arising
out of the Phoenix and Turtle
Dove's ashes.

O 'Twas a moving *Epicidium*!
Can fire? can Time? can blackest Fate consume
So rare creation? No; 'tis thwart to sense,
Corruption quakes to touch such excellence,

Competitive Intimacies in the Poetical Essays

> Nature exclaimes for Justice, Justice Fate,
> Ought into nought can never remigrate.[67]

This defiant reaction might seem to constitute shade, but it is both more direct and respectful than that. Lacking the obliqueness of shade, it is a forceful critical counterpoint that is much more like a 'read', albeit a gentle one. Marston's read of Shakespeare begins with a reassertion of terms: properly and traditionally, a 'most exact wondrous creature', a new phoenix, should arise from the ashes of the dead phoenix.[68] That this does not happen in Shakespeare's '*Epicedium*' (or funeral ode) is 'thwart to sense', illogical and implausible. 'Ought into nought can never remigrate': The phoenix, once forever gone, cannot 'remigrate' or 'go back again' to its former state, and that is unacceptable – its extinction constitutes an affront to physical as well as moral 'Nature', consisting of ethical abstractions such as 'Justice' and 'Fate'.[69] Shakespeare's poem, while 'moving', simply does not make sense, yet Marston is not ready to mock his idol; instead, he corrects course, noting the 'glorious issue' that rises from the ashes. He then proceeds to praise the Phoenix hyperbolically in a sequence of poems that fervently establish the continued existence of the fabled bird and that repeatedly stress its incomparable 'perfection'. In Marston, then, we see a continuation of Shakespeare's theme; it is merely as if Shakespeare had not waited long enough for '[s]o rare creation' to '[s]pring from yonder flame'.

Chapman, following Marston, does indeed introduce shade into the collection, and it is directed seemingly at everyone. Reminiscent of the lines signed by 'Ignoto', 'Peristeros' is pragmatic, earth-bound, and initially critical in tone. It begins by chiding 'idle Lovers' and those who

> Change their Affections with their Mistris' Sights,
> That with her Praise, or Dispraise, drowne, or flote,
> And must be fed with fresh Conceits, and Fashions;
> Never waxe cold, but die: love not, but dote:
> Loves fires, staid Judgements blow, not humorous Passions

Shakespeare's Queer Analytics

> Whose loves upon their Lovers pomp depend,
> > And quench as fast as her Eyes sparkle twinkles,
> (Nought lasts that doth to outward worth contend,
> > Al Love in smooth browes born is tomb'd in wrinkles).[70]

Long considered a bit of an oddity in this collection, and sometimes neglected, Chapman's verse seems in fact to respond to the significant themes we have traced thus far. In these lines Chapman takes issue with Marston's obsessive fascination and youthful passion, which 'must be fed with fresh Conceits, and Fashions'. Chapman is referring to Chester's 'fresh Conceit', that is, the Phoenix-Turtle motif itself. In what can be described as a preening and catty tone, he similarly inveighs against the Ovidianism of both Shakespeare's and Martson's poems, in which 'humorous Passions' govern love and poetic creation. If 'Al Love in smooth browes born is tomb'd in wrinkles', the fledgling Marston – only twenty-five years old in 1601 – best represents such a naïve disposition. His preoccupation with 'Fashions' and 'Lovers pomp' may lead perilously to false love, or else love that simply will not last long.

Though Chapman obviously wants none of this, he is left with a dilemma, because the phoenix – gussied up here by Chester with its 'fashionable' new mate – absolutely must be praised. He resolves the problem by taking on the role of analyst, using his judgement to produce verse arising from a 'constant heart'. In a surprising pivot towards the sincere and personal, Chapman directly likens himself to the dove and his mistress to the phoenix:

> She was to him th' *Analisde* World of pleasure,
> > Her firmenesse cloth'd him in varietie;
> Excesse of all things, he ioyd in her measure,
> Mourn'd when she mourn'd, and dieth when she dies.
> Like him I bound th' instinct of all my powers,
> > In her that bounds the Empire of desert[71]

In these lines, Chapman returns us to the sombre tone of Shakespeare's 'Phoenix' and to its conclusion that the phoenix and turtle die

Competitive Intimacies in the Poetical Essays

and do not reproduce. At the same time, he pointedly advances the conversation initiated in 'Phoenix' over the relationship between reason and desire, but flips the script: while these forces come into dramatic and irresolvable conflict in Shakespeare's poem, in 'Peristeros', reason and sound judgement conspire to allow for the form of unitive desire idealized yet ultimately destroyed in 'Phoenix'. While Chapman and Shakespeare part ways in terms of the pragmatic value each ascribes to reason, both insist on making the two forces meet and wrangle one another into a kind of resolution. It would appear that Chapman links his 'palmes' with the other 'elder' of our collection, Shakespeare; in 1601, they were, respectively, 42 and 37. Chapman thereby establishes a relationship of gentlemanly mutuality qua contrariety with Shakespeare, someone with whom he, or any literary man in 1601, would wish to be favourably compared – perhaps especially as an equal-but-opposite in an empyreal battle of wits. The Shakespeare-Chapman kinship takes on a structural meaning when one closely observes the Poetical Essays as a whole. Chapman and Shakespeare each contributed one poem to the Poetical Essays, while the younger Marston and Jonson each contributed four. So while Chapman rejects the Ovidianism of his younger colleague, he seems to embrace it in the form of Shakespeare's more tempered and solemn rendition. We see here a poet both critical of and deeply embedded within the hierarchical and social dynamics of early modern gentlemanliness.

Chapman, then, acts shady to most and more so to others, betraying similarities and kinships with his compeers while differentiating himself vis-à-vis a terse but profound aesthetic statement on the nature of love. His exclusionary attitude also carries the effect of implied inclusivity: like the allusive *ludus* Jonson forges using networks of private knowledge, Chapman serves up an early modern version of 'you can't sit with us' – a doctrine that implies a privileged 'we' that is admitted. Chapman extends his 'palmes' most overtly not to Shakespeare but to Jonson, whose stoic intellectual disposition most closely resembles his own. In his poem 'Epos', which follows his 'Praeludium', Jonson calls reason '*Affections* King' – a compliment rather than contrary to love.[72] Jonson's verse rides this theme across four poems, concluding the Poetical Essays and *Love's*

Shakespeare's Queer Analytics

Martyr as a whole on a thesis that extends the work of Chapman while earning him the title of *vates* with the loudest voice – more than half of all verse in the supplement is Jonson's. I think we can detect, in Chapman's poem, a certain weariness directed at his overbearing younger friend, too: His 'Peristeros' decries 'humorous passions', and at this time Jonson was most famous for 'humoral' comedies such as *Every Man in His Humour*. This remark could be a jab at Jonson or a compliment; it is difficult to say exactly what Chapman means by it, but it seems unlikely to signify nothing at all. Like Jonson's double-use of the royal we, functioning to welcome and shun his peers at the same time, Chapman's allusive ambiguity points to a pattern of semantic multivalence in *Love's Martyr* that has everything to do with the ludic scene and setting in which it was composed. In a volume that contains a seemingly endless series of authorial gestures and coterie references, Chapman's presence suggests a connection between shadiness and authorial elusiveness – a relationship between one's authorial attitude and one's attitude towards authorship. Indeed, if *Love's Martyr's* Poetical Essays were staged as a drag competition, then Chapman would easily win the ball. Saying more with fewer words than any of his fellow competitors – even if we hand him the 'Ignoto' verse in its entirety – Chapman stands out as shadiest king of this troupe.

By the conclusion of both *Love's Martyr* and the Poetical Essays, Chester's collaborators have put Chester in a bit of bind. His main narrative only rarely touches upon the intellectual questions broached by his famous friends, and it seems to require that the phoenix and turtle be reborn in physical form: otherwise, the collection takes on a depressing tone, and it is supposed to celebrate the knighthood of his friend and idol Salusbury. So, in his 'Pellican' and 'Conclusion' verse, Chester desperately but commendably reckons with the shock of the phoenix's death and accommodates the collection's late descent into philosophical obscurantism. In 'Pellican', he postulates:

> If that the Phoenix had bene separated,
> And from the gentle Turtle had bene parted,
> Love had bene murdered in the infancie,
> Without these two no love at all can be.[73]

Competitive Intimacies in the Poetical Essays

Chester thus brings the Platonism of the Poetical Essays into play in his own verse by describing the love between the birds as an inseparable two-in-oneness. He also seems invested in further developing the theme of gender speculation seen throughout the book. I mentioned in my previous chapter that Chester, in 'Pellican', refers to the possibility of the phoenix uniting with a '*second he*, / A perfect form of love and amitie', both birds burning together and yielding 'a more perfect creature'. The language is explicit: the phoenix is suddenly male, and it joins, hypothetically, with another 'he' in a fiery marriage of minds that, in verse if not in reality, produces a new creature – a 'child' combining the best features both of its parents. On the question of whether or not a new phoenix is born, Chester is adamant in his 'Conclusion' that follows: 'From the sweet fire of perfumed wood, / Another princely *Phoenix* upright stood'.[74] Subtext becomes text in the literal-minded Chester. Though G. Wilson Knight often describes feeling 'baffled' by the book's repeated gender confusions, there can be no confusion here: Chester is, at this moment, talking about a homosexual love between these birds that, to borrow Jonson's phrase, 'chastely die' and thereby reproduce the phoenix cycle, yielding another prince. Though Chester elsewhere uses female pronouns to describe the phoenix, no heterosexual reading of the poem can accommodate the notion of a 'second he' – not even, of course, a reading that would correct the pronoun to 'she'. Chester's seemingly proleptic but actually chronological reply to and summation of his peers is as explicitly queer as Renaissance poetry gets.

All of this leaves Shakespeare's poem itself still something of a mystery. While I began this chapter with an example of Shakespearean shade in the prologue to *Troilus*, I have focused my time here intentionally circling around his poem. As virtually every critic who has written at length about *Love's Martyr* or 'The Phoenix and Turtle' will tell you, setting Shakespeare's poem aside – giving it its own space in which to breathe – is necessary not only because its complexity requires dedicated space, but because its intimidating intellectualism threatens to absorb the attention of everything around it. This is not to say that the poem is not of a piece with the others in the collection; without *Love's Martyr*, to be sure, it would never have

97

been written, since it is here that he happens upon and transforms Chester's Phoenix-Turtle invention. But it is clear that Shakespeare's poem is unique among the others, not least because it is the only poem in which both the phoenix and turtle die and do not reproduce.

So, in the final part of this book, I read 'The Phoenix and Turtle' in context and in isolation, against the backdrop of the Poetical Essays and the intellectual history it so expressly invokes but with attention to its peculiar logical and grammatical structures. While Shakespeare's collaborators all demonstrate various levels of interest in the relationship between reason and desire, Shakespeare is most explicit in his argument that love and reason constitute mutually opposing forces. For him, reason is the critical force behind social order and is also, thereby, the greatest obstacle to personal desire; it is an artificial construct that consistently thwarts and threatens the realization of true love.

By reading this poem's critique of reason in terms of a more specific critique of binary logic, I extend this book's theorization of queer analytics to computational modes of thinking that precede mechanical computation per se – that is, to forms of ratiocination that anticipate the ways in which binary logic would come to be marshalled at scale, to shape social order. In this I resume my travels with G. Wilson Knight, who describes the 'mutual flame' in which the Phoenix and Turtle both bond and depart as a force that '[pierces] dimensions beyond earthly computation'.[75] Developing this offhand but compelling insight, I argue that the poem presents the first significant exploration of non-binary ontology written in English, and that its power is best understood in these seemingly anachronistic terms.

PART II
COMPUTING QUEERNESS

Logistica est ars bene computandi.

– John Napier, *De Arte Logistica*[1]

The phoenix riddle hath more wit
By us; we two being one, are it.
So, to one neutral thing both sexes fit.
We die and rise the same, and prove
Mysterious by this love.

– John Donne, 'The Canonization'[2]

CHAPTER 3
'NEITHER TWO NOR ONE WERE CALLED': QUEER LOGIC AND 'THE PHOENIX AND TURTLE'

And what impossibility would slay
In common sense, sense saves another way.
(2.1.176–177)

–All's Well that Ends Well

Reason is fundamental

The first half of this book has focused on ways to queer computation – how introducing the queer within the realm of the computational gets us to consider what is already queer about computation, and how thinking about computation in terms of queerness expands the interpretive possibilities of data. To conclude this book, I consider how computation, understood in an early modern context, may be said to generate forms of queerness. What do computationally adjacent or contingent concepts such as number, reason, and logic have to do with queerness? How might a conception of queerness rooted in computation elucidate the meaning of both categories?

Shakespeare's poem 'The Phoenix and Turtle' answers these questions by inaugurating a queer critical attitude that arises from its indictment of Aristotelian logic. In the poem, the phoenix merges with the turtledove in a profound synthesis that defies the laws of physics, prompting personified Reason to declare its death following a discussion with Property over its mysterious non-binary ontology.[3] The stakes could not be higher: The eternally recurring phoenix

Shakespeare's Queer Analytics

and its new mate, forged as one yet somehow retaining their own identities, are described in the final stanza as 'dead birds' enclosed in an 'urn' – a devastatingly grim picture of true love, far afield from the largely celebratory tone of the other poems in the Poetical Essays. By effectively negating this idealized but impossible bond, Reason shows itself to be incapable of understanding the subtleties of love, particularly when such love takes on an aberrant or non-normative cast. But why does Shakespeare put an end to the phoenix cycle, and what are the consequences of this decision?

The legendary difficulty of Shakespeare's poem has everything to do with the fact that the imperishable phoenix has died – but that it also appears to be alive.[4] In fact, in the opening stanza, the 'bird of loudest lay', perched atop the 'sole *Arabian* tree', may very well be the resurrected phoenix. By both killing off the phoenix and suggesting that it may have been reborn, the poem raises questions of temporality, futurity, potentiality, and possibility that have particular meaning in scholastic-Aristotelian thought. My claim, specifically, is that this poem about reason engages with the scholastic debate over idealized potentiality versus embodied possibility, placing this work at the very centre of twenty-first-century queer theory.[5] With its extinction of the phoenix, the poem posits perhaps no clearer demonstration of Lee Edeleman's influential antisocial or 'antirelational' thesis, which stipulates that queerness is all about an attempt to resist normative sociality and its tending towards 'reproductive futurity'.[6] The conjoined phoenix-turtle, called out by Reason for 'leaving no posterity' at the end of the poem, would seem to be the literal embodiment of this pessimistic view of queer potentiality: The non-normative desire binding these birds can neither survive societal pressures nor be sublated into something resembling 'the norm'. It posits, in this sense, the death of sociality and politics – a crystal-clear example of an Edelmanian rejection of futurity. At the same time, the poem's recursive nature, which asks one to consider the phoenix's rebirth, invites Jose Esteban Muñoz's claim that queerness is fundamentally utopic, all about what lies ahead; in his words, 'the rejection of a here and now and an insistence on the potentiality or concrete possibility for another world'.[7] In this light, the poem

102

Queer Logic and 'The Phoenix and Turtle'

may be read as a theoretical staging ground for the rational limits of idealized potentiality, which comes into conflict with embodied possibility. In his reading of Giorgio Agamben, Muñoz elucidates the classical distinction between these terms:

> Agamben's reading of Aristotle's *De Anima* makes the crucial point that the opposition between potentiality and actuality is a structuring binarism in Western metaphysics. Unlike a possibility, a thing that simply might happen, a potentiality is a certain mode of nonbeing that is [immanent], a thing that is present but not actually existing in the present tense.[8]

'Phoenix' appears not to reinforce this opposition, but rather, to betray the logical and existential limitations that such a binary imposes upon desiring bodies. That is, it makes an implicit claim that the phoenix – and so too, the merged phoenix-turtle – exists in potential as a recursive entity without end; if it somehow dies, it has been deprived of its rightful place in actuality. The poem therefore exposes the nature of the deviant logic that ought to give way, a multivalued logic of love, which is cancelled and overturned by dubious negotiations between Reason and Property. Violating Aristotelian laws of identity, the phoenix-turtle is thus a thesis unto itself on non-binary ontology and non-normative desire: it shows how that which is errant or 'impossible' must be understood as a component of the real, a potentiality that exists in violation of abstracted principles that dissociate desire from matter.[9]

I therefore focus in this chapter on how the poem is wired, how its differing versions of reason do and do not 'compute'. Such attention brings this poem, often read in exclusion from the other Poetical Essays, back into the fold of the book, but in a way that gets us to consider the kind of intellectual play we see in and beyond it. Like his collaborators, Shakespeare leans into the intellectual possibilities precipitated by Chester's phoenix-turtle invention, linking it to Platonic and scholastic themes and to a discussion on the nature of reason's relationship to desire.[10] We have already seen how Marston speaks of the phoenix in '*Metaphysicall*' terms and as a 'boundlesse *Ens*', referring to the Platonic notion of being; that Jonson follows Chapman in positing that

103

Shakespeare's Queer Analytics

reason is '*Affections* King', a stabilizing and socializing force that exists at one with love; and that Chester takes up the subject in his 'Pellican' verse, developing his ongoing theme of 'these two consumed in the fire, / Whom Loue did copulate with true desire'.[11] Shakespeare makes this shared concern with the socializing power of reason his central subject, driving home the insight that any incompatibility between love and reason is a function of a dysfunctional social order – one in which true potentiality is blocked and made actually impossible. His poem generates, through its unresolved extinction of the phoenix, a mode of errant or deviant rationality that asks us to critically evaluate and, if need be, condemn the reason of common sense, to refuse its limits and say, enough: No more will I accept your terms and definitions, no more will I accede to this nonsense framed as or taking the form of reason. Animating much of queer theory, this defiant critical spirit not only links the otherwise opposing views of Edelman and Muñoz, but also recalls Michel Foucault's claim that there is something particular to the early modern European mode of resistance, 'a kind of general cultural form, both a political and moral attitude, a way of thinking, etc. and which I would very simply call the art of not being governed or better, the art of not being governed like that and at that cost'.[12] To be queer is, on some level, to adopt this spirit of critical acuity and defiance, to forge a disposition that refuses the externally imposed authority if it does not 'govern' in ways that give some measure of authority back to the subject. I think of this stance not as one of mere abrogation of normativity but as a thinking and radically creative resistance, a resistance grounded in *poesis*.

Far from standing on its own, then, the poem's queer critique of normative reason directly hails early modern conversations on both the restrictive and generative effects of logic. The turn Foucault describes against externally imposed notions of the rational is, in fact, a hallmark of early modern resistance to scholastic-Aristotelianism. Though conventional Aristotelianism was alive and well in 1601, pockets of resistance to it infiltrated Europe and positively flourished in England, where the logical methods of Petrus Ramus held sway and deeply impacted poetic discourse. Ramus's views may be best summarized by the infamous dictum he may or may not have

Queer Logic and 'The Phoenix and Turtle'

uttered in his 1536 thesis defence, '*quaecumque ab Aristotele dicta essent, commentitia esse*' ('everything Aristotle had said was false').[13] The consequences of this anti-Aristotelian spirit were far-reaching, impacting domains from politics to philosophy to popular depictions

Figure 3.1 Master MZ, *Aristotle and Phyllis* (~1500).[14] The Art Institute of Chicago

Shakespeare's Queer Analytics

of the philosopher himself, as can be seen in the popular premodern meme of 'Aristotle and Phyllis' (see Figure 3.1).

Cultural distaste for things Aristotelian impacted logical discourse the most. The early seventeenth century was, in Rosemond Tuve's words, a period in poetics 'dominated by logic'; following the martyrdom of Ramus in the 1572 St. Bartholomew's Day massacre, '[i]t is scarcely necessary ... to give evidence for the currency and importance in England of Ramus's reorganization of what had been for centuries an educated man's chief tools of thought and expression.'[15] To ignore this popular movement and accompanying critical spirit, I believe, is potentially to misread or underappreciate the scholasticism of the 'The Phoenix and Turtle' and indeed, the scholastic language variously adopted by others in the *Love's Martyr* coterie. Shakespeare's scholastic terminology draws on a centuries-old intellectual tradition, but his deployment of that terminology reflects the serious opposition that tradition began to face from logicians, rhetoricians, and indeed poets of the period.

The reason of love

The originally untitled, 67-line poem now known as 'The Phoenix and Turtle' contains eighteen stanzas – fifteen quatrains followed by five tercets – and is organized into three sections, each containing and largely defined by a distinct rhetorical voice. The first five stanzas describe a gathering or invocation spoken by an unidentified voice that is the organizing principle of the poem's central act, an 'obsequy' (12) or 'Requiem' (16) to which certain birds described in these stanzas – those of 'chaste wing' (4) – are invited, and from which others – those of 'tyrant wing' (10) – are banished. This is followed by an 'Anthem' (21) seven stanzas long, sung either by the Swan or by the entire chorus of birds gathered at the funeral, in which the nature of love between the Phoenix and Turtle is articulated, then evaluated, by Reason. The poem concludes with a dirge or threnody in which Reason takes the stage and discusses the implications of the birds' deaths. The

Queer Logic and 'The Phoenix and Turtle'

separately titled 'Threnos', a lament spoken by Reason, appears on its own page elaborately decorated and flourished with the cursive inscription, 'William Shake-speare'.[16]

For the purposes of readability, I reproduce the poem below with modernizations adopted from the Duncan-Jones and Woudhuysen's transcription.[17] I also include images of the poem from the 1601 text held at the Folger Shakespeare Library (See Plates 2 and 3).

> Let the bird of loudest lay
> On the sole Arabian tree,
> Herald sad and trumpet be:
> To whose sound chaste wings obey.   4
>
> But thou shrieking harbinger,
> Foul precurrer of the fiend,
> Augur of the fever's end,
> To this troop come thou not near.   8
>
> From this session interdict
> Every fowl of tyrant wing,
> Save the eagle, feathered king:
> Keep the obsequy so strict.   12
>
> Let the priest in surplice white,
> That defunctive music can,
> Be the death-divining swan,
> Lest the requiem lack his right.   16
>
> And thou treble-dated crow,
> That thy sable gender mak'st
> With the breath thou giv'st and tak'st,
> 'Mongst our mourners shalt thou go.   20
>
> Here the anthem doth commence:
> Love and constancy is dead,
> Phoenix and the Turtle fled,
> In a mutual flame from hence.   24

Shakespeare's Queer Analytics

So they loved, as love in twain
Had the essence but in one,
Two distincts, division none:
Number there in love was slain.   28

Hearts remote yet not asunder;
Distance and no space was seen
'Twixt this turtle and his queen,
But in them it were a wonder.   32

So between them love did shine
That the turtle saw his right
Flaming in the Phoenix' sight;
Either was the other's mine.   36

Property was thus appalled
That the self was not the same:
Single nature's double name
Neither two nor one was called.   40

Reason in itself confounded
Saw division grow together,
To themselves yet either neither,
Simple were so well compounded,   44

That it cried, 'How true a twain
Seemeth this concordant one;
Love hath reason, Reason none,
If what parts can so remain.'   48

Whereupon it made this threne
To the Phoenix and the Dove,
Co-supremes and stars of love,
As chorus to their tragic scene.   52

Threnos
Beauty, truth, and rarity,
Grace in all simplicity,
Here enclosed, in cinders lie.   55

Queer Logic and 'The Phoenix and Turtle'

Death is now the Phoenix' nest,
And the Turtle's loyal breast
To eternity doth rest.   58

Leaving no posterity,
'Twas not their infirmity,
It was married chastity.   61

Truth may seem, but cannot be;
Beauty brag, but 'tis not she;
Truth and beauty buried be.   64

To this urn let those repair
That are either true or fair;
For these dead birds sigh a prayer.   67

There is no serious question over the authorship of 'The Phoenix and Turtle', but this is not to say that authorial matters are irrelevant to a discussion of it. Thinking about authorship can also mean thinking about how writers situate themselves in their works – how, if at all, we see the author's intended views reflected.[18] In the first five stanzas of the poem, we detect a distinct personality that stands in sharp contrast to what follows. Sometimes overlooked in discussions of 'Phoenix', the invocation initiates a discussion on logic essential to an understanding of the poem's queer critique of reason. The lines begin in the *irrealis* or literally 'unreal' mood to establish a set of conditions for events that are presumably to follow. The four-line *abba* structure of the first stanza is preserved throughout the poem until we reach 'Threnos', which is composed in tercets. The first line, typical of those that form the poem's first thirteen quatrains, contains seven syllables and four accents. In a voice that is both hieratic and judgmental, taking on the role of *maestro ceremonial*, the invocation proceeds entirely with commanding imperatives: 'Let the bird of loudest lay', perhaps the risen phoenix, do its work in gathering the mourners; 'To this troop come thou not near', says the speaker to the owl, 'shrieking harbinger' of death. This discerning voice is as close as we get to an authorial presence in this poem – an insight into how

Shakespeare's Queer Analytics

the poet himself wants us to understand his work, an occult reading protocol of sorts.[19]

Though this opening section lacks any explicit reference to the scholastic imagery with which I am most concerned, its content is far from irrelevant. Namely, this introductory material establishes conditions for attendance among the birds revealing a logic that will have us question how the speaker of these lines feels about the ensuing event, in which the phoenix's death is detailed. These lines also, in themselves, establish a structure critical to a comprehensive understanding of the multiple 'reasons' we encounter in the poem; even before 'reason' is expressly invoked, we can intuit already traces of the more thoroughgoing critique of reason in the poem's next section. The invocation, specifically, presents two logical quandaries that confront the reader. The first, already touched upon, involves the identity of the 'the bird of lowdest lay' in line one. Volumes of scholarship have been dedicated solely to the question of who or what is represented by it. Standing on 'the sole *Arabian* tree', it appears, at first, to be the phoenix, but this is later shown to be impossible: the Phoenix is dead before the poem begins, its remains 'enclosed' in an 'urn' around which the 'chaste wings' described in the invocation have gathered. Some critics argue that the poem's ambiguities and paradoxes allow one to place the Phoenix of this poem in these opening lines. This interpretation is supported by what we know about the phoenix myth: in it, traditionally, the notably Arabian bird revivifies after consuming itself in a fire. In *The Tempest*, Sebastian, awed by Prospero's magical talents, demonstrates Shakespeare's familiarity with the myth and more importantly the terms he uses to describe it:

> Now I will believe
> That there are unicorns; that in Arabia
> There is one tree, the phoenix' throne, one phoenix,
> At this hour reigning there.

$$(3.3.21–24)$$

The bird appears again in *Cymbeline*:

> All of her that is out of door most rich!
> If she be furnish'd with a mind so rare,

Queer Logic and 'The Phoenix and Turtle'

> She is alone the Arabian bird, and I
> Have lost the wager.
>
> (1.6.620–623)

The association of the phoenix with a singular 'Arabian bird' resting upon a tree is unmistakable (see Plate 5). Within the pages of *Love's Martyr*, the connection is repeatedly made.[20] So, is the 'bird of loudest lay' an earthly replacement for the dead phoenix, or has the original phoenix itself returned from the dead – bizarrely, to perform the role of 'herald sad and trumpet' at its own funeral, before it has been announced to be dead? If the phoenix is still alive, what is the purpose of the swan's song, or Reason's lament? If it is reborn, then Reason is acutely mistaken in grieving its loss. Shakespeare's 'moving Epicidium' might therefore be, as a minority of scholars have suggested, a 'leg pull', or even a comedy.[21]

While these questions may dart through the reader's mind, 'Threnos' confirms over and over that the Phoenix and Turtle, allegorized Love and Constancy, are 'dead', finally and forever. It is said metaphorically:

> Death is now the Phoenix' nest,
> And the Turtle's loyal breast
> To eternity doth rest.
>
> (56–58)

metaphysically:

> Truth may seem, but cannot be,
> Beauty brag, but tis not she,
> Truth and Beauty buried be.
>
> (62–64)

And, in the poem's final line, emphatically:

> For these dead birds, sigh a prayer.
>
> (67)

Nothing could be more final, more physically concrete and less philosophically abstract, than the words 'dead birds'. Seemingly, then, the bird of loudest lay cannot be the dead phoenix. But what else

Shakespeare's Queer Analytics

could it be? Some have argued that it could be the nightingale, often said to have a loud, melodic voice; more have allowed that the poem's ambiguities ask one to consider the possibility that the phoenix is in fact resurrected here, though no satisfactory explanation for its duplication within the poem has been submitted. The answer would seem to depend on some combination of the reader's knowledge and understanding: for a coterie reader, who would certainly be familiar with references outside of this poem to the phoenix as a 'sole' Arabian bird, none other than the phoenix itself could be alluded to. Such a reader, in the process of having read this poem for the first time, likewise has no reason, passing through stanzas one through five, to reject this definitive association, as the bird has not yet been proclaimed dead. So: it is alive for now in the reader's mind through the end of the poem's invocation. The fact that it is later declared dead requires the reader to question what they know to be true both in terms of their readerly attentiveness and literary learnedness. This particular logical problem therefore is not a problem at all until we reach the blunt proclamation that 'Love and Constancy is dead, / Phoenix and the Turtle fled' in the sixth stanza. Here on, the question of the phoenix's death and apparent revival becomes the central and most problematic question raised in this poem, one that appears to have demanded mitigating responses from both John Marston and Robert Chester.[22]

The other puzzle in the invocation, which unlike the first has gone largely unexplored, focuses on the logic according to which various fowl may or may not attend the ceremony. We observe that the poem excludes birds of 'tyrant wing' while welcoming those who are 'chaste'. The swan of stanza four is the easiest of all to place within this schema: Its undoubtedly chaste presence is required due to its 'death divining' properties, making it the perfect bird to lead the funerary proceedings with its song. The owl of stanza two, in keeping with tradition established in medieval and early modern avian bestiaries, is the 'shrieking harbinger' of death, an annoying and pestilent presence that is programmatically shunned. Among 'every fowl of tyrant wing', only the eagle, 'feath'red king', is permitted access. The reasoning behind this makes a certain kind of practical, if not logical,

112

Queer Logic and 'The Phoenix and Turtle'

sense: though the operative binary dyad of chastity / tyranny would seemingly require its banishment, the logic of the authorial voice suggests a certain awareness of social conventions is needed in order to make judgements as to who or what may be included in or excluded from the makings of the poem's social order. A rational valuation, underwritten by a logic of exception, permits the ruling that the eagle should of course be present. A mixture of chaste and tyrant, the eagle may attend precisely because it is 'King' – without its presence, sociality itself would be incomplete. So, it doesn't matter if the eagle is tyrant; pragmatism unproblematically trumps logic. The reader passes over this stanza without a second thought, because it should not matter, and ultimately does not matter, if the eagle operates as if in a position of exclusion from the rest of the troupe. Its attendance at the ceremony presents us with the second clue that a peculiar logical riddle is afoot in these opening lines – that the 'reason' at work here is something we should neither take prima facie nor treat as absolute or uncontestable.

This logic of exception migrates into the final stanza of the invocation, where the speaker encounters the crow. Reaching this stanza, which mirrors the structure of stanza two containing the banished owl, we fully expect to see the 'treble dated' crow ejected from the proceedings – the crow is if nothing else a tyrant bird, and 'treble dated' implies only that it is uncommonly old, or ancient.[23] Like the owl, it carries strongly pejorative associations in the literature of Shakespeare's time; in a typical image, Gascoigne calls it a 'lothsome beast … [that] The devil resembleth playne'.[24] Our expectations are reversed: the crow takes a privileged seat 'mongs't our mourners'. It appears that the crow receives dispensation for its tyranny because of its unusual form chastity, as it was popularly thought that the crow reproduced with its beak through an exchange of breath with another crow. Thus, the crow's 'sable gender' must be understood to have been produced asexually: for if the crow is in any way 'chaste' – as it must be in order to attend – it is so in these (a)sexual terms. The fact that the speaker pardons the crow suggests a certain subtlety to its reasoning, a feeling that an individual consciousness, and not some abstraction divorced from earthly and human affairs, has made these

Shakespeare's Queer Analytics

studied determinations. The speaker's judgement suggests, moreover, an organizational rationale animated by an appreciation of non-normative sexuality and desire – a voice that, while stern and clear in conviction, is also attentive to the oddities and errancies that comprise the natural world.

What, then, to make of the logic at play in these opening stanzas? First of all, the speaker of these lines seems unconcerned with defying the Aristotelian notion of identity, which dictates that a thing must be only itself (P = P) and nothing more. The duplicated phoenix clearly defies this law, a fact that enters the reader's awareness as the poem unfolds and certainly by its conclusion. The crow and eagle, too, present the reader with troubling juxtapositions between allegorical or potential and actual being; what should be, what we would expect to be, does not necessarily match up with what is permitted to occur. The speaker presents a double disjunction between convention and permissibility: The eagle by convention is exalted and welcomed despite its noted tyranny, while the crow is by convention unwelcome but invited due to the speaker's admiration of its chaste sexuality. The invocation thus announces a set of poetic conventions that both rely upon and depart from classical associations and casts reason in a state of casuistic ambiguity, even as the voice making these declarations proceeds with utmost confidence. In short, we trust the speaker of these lines about what it is saying, which is to say that we trust its powers of reasoning, even though it does not appear to be following a logical script or method.

I would argue that we trust the speaker precisely because it follows no such script but rather its own assured conscience, which is to protect those among its jurisdiction ('Keep the obsequy so strict') and fend off death and negativity ('Augur of the fever's end'). We get the distinct impression that the speaker of these lines operates from a position of moral authority. The rational ambiguities it introduces seem indeed to have epistemic roots outside of the world of the poem – it is as if the poet himself has entered the magic circle and brought with him a set of views and methods of interpretation that we, as readers, are meant to abide by and respect, if not adopt. The speaker wants us to believe in the reality of a duplicated phoenix, a world in which its simultaneous

Queer Logic and 'The Phoenix and Turtle'

absence and presence is both possible and morally unproblematic – a world, that is, governed by the protective and empathic 'reason' of love itself. In these five brief stanzas, the poem thus establishes a logical and moral counterpoint to the logic of Reason soon to follow. The poem's utopic queer potentiality lies dormant in these opening stanzas, waiting to be rediscovered and reactivated upon our realization that the Phoenix does not need to die after all.

Shakespeare's queer analytics

The terms of the invocation having been met, the speaker and its imperative tone disappears as the poem's 'Anthem' begins. In the first of these stanzas, the imperative mood is dropped and the indicative mood deployed to describe an event that has already passed. Unlike the poised language of the invocation, the anthem is disputatious and paradoxical: words like 'appalled', 'confounded', and 'cried' suggest that a drama is taking place in these lines. Most surprisingly, it contains words like 'essence', 'division', 'number', and 'property' – words that distinctly reference scholastic terms and concepts. Those interested in the poem's scholastic terminology generally focus on what takes place in these lines. Too often the discussion merely begins here, treating the invocation as if unrelated to what actually matters in the poem. In fact, the speaker's logic and conviction of tone have everything to do with how the reader reckons with the ensuing paradoxes. In his classic 1955 study, J.V. Cunningham provided the most influential explanation of what is happening in the anthem, inspiring two generations of criticism focused on the poem's Neoplatonic elements:

> The central part of the poem [the anthem] refines in exact, technical, scholastic language the relationship of the lovers. They are Love and Constancy, Beauty and Truth, Phoenix and Turtle. The nature of their love was such that love in each had the essence (the defining principle by which anything that is, is what it is) only in one. Obviously, then, the effect of their love was unitive. But in terms of what scheme of ideas is this union conceived? It is not

115

Shakespeare's Queer Analytics

unlike, of course, the Neo-Platonic union, in which the soul, being reduced to the trace of the One which constitutes its resemblance to it, is absorbed, submerged, and lost in the presence of the One. There is no more distance, no doubleness, the two fuse in one.[25]

James Bednarz largely concurs with Cunningham, arguing for a 'poetic theology' that underscores the poem's interpretation of love: '[H]e presents lovers, like the persons of the Holy Trinity, who are godlike in being simultaneously and apart.'[26] Since my concern here is less with the precise 'nature' of love between these birds than the form of logic they hail into presence, I do not reject this view, yet I am not convinced that it best characterizes the tone of the anthem, in which scholastic terminology is elegantly applied to describe the idealized love of the birds yet is also linked by association to Reason's 'confounded' discourse. That is, I do not believe that engaging the poem's scholastic terminology requires one to accept that 'only Trinitarian theology can adequately describe the anthem's ideal.'[27] If the form of ideal love represented by the Phoenix and Turtle is Trinitarian, on what grounds would it be disqualified by Reason? Reason, a character that may be a virtual stand-in for 'university-trained theologians, the schoolmen of "Dunces" … who were said to pursue fruitless and self-defeating arcane gestures', has given us little reason to trust what it has to say, but it should know not to take shots at the holy trinity.[28] In my view, what is most important about this love is not what it comprises metaphysically, but the fact of its categorical rejection by Reason.[29] That this matter-defying love cannot be sustained on earth, in reality, in a world in which Reason has the final word is precisely what lends this poem its tragic heft while also providing sly yet blistering commentary on those rational-taxonomical impulses that would reject as imperfect something that is so obviously the very embodiment of perfection, as Marston's set of Poetical Essays repeatedly point out.[30]

Here, a turn to Ramist critique elucidates this emphasis not on metaphysics per se but on the logic that rushes in to categorize, name, and define from without, in socio-rational terms that simply do not apply to the example at hand. The poem seems to be aware of the Ramist emphasis on practical effects: the real-world uses to

Queer Logic and 'The Phoenix and Turtle'

which reason may be put rather than meaningless conjecture over the 'nature' of things, as in the scholastic debate over how many angels might be said to sit on the head of a pin.[31] Ramus himself totally rejects metaphysics as a division of philosophy, since for him logic – an inspection of things from the general to the particular – can explain all truths; metaphysics becomes utterly superfluous.[32] This move had consequences for both the prestige of metaphysics and the importance post-Ramist philosophies would place on it. Despite the shallowness of Ramist reforms, as Walter Ong and others have described them, his push towards curricular change and privileging of pedagogy redirected the aims of philosophy towards the practical, the earthly, and the accessible; in short, towards a reckoning of what comprises 'common sense' itself. Under Ramism, to be sure, no longer did scholastic logic hold the power to make absolute sense of the physical world.

This context requires me to depart from Trinitarian readings of 'Phoenix' in one additional respect. Interpretations of the poem that stress its indebtedness to scholastic-as-Trinitarian models focus on the poem's psychological or 'intersubjective' drama, either implicitly or explicitly rejecting the actual bodies of these birds as extraneous. If the form of desire these creatures summon into being is immaterial in nature, what threat does it pose to 'Property', which in this poem carries distinct associations with physical matter? '[A]ppalled' that 'the self was not the same', Property rejects the fabulously conjoined being as ontologically impossible, thereby prompting Reason to declare, 'Loue hath reason, Reason none, / If what parts, can so remain'. While one may insert the Christian trinity in these lines, my reading attempts to approximate what I believe G. Wilson Knight's alludes to in his assessment that the phoenix 'enjoys a certain immediacy of physical impact peculiar to a period when the divine was felt as incarnate'.[33] There is something potentially fleshly and earthly about this love, something unsettlingly but precisely *actual*, that disgusts 'Property' and unmoors Reason. The very fact that 'these dead birds' appear in an 'urn' by the poem's close strongly urges us, on at least one register, to consider the corporeal dimensions of intersubjective desire. In other words, the poem necessitates a consideration of non-

117

Shakespeare's Queer Analytics

binary physicality, a two-in-oneness that bears explicitly on notions of gender hybridity and multiplicity. The poem seems to hint not merely at some Neoplatonic abstraction of two-in-one completeness, but rather at gender nonconforming bodies themselves – individuals who, like the Phoenix-Turtle, enact the principle that 'Single nature's double name / Neither two nor one was called'.

I therefore propose a method by which to perform a logical rereading of the poem's anthem that hails its scholastic features as well as the urgency of the poem's critical message. In a pointedly post-Aristotelian turn, 'Phoenix' yields no single avenue of interpretation, since no single voice of reason can be said to exist. This point is best understood by turning to Aristotle himself. In the *Metaphysics* IV, Aristotle quibbles of his opponents:

> There are some who … assert that it is possible for the same thing to be and not to be, and say that people can judge this to be the case … But we have now posited that it is impossible for anything at the same time to be and not to be, and by this means have shown that this is the most indisputable of all principles.[34]

These principles form the tenets of propositional logic, which demand observance to three laws, paraphrased here:

> Law of Identity: P must equal, and equal only, P (P = P)
> Non-Contradiction: P must not equal not-P (P ≠ -P)
> Excluded Middle: for any proposition, either P is true its negation is (P or –P)[35]

Computer scientist Bart Kosko, a theorist of fuzzy or multivalued logic, describes what is at stake in uncritically upholding these laws:

> All around us things change their identities … Things flow smoothly to nonthings … We can put black-and-white labels on these things. But the labels will pass from accurate to inaccurate as the things change. Language ties a string between a word and the thing it stands for. When the thing changes to a nonthing, the string stretches or breaks or tangles with other strings.[36]

Queer Logic and 'The Phoenix and Turtle'

The matter of when a given thing crosses over into 'nonthing' – the precise moment at which it violates the law of non-contradiction – may seem like a meaningless scholastic preoccupation, but the stakes could not be higher for non-normative or gender-nonconforming bodies. Early modern people were in fact fascinated by the ways in which non-normative genders could subvert logic, especially in the figure of the hermaphrodite, which represents 'the vanishing point of all binary logics, a figure which embodies the dissolution of male and female as absolute categories'.[37]

Equal parts self and non-self, male and female, Shakespeare's merged Phoenix-Turtle audaciously rejects Aristotle's binary-enforcing laws, which is why it so threatens Reason. Reason's judgement arises from Property's complaint, which warrants a closer look.

> Property was thus appalled
> That the self was not the same:
> Single Nature's double name
> Neither two nor one was called.
>
> (37–40)

Property, 'appalled' that 'the self was not the same' ($P = -P$), issues a complaint to Reason: the Phoenix-Turtle, 'single nature's double name', exists in violation of the law of Identity ($P = P$) and Non-Contradiction ($P \neq -P$). Impossibly, 'Phoenix' equals 'Phoenix-Turtle', and vice versa. Reason reacts:

> Reason in itself confounded
> Saw Division grow together;
> To themselves yet either-neither,
> Simple were so well compounded.
>
> (41–44)

Reason's observation, 'To themselves yet either-neither', accords with Property's complaint. The idea is impossible because 'neither' requires two reference points whereas only one, the Phoenix-Turtle, now exists; as one critic put it, this creates 'an Escher-esque impossible logic circuit, recreating the implosion of Reason in the reader's confusion'.[38] 'Division', too, wades into unrealizable territory,

Shakespeare's Queer Analytics

violating logic by way of mathematics: It '[grows] together' as the two beings become one. The unitive love between the Phoenix and Turtle dissolves the proper boundaries of Property. Reason, 'confounded', carries Property's complaint to its logical conclusion: 'Love hath reason, Reason none, / If what parts can so remain' (47–8). Why must Love's version of reason, yielding 'a concordant one' (46), 'simple' and 'well compounded', not 'remain'? As described in a dazzling specular metaphor in stanza nine, the love between the two birds resists logical categorization or containment:

> So between them love did shine,
> That the Turtle saw his right
> Flaming in the Phoenix' sight;
> Either was the others mine.

> (33–36)

Love, if it 'hath reason', would express it thus: 'Phoenix' is 'Phoenix-Turtle' or 'Turtle' is 'Phoenix-Turtle' ('either was the others mine'). The chain of logic reads: if 'Phoenix' is 'Phoenix-Turtle', then 'Phoenix' must be 'not-Phoenix' ($P = -P$) and 'Turtle' must be 'not-Turtle' ($P = -P$). Therefore, according to the 'reason' of Love, Aristotle's Law of Identity ($P = P$) is false. 'Neither two nor one were called': the Phoenix-Turtle, defying the laws of Identity and Non-Contradiction, and so too the Excluded Middle (either P or -P; 'Phoenix' is 'Phoenix', 'Turtle' is 'Turtle'), is a third or non-binary object, something empirically observable yet utterly indescribable in Aristotelian terms. The creature is an error insofar as it cannot be comprehended in terms that satisfy prevailing conceptions of reason. Yet, the form of non-normative love that unites the Phoenix with the dove, along with the shocking unreasonableness of their demise, debunks the computationally derived laws dictating the ways in which their bodies have been identified and subsequently eviscerated. By introducing the conjoined Phoenix-Turtle as an actuality within a universe governed by binary logic, the speaker of this poem – having sent the dead Phoenix back into the poem's world, alive – flagrantly 'disproves' Aristotelian logic itself.

I indulge this notational practice not to argue that Shakespeare himself would be interested in such bald diagrammatics, but because

Queer Logic and 'The Phoenix and Turtle'

his poem reveals the limitations of such quasi-computational schemas when attempting to grasp the quality of a being that resists normative taxonomical rationality. The unintelligible but still actual forms of identity and desire precipitated by the merging of the birds initiates a logical crisis that is also deeply existential. This is precisely how computation begets queerness: it arises in response to the algorithm, the script, as a critical reaction to its normativizing impulses. In terms of a trans or non-binary theory of identity, the poem militates less against the possibility of knowing and naming the taxonomically resistant being than in asking: To what end exactly is this analysis directed? Who or what is being served in making this kind of articulation? Why, in short, must what exists in potential be subjected to the laws of an arbitrary real that then determines what is permissible within the actual?[39] The speaker's invocation, we recall, heralds a subtle but pointed notion of non-binary intelligibility in granting the crow and eagle (each containing traces of both chastity and tyranny) places at the session; in the grasp of Reason, whose job it is to interrogate its subjects through cycles of analysis that determine what is allowed to exist, such subtlety of thought is simply incomprehensible. Reason behaves exactly like a computational script, using a language of binary signals to detect what can or cannot stand within its program; 'confounded', it simply rejects, despite itself, that which does not pass its conditional judgements ('If what parts can so remain'). While Reason is sympathetic, it seems fundamentally incapable of understanding that which does not behave according to its algorithmic decrees. The consequences of Reason's profoundly unsubtle reasoning devastates both Reason itself and the universe over which it holds rational sovereignty.[40]

That Reason's immutable tenets dictate the parameters of desire and existence for bodies is the focus of the poem's critique is made apparent when one examines the nature of the birds' 'infirmity', detailed in the anthem:

> So they lov'd, as love in twain
> Had the essence but in one;
> Two distincts, division none:
> Number there in love was slain.

Shakespeare's Queer Analytics

> Hearts remote, yet not asunder;
> Distance, and no space was seen
> 'Twixt the turtle and his queen;
> But in them it were a wonder.

(25–32)

Love, assuming 'essence' not merely metaphysically but bodily 'in twain', disgusts Property, which holds not only sovereignty but also an acute sense of judgment over the material realm. Again, given this crucial distinction, the pressing intellectual dilemma of 'Phoenix' cannot be consigned wholly to Neoplatonic discussions on the nature of unity in love. If that were the case, there is no logical reason why the actual bodies of the birds must perish. But Shakespeare's version of Reason, meddling clumsily in affairs of the heart in language that cannot begin to account for its infinite subtleties, poses a parallel that results in nothing less than the death of 'Beauty, Truth, and Rarity'. With the death of the inosculated Phoenix-Turtle, the poem effectively declares the death of embodied potentiality itself. Reason commits a most profound error in judgement, for which the Phoenix-Turtle, once-living proof of the fallibility of Aristotle's syllogism, must perish. Reason's decision places reason – and also 'Reason' itself – in jeopardy. Absurdly, following its conclusion ($P = -P = false$), Reason piously laments the birds' deaths then proceeds to expose their 'infirmity' (60). If, as Marston exclaims in his response to this poem, Reason makes any sense at all, it is difficult to locate the kind of sense it is making. In stark contrast with the assured voice of the invocation, Reason's tone is best characterized by how 'confounded' it is by its predicament. Reason's reason simply does not compute.

The poem's critique of reason, however, does not end with this blatant attack on Aristotelian logic. I believe that it may also be taking aim at Ramism itself. Ramus inveighed against Aristotelian logic as being 'unnatural' in that it requires the use of 'two logics', one for rhetoric and one for dialectic. 'Phoenix', I have been arguing, levies a critique of logic on the basis that it should not be applied to real-world scenarios that may defy logical explanation. But Aristotelianism, in fact, offers a parallel if deeply flawed logic to deal with precisely

Queer Logic and 'The Phoenix and Turtle'

this problem; it is under Ramism that the two logics collapse into one 'method', which is said to be the universal means by which any problem might be solved. The poem, which doubles reason, is therefore as critical of Ramistic reform as it is of misapplied or shallow deployments of Aristotelianism: neither approach is sophisticated enough to make totalizing claims about the physical world. Reason, 'in itself', whatever form it may take, is precisely what is at stake. The poem seems to say, Keep your Reason off my body, because it cannot begin to understand me. Reason the character is not just a caricature of Aristotle or Aristotelian-scholastics, but of their critics, too – a recognition that Ramus's gutting of metaphysics merely replicates the problem in another form. Though the speaker of the opening lines of the poem does not address Reason, it seems intuitively to want it gone, for it to join the 'shrieking harbinger' of stanza two and simply buzz off. It effectively performs a 'read' of the logical traditions represented by Reason without referencing Aristotelianism or Ramism directly, throwing shade at Reason and leaving it dumbfounded by its own incompetence.

A natural perspective, that is and is not!

The malleability and multiplicity of Reason's 'reason' reaches its apex when we turn to its final determinations in 'Threnos'. Composed in the same seven-syllable line as the first thirteen quatrains, Reason's verse condenses poetic form by eliminating the binary couplet, the separate but unified structural centre of the poem's stanzas prior to this sombre concluding section. In 'Threnos', the couplet, and all discussion or appreciation of union-in-binaries, disappears as the voice of Reason commences a dirge in a succession of five cascading tercets.[41] It contains the poem's second-most puzzling stanza:

> Leaving no posterity,
> 'Twas not their infirmity;
> It was married Chastity.

(59–61)

Shakespeare's Queer Analytics

Ronald Bates observes that the lines 'sound almost like a Falstaffian quip at some over fanatic Puritan pair. The double-rhyme, extended for three lines, could scarcely help hovering on the verge of comic.'[42] Using simple, unadorned language, Reason reveals the explicit nature of the birds' 'infirmity', arguing in enthymeme: 'Leaving no posterity / 'Twas not their infirmity'; then it is something else, 'married chastity'. Earlier in the poem, in the invocation, chastity receives a positive valuation by the speaker; it is the very moral principle around which the poem's social order is organized. How, then, does it become associated in these lines with 'infirmity'? While generations of critics have struggled to wrangle this stanza into sense, I would argue that Reason here actually does not and cannot make sense – that it has reached the apex of its absurdity. The point here is not that Reason's lament contains a cryptic hint at the 'nature' of the birds' infirmity, but rather, that Reason has made a mistake in attempting to label and confine it whatsoever. The contradiction it poses is patently ridiculous and is supposed to stand as such; the poem wants us to view this judgement over and against the ethical determinations of the authorial voice of the invocation, to which the reader is compelled by design to return upon the realization that the Phoenix may be revived in its opening lines. In contrast with the speaker's positive, uncontroversial valuation of 'chaste wings' (4), Reason's conclusion that 'married chastity' constitutes some obscure cosmic 'infirmity' yields the insight that sense can lead to nonsense, which can in turn lead to needless death and destruction.

Upon examining the nature of the 'Infirmitie' through an Aristotelian lens, we are left with a poem that prevails upon logic to demand ambiguity. Just as there is no single 'bird of loudest lay, / On the sole *Arabian* tree' (1–2), there is no one version of Reason, Property, or Beauty to be understood. Knight, again, brilliantly captures the queer sprit of this poem: 'Neither duality nor unity, both being "numbers," properly exist. We have not merely a transcending of duality: rather the duality-unity dualism is itself transcended. Division is now unity, unity division, the self no more the self and reason the only irrationality.'[43] In its announcement, 'Truth may seem, but cannot be', Reason effectively abdicates the throne of reason. If there is

Queer Logic and 'The Phoenix and Turtle'

no truth, Reason is just an absurdity, a stage-presence, a clever myth-giver, as sincere and as foolish – and as paradoxically self-eviscerating – as Falstaff, the archetypal clown or court jester whom Shakespeare casts in moments of epistemological crisis. Right up to the revelation that the Phoenix is reborn in stanza one, the only force that retains its constancy in 'Phoenix' is love, carried on through a 'sigh', a spectral immateriality to which Reason and Property turn with a jolting mix of admiration and repugnance.

What, then, is the authorial voice of this poem saying about reason, and do we see evidence of this queer critical attitude elsewhere in Shakespeare? In my last chapter I claimed that Shakespeare was not alone in his views on reason, that he finds in Marston and Chester kindred spirits on the topic of reason's relationship to desire. In their contributions to the Poetical Essays, love unproblematically contradicts reason. While this determination comes as no surprise – few today would argue that love and reason should be included in the same sphere of discussion – this was not always the dominant view; we have seen, for example, Chapman and Jonson espousing the notion that true love requires the mediating presence of reason. The modern view that love is basically irrational is indeed a Shakespearean notion, and it is articulated across the canon. Such a perspective positively animates the romantic tragedies but also rears its head in non-romantic contexts, as in *Lear* (Edgar, horrified by Lear's speech and his crown of weeds and flowers, exclaims in an aside: 'O matter and impertinency mixed, / Reason in madness' [4.6.170–171]), and in moments of high comedy, as in *A Midsummer Night's Dream*. After Puck erroneously applies Oberon's eye-elixir to Lysander, the youth awakens beside Helena and finds himself suddenly enamoured of her instead of the woman he fled from Athens to marry: 'The will of man is by his reason swayed, / And reason says you are the worthier maid' (2.2.119–120).[44] Binary logic, too, is almost always invoked in order to be unmasked and deconstructed, as in offhand but loaded moments in *Troilus and Cressida* ('This is and is not Cressid.' [5.2.153]) and *Twelfth Night*, where a befuddled Orsino declares of Viola and Sebastian, 'One face, one voice, one habit and two persons: / A natural perspective, that is and is not'! (5.1.212–213).

125

Shakespeare's Queer Analytics

Of course, Shakespeare's critique of reason in 'Phoenix' need not be understood in this broader theatrical context in order for it to be intelligible. But these examples show how Shakespeare's queer analytics – his reckoning of how the computational begets the queer – animate more than just this tiny poem, though no other work of his puts this idea into effect so spectacularly. More than anything else Shakespeare wrote, the poem is a veritable a nexus of tensions regarding the function of reason in its moment of production. In the poem's anthem, we recall, Reason stands 'confounded', outside the very bounds of comprehension. The idea that as the Phoenix doubles, reason splits, is reinforced upon turning to the poem's original orthography, which I duplicate here:

> Reason in itselfe confounded,
> Saw Diuision grow together,
> To themselues yet either neither,
> Simple were so well compounded.
>
> That it cried, how true a twaine,
> Seemeth this concordant one,
> **Loue hath Reason, Reason none,**
> If what parts, can so remaine.

(45–52, emphasis mine)

What are the interpretive stakes of insisting upon a return to the original typographic context of the second to last line? According to most editors, lower-case 'reason', a concept or mode, is explicitly contrasted here with 'Reason', the character who presides over the funeral and issues the series of judgments that lead, one must presume implicitly, to their inexplicable and unexplained deaths. What might be the implications of asserting, as the original language of the text seems to do, that 'Love *hath* [upper-case] *Reason*', the personified, speaking figure of this poem, and not merely 'reason', the attendant but categorically distinct cognitive mode? In other words, might 'Love's' grasp of 'Reason in itself', in the face of the dazzling paradoxes presented in the poem's anthem, have altered its character – changed its very essence – thereby enabling it to declare its own annihilation

Queer Logic and 'The Phoenix and Turtle'

in 'Threnos'? If so, might then the very 'reason' of 'Love', and the rhetoric of purposiveness and futurity appointed to a heteronormative conception of the term, have become destabilized in these lines?

These are admittedly speculative questions. Yet, the poem's concerns with problematizing categories underwritten by Aristotelian binaries requires one to imagine a poet keenly aware of the intellectual, erotic, and existential consequences of adopting terms such as 'reason' in any neutral sense. Such a reading has implications for the poem's form as well as its temporal structure. We recall that the first part of the poem, written in the conditional, concerns an event that is about to happen; the anthem, occurring in the present tense, takes place in real time, as the reader encounters these words, though the substance of the anthem is in its description of an event that has already transpired; and 'Threnos', spoken by Reason, is an event supposed at first to be occurring in the present but which, upon closer inspection, is the chronological conclusion to and continuation of the narrative established in the anthem, revealed by the lines 'Whereupon [Reason] made this Threne … As chorus to their tragic scene'. The anthem tells us in no uncertain terms that the Threne is embedded within the swan's song, so it technically is not a performance unto itself, even if it is typographically represented as such. The poem, then, exhibits a bizarre atemporality, by which I mean that it does not possess a moment or secure its own presence in time; its 'momentousness' is contained entirely in a description of events that occurred in the past, as related by observers. The sequence suggests that the character Reason is never actually present: its quoted speeches in the anthem have not been uttered in real-time but reconveyed for the sake of the audience, the community of the living granted allowance to attend the ceremony. The poem's very isness, its actuality in time, therefore belongs not to Reason but to the speaker, the convener of community, the poet himself and so too, the reader listening to his words. Markedly, the voice of the invocation, with its strident tone and concern with the social order and rank of the attendants, its lofty proclamations and decrees, contrasts both with Reason's befuddled posturing in 'Threnos' and the mathematical lyricism of the anthem. Its language and tone recalls Genesis, and in Shakespeare, can be

127

Shakespeare's Queer Analytics

found in the rousing military speeches of the Henriad. It is a voice in clear possession of its rational capabilities, demonstrating in its subtle deployment of reason that the categories through which we make sense of the world do not always conform to a formula that may be universally or indiscriminately applied.

The poem's temporal qua existential dilemma is most thoroughly envisioned in stanza seven, sitting at the precise midpoint of the thirteen quatrains preceding 'Threnos'.

> So they loved as love in twain,
> Had the essence but in one;
> Two distincts, Division none:
> Number there in love was slain.

(25–28)

That two contradictory voices dominate the first thirteen quatrains and markedly contrast each other in tone and intent may be demonstrated, amusingly, by severing the quatrains in half. At the exact mathematical centre of these 54 lines, we find the couplet: 'Had the essence but in one, / Two distincts, Diuision none', followed by the line: 'Number there in loue was slaine'. Here it is instructive, again, to consult the 1601 edition of the poem, which graphically reifies the idea that this kind of 'Diuision', while 'logical', has nothing to do with physical reality; at precisely this point, between lines 26 and 27, the page splits.[45] The speaker's invocation and the swan's anthem are absorbed and conjoined by the couplet, which refuses to 'divide' even when severed in two. 'Threnos', composed in meandering, mock-syllogistic tercets free of binary couplets, dissipates into a sigh of relief. Truth and Beauty dead, Reason no longer has a reason to exist, unless it is to contemplate the mysteries of $P = -P$ before the cinders of love's undying offspring, a tedious metaphysical project that Shakespeare would rather leave to the dunces.

* * *

I began this chapter by relinquishing the arsenal of digital tools that have driven the other parts of this book, but I want to conclude by returning briefly to data I present in chapter 1. It may offer another

Queer Logic and 'The Phoenix and Turtle'

way of understanding the recursive method of 'The Phoenix and Turtle' – a heuristic that takes us outside of the poem and even the Poetical Essays itself. I believe that 'Phoenix' may offer a hint at its relationship to the larger book, and potentially even to Shakespeare's meddling of Chester's verse, with its final line: 'For these dead birds, sigh a prayer'. 'Prayer' is a strange word with which to conclude a poem – it suggests new beginnings, new vistas, possibilities beyond what is circumscribed by the present and actual. We have seen how this line prompts the reader to return to the beginning of the poem, where a bird on 'the sole *Arabian* tree', undoubtedly the Phoenix, blasts its 'trumpet' to convene the poem's social order. I want to suggest that it may also refer to a critical section of verse in *Love's Martyr* that, per stylometric results in Chapter 1, carries a distinctly Shakespearean signal: a part of the book containing a brief sequence titled 'An Introduction to the Prayer' followed by 'A Prayer *made for the prosperitie of a* siluer coloured Doue, applyed to the *beauteous Phoenix*' (segment 4). It is here that we find an impassioned conversation between Nature and the Phoenix that begins with the Phoenix's complaint, 'O stay me not, I am no *Phoenix* I, / And if I be that bird, I am defaced', since the Phoenix can no longer perform its task of self-renewal; 'Vpon the *Arabian* mountaines I must die', she claims, because 'Such operation in me is not placed'.[46] The dysfunctional bird of this early verse distinctly recalls the Phoenix of Shakespeare's poem, which not only '[leaves] no posterity' but also suffers an acute identity crisis leading to its death. The literary parallels between the saturnine Phoenix of this early verse and Shakespeare's tragic protagonist are striking, and this verse is easily among the most lucid and compelling of anything signed by Chester.

The 'prayer' that concludes 'Phoenix' therefore hails the prayer that opens the book, perhaps guiding us to reread the entirety of *Love's Martyr* – and not just 'Phoenix' itself – in a recursive light, with a renewed consideration of the potentialities that have been and will be foreclosed in one way but also opened up in another. If, as the King of France surmises in *All's Well that Ends Well*, 'what impossibility would slay / In common sense, sense saves another way', then this splintered-off 'sense' achieves its goal by taking on a form that cannot be corrupted or destroyed by that which is held in 'common'. The

129

Shakespeare's Queer Analytics

queer love between the Phoenix and Turtle may lead to their deaths on one register – the sense ordained by the logic of normative sociality – but at the same time, or perhaps in parallel time, lives on, defying the world in its radiant and unapologetic queerness.

This is precisely how 'The Phoenix and Turtle' both generates and resolves the antisocial and utopic tensions in queer theory. Its doubly recursive structure suggests both the end of futurity and the opening of an entirely new order: a formal and perceptual revolution grounded in an eschatological poetics that requires one to imagine the very destruction of reason as commonly understood. At once utopic and apocalyptic, hopeful and anti-relational, 'Phoenix' posits a conception of logic that makes Reason look nonsensical – and a conception of love that quite literally creates or 'makes sense'.

AFTERWORD

Speaking of the rift between Renaissance studies and black feminism, Kim Hall famously attempted 'to join together, often with ragged edges, fields that are, for the most part, invisible to each other'.[1] In a similar critical sprit, I have essayed in this book a synthesis of queer and computational methods to chart a path towards reimagining *Love's Martyr*'s stylistically as well as erotically disruptive properties. The result, I hope, is a somewhat enlarged view of Shakespeare's collaborative activity at a time when he is thought to have been working largely in isolation. In this modest way, I have duly hailed the spirit of Hall's critical injunction. Yet in another, more important sense, this book just barely scratches the surface. To put it baldly: Too many of the critics and theorists I have cited are white, heterosexual men. In a large sense, the book is a product of its chosen areas of focus and figures of study. With continued critique and self-examination, though, we might imagine a future for early modern computational scholarship where black, queer, and queer of colour voices figure both more centrally and more prominently. The reason for such advocacy, of course, is more than merely symbolic or axiological: Critical conversations occurring outside of 'early modern studies' or 'computational studies' or 'queer studies' offer ways to revitalize these fields and to reassess how we have been trained to look at and care for them. Without queer of colour critique, my second chapter, with its focus on 'shade', would never have been possible. I hope then at least to have touched on the interpretive potentiality of integrating marginalized voices and perspectives within the fields I have brought together – fields that are perhaps the whitest and most self-consciously elite of any that routinely brush up against the early modern.

Shakespeare's Queer Analytics

This concern brings me to a claim made in my introduction over the epistemological power of the queer outlier. Computation is already queer, I have claimed, insofar as it gives us insight into aspects of a text that may otherwise go ignored; it is also, though not always, particularly attuned to aberrant or outlying data. But we can bring the queer and the computational into even closer proximity by examining data that threatens to disrupt *our own* assumptions about a given object – data or knowledge that would trouble a long-standing narrative that has, through traditional criticism or empirical methods, become calcified and entrenched. Queerness in this sense is not just about resisting or rejecting an externalized notion of the norm, some telos that we identify as existing outside of ourselves, but rather about looking at how normativities emerge from and multiply within – especially, in our writing and our arguments. Sometimes, perhaps, we need to turn against ourselves, our very claims and intuitions, in order to avoid becoming unwitting participants in larger homogenizing and normativizing stories. Computation, with its outstanding ability to undermine our ideas and expectations exactly as we articulate them, offers one methodological way to enact this form of queer critical address. Unlike a textual passage we might simply ignore because it does not conform to our argumentative plans, a computational result that butts up against our ideas may threaten to reduce them to cinders. In this way computational data can be perilous, taxing, and profoundly revealing, forcing us to examine the most intimate and ingrained aspects of our very function as critics.

Of course, understandably, this process may be too stressful for some or outright uninteresting to others – to be sure, not all studies require the presence or even suggestion of computation. Even so, as I hope to have shown in my chapter on 'The Phoenix and Turtle', to think about literature in terms of computation need not require a capitulation to large-scale quantitative processes. As the exciting field of early modern mathematics shows us, we do not need to be computer programmers in order to explore computational analogies, metaphors, plot points, and formal considerations. In the early modern period and well beyond, literature percolates with unsettling and strange computational activity; we see it in the fantastic geometry

Afterword

of Lewis Carroll, the aphoristic postulations of Ludwig Wittgenstein, the punishing logical paradoxes of M. NourBese Philip and Jamaica Kincaid. A queer analytical study might examine, for instance, Wittgenstein's *Tractatus* as a work of queer theory or Gertrude Stein's *Three Lives* as a critique of Aristotelian logic. It might consider relationships between the multivalent logics animating Virginia Woolf's *To the Lighthouse* and *Orlando* – how does her thinking about the relationship between number and identity evolve over these projects? It might look, too, at poetic forms such as the sestina or line arrangements such as trochaic tetrameter in terms of something like queer algorithmic activity.[2] The possibilities, as they say, are infinite.

With its anti-normative impulses and tendencies, its resistances to positivist and mechanistic ways of ordering the world, queerness might be the exact logical counterpoint to computation – that very constitutive absence without which its binarily opposed term would signify. Each term is epistemologically embedded in the other. The queer is the very category that escapes, destroys, undermines, mocks, or critiques computation, which means precisely that it depends upon computation for its existence and power. It may therefore offer singular insight into some of the most disquieting and threatening aspects of computational culture, from 'the neoliberal drive toward the capture and exploitation of the self by technology' to 'the demands of pervasive visibility by means of always-on devices'.[3] Or, it might help us see how '[d]ata, much like the figure of the child evoked by Edelman, is a political trope through which we are coerced into the promise that more data collected now will lead to a better and brighter future'.[4] Queerness may offer a way out of these dilemmas that is also an insidious way back in, that is, the means by which to enter through the rear in order to corrupt, recalibrate, and redirect the neoliberal telos of 'compulsory data production' towards something fuzzy, sexy, and liberatory – something indeed like the radical promise of Jose Esteban Muñoz's queer utopia.[5] Arising from the very act of living at odds with itself, the queer 'gives life' by making joy out of trouble. It consumes itself over and over, in an endless cycle of agon and ecstasy, so that it may be reborn and thereby 'sigh a prayer' and 'live [its] truth', whatever form this may take.

APPENDIX 1
TECHNICAL APPENDIX

This appendix contains important data and information deemed either too specific or too general to be included in the preceding chapters. Issues addressed include text processing steps, text processing methods, technical information on Robert Chester's "Pellican" verse and "Conclusion," and tables of data referred to earlier in the book.

Text preprocessing steps

The corpora tested in this study were compiled using the following pre-processing steps. These steps are fairly typical of those performed in attribution and other computational tests: (1) copy the text from *Early English Books Online* (EEBO) into a UTF-8 Unicode file format (a .txt document); (2) remove transcription artefacts; correct errors or supply missing information from EEBO's *Text Creation Partnership* (TCP) sourced from facsimile or critical editions that retain original spelling; replace hyphens with a space; (3) normalize and expand symbols and diacritics ('&' changes to 'and', 'ö' changes to 'o', 'æ' changes to 'ae', etc.); (4) perform 'scrubbing' (make all letters lowercase, remove digits, remove punctuation, remove line breaks and formatting); perform 'tokenization' (each word is represented as a 1-gram feature); (5) perform 'chunking' (divide the text into even length segments of words, e.g. 1500, 2000, 2500, etc.);[1] and (6) create a frequency table for most frequent words to be used in analysis.[2] This data in turn may be visualized a number of ways, as in the dendrograms of Chapters 1 and 2. This same data was also used for Network Analysis (Plate 10) and other methods, as described below.

---

[1] See Maciej Eder, 'Does Size Matter? Authorship Attribution, Small Samples, Big Problem', *Digital Scholarship in the Humanities* 30.2 (2015): 167–82 and 'Short Samples in Authorship Attribution: A New Approach,' *DH* (2017).

[2] Texts not sourced from EEBO include Chester's and Salusbury's poems in Christ Church manuscript 184 sourced from Carleton Brown, which were keyboarded *ad literatim*. Poems attributed to Salusbury by Brown but disputed by G. Blakemore Evans

Technical Appendix

Processing methods

We chose Classic Delta as the distance metric since 'this measure relies on z-scores – –i.e. normalized word frequencies', which were considered when creating the table of frequencies from normalized samples.[3] We also used a 'culling' percentage to increase the likelihood of similar comparisons. The 'culling' percentage refers to the process of removing words from the table of frequencies that do not appear in the chosen percentage of texts.[4]

The corpora were assessed using various stylometric tools provided by the *stylo* package for the programming suite R, and for the network analysis we used the visualization tool, Gephi.[5] The analysis methods include: Hierarchical Cluster Analysis (CA), Principal Component Analysis (PCA), Bootstrap Consensus Trees (BCT), Network Analysis, Rolling Stylometry, and supervised machine learning classifiers Support Vector Machines (SVM), and Nearest Shrunken Centroids (NSC).

Hierarchical Cluster Analysis (CA) is a method for building a hierarchy of clusters based on a metric (or a measure of distance between pairs of observations) and a linkage criterion, which specifies the dissimilarity of sets as a function of the pairwise distances of observations in the sets. The clusters are shown in a dendrogram, or a visualization of the clusters.[6]

Principal Component Analysis (PCA) 'is a method of condensing multiple features into "principal components," components that represent, somewhat closely, but not perfectly, the amount of variance in the data'.[7] This method reduces the dimensionality of datasets thereby increasing the interpretability of the graph. PCA results upheld our other findings, but were not suited for meaningful reproduction in this book.

---

in favour of authorship by Robert Parry were not included in this study. See Brown, *Poems by Sir John Salusbury and Robert Chester*, xl–xlvii and Evans, *The Poems of Robert Parry* (Tempe: Arizona Center for Medieval and Renaissance Studies, 2005), 10–23.

[3] Maciej Eder, Jan Rybicki, and Mike Kestemont, '"Stylo": A Package for Stylometric Analyses', *Computational Stylistics Group* (2018): 16.

[4] Ibid., 13.

[5] Ibid., 27–8.

[6] For issues related to cluster analysis see Maciej Eder, 'Visualization in Stylometry: Cluster Analysis Using Networks', *Digital Scholarship in the Humanities* 32 (2017): 53–5.

[7] Matthew L. Jockers, *Macroanalysis: Digital Methods and Literary History* (Urbana: University of Illinois Press, 2013), 67.

Technical Appendix

Bootstrap Consensus Trees (BCT) are the output of a statistically justified 'compromise' among several virtual cluster analyses from various parameters such as MFFW and culling values. The linkages appear based on the consensus tree strength value – in our case a setting of 50 % – which means that a linkage between two texts are made if that same link shows up in at least 50 % of the virtual cluster analyses. Maciej Eder explains that this method is a 'partial solution of the cherry-picking problem' associated with cluster analysis.[8]

Network Analysis plots visualize textual relations with text segments represented as the nodes and their relations represented as links between the nodes. Eder explains that the linkage is computed by two algorithms: one computes the distance between texts, establishing its strongest connection to its most similar text and the next two runners-up; the second algorithm uses the feature sets – in this case MFWs – and at what percentage they show up as a whole.[9] These connections produce 'snapshots' and are added into a consensus network ready for visualization through Gephi, software for graph and network analysis.[10]

For a network visualization of the works of all players involved in this study, see Plate 10.

Supervised machine learning methods for authorship attribution, specifically Support Vector Machines (SVM) and Nearest Shrunken Centroids (NSC), are classification methods not specifically built for authorship attribution but have been shown to be effective in authorship attribution problems.[11] These classifiers use a 'training set' of texts by known authors and a 'test set' of texts. The models use tuning parameters and differ on how the features used to determine authorship are selected and processed. SVM 'has a single tuning parameter, which determines the cost of violating the constraints', whereas NSC 'has one

---

[8] Eder, 'Visualization in stylometry', 55.

[9] Eder, (et al.), '"Stylo": A Package for Stylometric Analyses', 27–8.

[10] Mathieu Bastian, Sebastien Heymann, and Mathieu Jacomy, 'Gephi: An Open Source Software for Exploring and Manipulating Networks', *International AAAI Conference on Web and Social Media* (2009).

[11] See Matthew L. Jockers and Daniela M. Witten, 'A Comparative Study of Machine Learning Methods for Authorship Attribution', *Literary and Linguistic Computing* 25.2 (2010): 215–23.

Technical Appendix

tuning parameter, which controls the number of features used.'[12] We used these supervised machine learning classifiers in combination with Eder's 'rolling.classify' and 'classify' functions of the 'stylo' package.[13]

Authorship of *Love's Martyr's* 'Pellican' and 'Conclusion' (segment 29)

As discussed in Chapter 2, the final dialectical turn introduced in the Poetical Essays appears some 40 pages before it, in Chester's

Table A1.1 'Pellican' and 'The Phoenix and Turtle' stylistic similarities[14]

Chester's 'Pellican'	Shakespeare
'With what a spirit did the *Turtle* flye	'*Phoenix* and the *Turtle* fled,
Into the fire … And both together in that fire do burne.'	In a mutuall flame from hence.'
'Because that two in one is put by Nature.'	Single Natures double name, Neither two nor one was called.'
'If that the *Phoenix* have bene separated, And from the gentle *Turtle* had bene parted,	So they loued as loue in twaine, Had the essence but in one, Two distincts, Diuision none,
Loue had bene murdred in the infancie.	Number there in loue was slaine.'
Without these two no loue at all can be.	'Truth may seeme, but cannot be.'
Let the loue wandring wits but learne of these, To die together, so their griefe to ease.'	'To this vrne let those repaire, That are either true or faire, For these dead Birds, sigh a prayer.'
'Though as these two did, deaths arrest they proue.'	'If what parts, can so remaine.'

[12] Jockers and Witten, 'A comparative study of machine learning methods for authorship attribution', 217.

[13] See Maciej Eder, 'Rolling Stylometry', *Digital Scholarship in the Humanities* 31.3 (2016): 457–69.

[14] This chart appears in Matchett, *The Phoenix and the Turtle*, 81.

138

Technical Appendix

'Pellican' poem and his 'Conclusion', which immediately precede the volume's Cantos. William Matchett demonstrated that 'Pellican' bears a great number of stylistic similarities with Shakespeare's 'Phoenix'; I reproduce his chart above (Table A1.1).

These parallels, of course, are too numerous and strong to be mere coincidence; as Matchett puts it, '[t]he similarities of idea and diction in Shakespeare's poem and Chester's "Pellican" force us to conclude that the relationship is direct … the cumulative effect of the common details is inescapable'.[15] The connections suggest either that Shakespeare, who we already know must have read some of Chester's poem, picked up these terms and notions from Chester and used them as the basis for 'The Phoenix and Turtle', or perhaps the influence was the other way around. Matchett, whose opinion of Chester is particularly low, supposes that given 'Chester's proclivity toward literary packratting', he 'was unable to resist appropriating and setting forth over his own signature as many of the ideas he could incorporate into a further comment'.[16] Computational tests performed on 'Pellican' and Chester's brief two-stanza 'Conclusion' using most frequent words illuminate this discussion in two ways (Figure A1.2).

Tests comparing *Love's Martyr* to Shakespearean material outside of the book consistently indicate dissimilarity between his work and segment 29, containing both 'Pellican' and 'Conclusion' (e.g. see Figure A1.1). In fact, in other graphs, tests variously show affiliations between segment 29 and work by Chapman and Jonson. In Figures A1.2 (a snapshot of a larger dendrogram containing works by all the contributing poets) and A1.3 (a dendrogram of *Love's Martyr* compared with Chapman's poetry), the verse appears closely aligned

---

[15] In a footnote, Matchett adds, '[t]he poems share … identical words used in unrelated ways ("grace" and "breath"); related though not identical forms ("wondrous" and "wonder," "true" and "Truth," "pleasant wings" and "chaste wings," "mourne" and "mourners," "sadnesse" and "sad"); and finally the key words, "beautie," "loue," "constancie," "chastitie" and "raritie."' Matchett, *The Phoenix and the Turtle*, 81.

[16] Matchett, *The Phoenix and the Turtle*, 82–3.

139

Technical Appendix

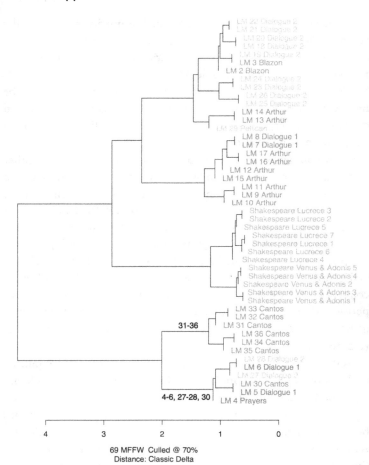

Figure A1.1 Dendrogram of *Love's Martyr* and *Venus and Adonis* and *Rape of Lucrece*

with Chapman's work; here, too, segment 2 of *Love's Martyr*, containing Chester's blazon, also appears Chapmanian.

The 'Pellican' verse is statistically aberrant or queer in that it departs from the patterns we might expect – it is the only segment of text between contiguous segments 27-28 (the Dialogue) and 30-36

Technical Appendix

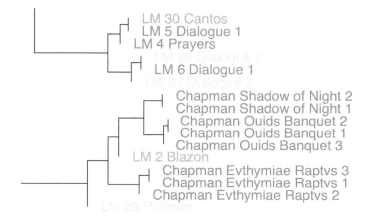

Figure A1.2 'Pellican' snapshot

(the Cantos) that falls into a different clade structure. Since 'Pellican' behaves so oddly in our tests and is, on its surface, perhaps the most obvious example in all of *Love's Martyr* of authorial transplantation, the results are at best inconclusive – there is simply too much noise, too much stylistic queerness, to make any kind of positive determination. However, the data should not then be regarded as altogether useless, as it seems to rule out Shakespeare as having contributed to this section in any meaningful way. In all, then, I am inclined to consider Chester's 'Pellican' and 'Conclusion' as of a piece with the other collaboratively written verse in the book – a poem written and signed by Chester but which nonetheless bears the multiple impressions of his 'best-minded friends'. Chester's additions, are probably best understood to be 'comments on the contributed poems' – poems that could not have been completed without the rest of the poetic coterie, but which ultimately betray, again to use Fred Moten's term, a Chesterian singularity.[17] Figure A1.3 indicates, again, the strange connection between 'Pellican' and Chapman's verse.

---

[17] Matchett, *The Phoenix and the Turtle*, 82.

Technical Appendix

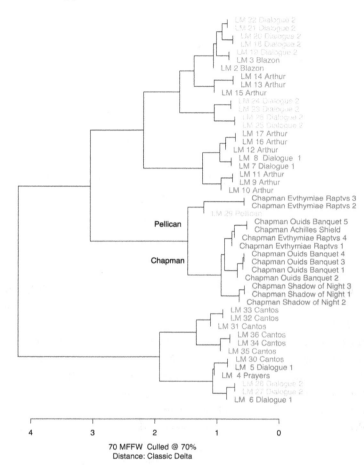

Figure A1.3 Dendrogram of *Love's Martyr* and Chapman's poetry

Table of 'Arabian' in *Love's Martyr*

When the word 'Arabian' appears in *Love's Martyr*, it is almost always preceded or followed by phoenix imagery. The connection between the phoenix and a bird setting upon the 'sole Arabian tree', as in Shakespeare's 'The Phoenix and Turtle', is unmistakable. See Chapter 3 for other examples in Shakespeare's plays.

Technical Appendix

Table A1.2 Table of 'Arabian' in *Love's Martyr*

LM	Left Context	Keyword	Right Context
2	Far whiter then the milke-white lillie flower. O might	*Arabian*	*Phoenix* come inuisible, And on this mountaine build a glorious bower.
3	And her rich beauty for to equalize: The	*Arabian*	fiers are too dull and base, To make another spring within her place.
3	Looke on that painted picture there, behold The rich wrought *Phoenix* of	*Arabian*	gold. *Ioues* eyes were setled on her painted eyes,
3	*Nature* go hie thee, get thee *Phoebus* chaire, Cut through the skie, and leaue	*Arabia,*	Leaue that il working peece of fruitlesse ayre,
3	Bringing increase from one to number twentie, As Lycorice and sweet	*Arabian*	spice: No place is found vnder bright heauens faire blisse,
5	And if I be that bird, I am defaced, Vpon the	*Arabian*	mountaines I must die, And neuer with a poore yong Turtle graced;
6	Banisht for euer comming any more: But in	*Arabia*	burnes another Light, A darke dimme Taper that I must adore,
21	From their fresh springing loines there shall arise. Theres *Rosemarie,* the	*Arabians*	justifie, (*Phisitions* of exceeding perfect skill,) It comforteth the braine and Memorie.
27	Already buried in the graue of wo. *Phoenix*: Why I haue left	*Arabia*	for thy sake, Because those fires haue no working substance,
40	Let the bird of lowdest lay, On the sole	*Arabian*	tree, Herauld sad and trumpet be: To whose sound chaste wings obay.

Technical Appendix

G. Wilson Knight Comparison Table

The following table contains comparisons made by G. Wilson Knight between *Love's Martyr* and Shakespeare's works. On the left, you will see the segment number in which the verse may be found. See our ribbon diagram (Plate 7) for comparison. Note, our stylometric tests indicate that segments 4-6, 27-28, and 30-36 carry a certain Shakespearean signal. See Chapter 1 for further analysis.

Table A1.3 G. Wilson Knight comparison table

LM	*Love's Martyr*	Knight's Shakespearian Connections
2	Her breasts **two crystal orbes of whitest white**.(4/12)	*The Rape of Lucrece* 407 Her breasts like **ivory globes** circled with blue.
5	*Nature*: Tell me (O Mirrour) of our earthly time, Tell me sweete *Phoenix* glorie of mine age, Who blots thy Beauty with foule *Enuies* crime, And locks thee vp in fond *Suspitions* cage? Can any humane heart beare thee such rage? Daunt their proud stomacks with thy piercing Eye, Vnchaine Loues sweetnesse at thy libertie. (18/26)	'The poetry is often powerful; some of it is reminiscent, and parts not unworthy, of Shakespeare; and whatever be the exact meaning, the Sonnets are continually recalled.' (Knight, 158)
27	*Phoenix*: Haile **map of sorrow**: *Tur*: Welcome *Cupid's* child. (125/133)	Sonnet 68 Thus is his cheek the **map of days** outworn, When beauty lived and died as flowers do now.

Technical Appendix

27   Come poore lamenting soule,
come sit by me,
We are all one, thy sorrow shall
be mine,
Fall thou a teare, and thou shalt
plainly see.

                  (125/133)

Antony and Cleopatra III.ix.70-71
ANTONY: **Fall not a tear**, I say;
one of them rates
All that is won and lost …

29   O fond corrupted age, when
birds shall show
The world their dutie, and to let
men know
That no sinister chaunce should
hinder loue,
Though as these two did, **deaths
arrest** they proue.
(133/141)

Hamlet, The Folio V.ii.291-92
Had I but time (**as this fell
sergeant Death
Is strict in his arrest**) …
Sonnet 74
But be contented when **that fell
arrest
Without all bail** shall carry me
away.

30   **Gold beautifying** *Phoenix*, I
must praise thee,
Graunt gracious heauens a
delightsome **Muse**,
Giue me **old** *Homers* **spirit**, and
Ile raise thee,
Gracious in thought do not my
Loue refuse,
Great **map of beauty** make thou
no excuse,
Gainst my true louing spirit do
not carpe,
**Grant me to play my Sonnet on
thy Harpe**.

                  (136/144)

'The "gold beautifying Phoenix"
is, as in Shakespeare's Sonnets,
the poet's "muse", able to give him
"old Homer's spirit."'

                  (Knight, 163)

Richard II V.i.11-13
Ah, thou, the model where old
Troy did stand,
Thou **map of honour**, thou King
Richard's tomb,
And not King Richard! …

30   **Looke** *Phoenix* **to thy selfe do
not decay**.

                  (137/145)

**Not being gathered in her
chiefest beauty,
Neglecting time it dies with
infamy**.

       (137/145-138/146)

'Phoenix is a rose which, if not
gathered at the time of "chiefest
beauty", will be thereafter
neglected.
All this recalls Shakespeare.'

                  (Knight, 174)

Technical Appendix

30	**Quite captiuate and prisner at thy call**. (138/146)	*Venus and Adonis* 110 **Leading him prisoner in a red-rose chain**.
		Sonnet 5 **A liquid prisoner pent in walls of glass**.
30	**Remember how thy beauty is abused, Ract on the tenter-hookes of foule disgrace**. (138/146)	'Even the circumstances of the Sonnets appear to be recalled. Shakespeare's Fair Youth was repeatedly charged with growing "common" and losing his good name, so that people are "making lascivious comments" on his "sport", and so on ([Sonnets] 69, 94, 95).' (Knight, 173)
30	**Shame is ashamed to see thee obstinate**. (139/147)	*Romeo and Juliet* III.ii.91-92 He was not born to shame; **Upon his brow shame is ashamed to sit …**
30	**Singing thy pride of beauty in her height**. (139/147)	*Sonnet 16* **Now stand you on the top of happy hours**.
		Sonnet 3 So thou through windows of thine age shalt see, Despite of wrinkles, **this thy golden time**.
		Sonnet 115 Alas, why, fearing of time's tyranny, Might I not then say, 'Now I love you best', When I was certain o'er uncertainty, **Crowning the present**, doubting of the rest?

Technical Appendix

		Sonnet 2
		Thy **youth's proud livery, so gazed on now**,
		Will be a tattered weed of small worth held.
30	**Thou art a** *Turtle* **wanting of thy mate**.	*The Winter's Tale* V.iii.131-34
	(139/147)	I, an old **turtle**,
		Will wing me to some withered bough, and there
		My **mate, that's never to be found again**,
		Lament till I am lost.
30	**To thy sweete selfe** thou canst not find another.	Sonnet 114
	(139/147)	Such cherubins as **your sweet self** resemble.
		Sonnet 126
		Who hast by waning grown, and therein show'st
		Thy lover's withering, as **thy sweet self** grow'st.
31	**My loue-layes in my Loues praise alwayes written**.	Sonnet 76
	(143/151)	O know, sweet love, **I always write of you**,
		And **you and love are still my argument**.
		Sonnet 108
		What's in the brain that **ink may character**
		Which hath not figured to thee my true spirit?
		What's new to speak, what new to register,
		That may express my love, or thy dear merit?
		Nothing, sweet boy; but yet, like prayers divine,
		I must each day say o'er the very same,

147

Technical Appendix

31 Disgrace be banisht from thy
    heauenly brow, Not entertained
    of thy **piercing eie**.

    (145/153)

32 The **ey-bals** in your head are
    Cupids **fire**,
    Darting such **hot sparkles** at my
    brest.

    (146/154)

32 Within the circuit of a **Christall
    spheare**,
    Thy **eyes** are plast, and
    vnderneath those **eyes**,
    Brest of **hard flint**, eares that do
    scorne to heare
    My dayes sad gronings, and night
    waking cries,
    Hart sore sicke passions, and
    Loues agonies,
    Doth it become thy beauty? no,
    a staine
    Rests on thy bright brow
    wrinckled with **disdaine**.

    (148/156)

Counting no old thing old; thou
mine, I thine,
Even as when first I hallowed thy
fair name.

Henry VI Part II III.i.154
Beaufort's **red sparkling eyes** blab
his heart's malice.

Henry VI Part II III.ii.317
Upon thy **eyeballs murderous
tyranny**
Sits in grim majesty to fright the
world.

Henry VI Part II III.ii.317
Mine **eyes** should **sparkle** like the
beaten flint.

Sonnet 119
How have mine **eyes** out of their
spheres been fitted
In this distraction of this
madding fever?

Sonnet 88
When thou shalt be disposed to
set me light
And place my merit in the **eye of
scorn**.

Venus and Adonis 240-41, 251-52
At this Adonis smiles as in
disdain,
That in each cheek appears a
pretty dimple:
…
Poor queen of love, in thine own
law forlorn,
To love a cheek that smiles at thee
in **scorn!**

Technical Appendix

32 My care to haue my blooming
Rose not wither,
Selfe-louing Enuie shall it not denie,
And that **base weed** thy growth
doth seeke to hinder,
Mine hands shall pull him vp
immediatly,
Are they not enuious monsters in
thine eie,
Always with vaine occasions to
inclose
Thine euer growing beautie, like
the Rose?

(145/153)

'Exactly so Shakespeare wrote of
his Fair Youth being trammeled
by various dangers in Sonnets 69
and 70.'
(Knight, 173)

Sonnet 94
The **basest weed** outbraves his
dignity:
For sweetest things turn sourest
by their deeds;
**Lilies that fester smell far worse
than weeds**.

32 Being enamored of rich Beauties
pride,
Absent, **I freeze in Winters
pining cold**.

(147/155)

Sonnet 97
How like a **winter hath my
absence been**
From thee, the pleasure of the
fleeting year!
What **freezings** have I felt, what
dark days seen,
What **old December's bareness
everywhere**!

Richard II V.i.76
KING RICHARD: … I towards
the north,
Where shivering **cold** and
sickness **pines** the clime.

32 **Die periur'd Enuie for thy late
offence**.

(147/155)

'Lines start up in Shakespearian
rhythm … '

(Knight, 172)

32 **Eye-dazling Mistris**, with a
looke of pittie,
Grace my sad Song, and my
hearts pining Dittie.

(147/155)

Your **eye-bals** do enwrap my
destinie.

(147/155)

149

Technical Appendix

33 You are my **Sunne**, my dayes
delightsome Queene,
I am your haruest laborer almost
mad,
Had I not my **glorious commet
seene**.

(150/158)

34 My *Phoenix* hath **two starre-
resembling Eyes**,
Heart full of pittie, and her
smiling looke.

(154/162)

Sonnet 119
How have mine **eyes** out of their
spheres been fitted
In this distraction of this
madding fever?

35 And from my faith that's
vnremoueable,
Fauour be seated in thy **maiden
eie**,
None can receiue it loue more
acceptable
But I my selfe, waiting thy
pittying mercie:
Me hast thou made the substance
of delight,
By thy faire **sunne-resembling**
heauenly sight.

(161/169)

Sonnet 147
Past cure I am, now reason is past
care,
And **frantic mad** with ever more
unrest.

33 My inward *Muse* can sing of
nought but Loue,
Thoughts are his Heralds, flying
to my breast.

(151/159)

Romeo and Juliet II.v.4-5
**Love's heralds should be
thoughts**,
Which ten times faster glides than
the sun's beams.

33 **Thou art that All-in-all that I
loue best**.

(151/159)

Sonnet 109
For nothing this wide universe I
call,
Save thou, my rose; in it **thou art
my all**.

Technical Appendix

33   Me thinkes it were your glorie for to find
Iust measure at my hands, but you to blame
Haue from the deepest closet of your heart,
Knowne my pure thoughts, and yet I **pine** in smart.

(152/160)

Sonnet 48
Thee have I not locked up in any chest,
Save where thou art not, though I feel thou art,
Within the gentle closure of my breast.

33   For in my bosomes chamber, I enroule
Your deepe **loue-darting eie**, and still will be
Owne of your owne, despight **extremitie**.

(152/160)

Romeo and Juliet III.ii.45-47
Hath Romeo slain himself? Say thou but 'Ay',
And that bare vowel 'I' shall poison more
Than the **death-darting eye** of cockatrice.

Sonnet 108
Counting no old thing old; **thou mine, I thine**,
Even as when first I hallowed thy fair name.

Pericles V.i.140
Like Patience gazing on kings' graves and **smiling**
Extremity out of act …

33   If adoration euer were created,
I am a **Maister** of that holy Art,
You my aduotrix, whom I haue admired,
Haue of my true deuotion bore a part …

(149/157)

A Lover's Complaint 246-52
"'O pardon me, in that my boast is true;
The accident which brought me to her eye
Upon the moment did her force subdue,
And now she would the caged cloister fly,
Religious love put out religion's eye;
Not to be tempted would she be immured,

Technical Appendix

And now to tempt all liberty procured.

Sonnet 31
How many a holy and obsequious tear
Hath **dear religious love** stol'n from mine eye.

36 Most reuerend **Mistris** honor of mine eie,
Deuine, most holy in **religious loue**,
And **Lord** itselfe of my hearts emperie,
Sacred in thoughts admitted from aboue.

(165/173)

All's Well That Ends Well
I.iii.197-203
Helen
I know I love in vain, strive against hope;
Yet in this captious and intenable sieve I still pour in the waters of my love
And lack not to lose still. Thus, Indian-like,
Religious in mine error, I adore
The sun that looks upon his worshipper,
But knows of him no more ...

Sonnet 20
'A woman's face with nature's own hand painted
Hast thou, the **master mistress** of my passion.

35 **So that thou smile on me and be my loue.**

(158/166)

35 Death is amazed, viewing of thy beautie,
Thinking thy selfe perfect eternitie.

(159/167)

Sonnet 29
When in disgrace with fortune and men's eyes ...

'Nowhere in the Sonnets is their whole theme so
exquisitely and compactly expressed.'

(Knight, 177)

Technical Appendix

35 Hell round enwraps my bodie by
disdaine,
And then a heauen if thou loue
againe.

(159/167)

30 Note but the **fresh bloom'd Rose
within her pride**.

(137/145)

32 **Thine euer growing beautie,
like the Rose?**

(146/154)

36 Yet my soules life to my deare
lifes concluding,
Nere let Absurditie that villaine,
theefe,
The monster of our time, mens
praise deriding,
Lesse in perseuerance, of small
knowledge chiefe,
Keep the base Gate to things that
are excelling,
Thou by faire vertues praise maist
yeeld reliefe,
My lines are thine, then tell
Absurditie,
Hart of my deare, shall blot his
villainie.

(163/171)

'This is pure Shakespeare … So
are certain impressions of the
rose.'

(Knight, 173)

Sonnet 2
Thy **youth's proud livery, so
gazed on now**,
Will be a tattered weed of small
worth held.

Sonnet 121
'Tis better to be vile than vile
esteemed,
When not to be, receives reproach
of being,
And the just pleasure lost, which
is so deemed
Not by our feeling, but by others'
seeing.
For why should others' false
adulterate eyes
Give salutation to my sportive
blood?
Or on my frailties why are frailer
spies,
Which in their wills count bad
what I think good?
No, I am that I am, and they that
level
At my abuses, reckon up their
own;
I may be straight, though they
themselves be bevel.
By their rank thoughts my deeds
must not be shown,
Unless this general evil they
maintain:
All men are bad, and in their
badness reign.

Technical Appendix

36   Till that **leane fleshles cripple, pale-fac'd Death**,
 Thy louely Doue shall pierce with his fell dart.

(164/172)

Romeo and Juliet V.iii.94-6, 102-5
 Thou art not conquered. Beauty's ensign yet
 Is crimson in thy lips and in thy cheeks,
 And **death's pale flag** is not advanced there.
 ...
 Why art thou yet so fair? Shall I believe
 That unsubstantial death is amorous,
 And that the **lean abhorred monster** keeps
 Thee here in dark to be his paramour?

36   Be thou **my Saint, my bosomes Lord** to proue,
 Scorned of all, Ile be thy truest loue.

(166/174)

Romeo and Juliet V.i.1-5:
 If I may trust the flattering truth of sleep,
 My dreams presage some joyful news at hand.
 My bosom's lord sits lightly in his throne,
 And all this day an unaccustomed spirit
 Lifts me above the ground with cheerful thoughts.

36   Where two harts are vnited all in one,
 Loue like a King, a Lord, a Soueraigne,
 Enioyes the throne of blisse to sit vpon,
 Each sad heart crauing aid, by *Cupid* slaine:
 Louers be merrie, Loue being dignified,
 With what you will, it shall not be denied.

(167/175)

Sonnet 26
 Lord of my love, to whom in vassalage
 Thy merit hath my duty strongly knit:
 To thee I send this **written embassage**.

Sonnet 57
 Being your **slave**, what should I do but tend
 Upon the hours and times of your desire?
 ...

Technical Appendix

		Whilst I, my **sovereign**, watch the clock for you, Nor think the bitterness of absence sour When you have bid your **servant** once adieu.
40	So they loued as loue in twaine, Had the essence but in one, Two distincts, Diuision none, Number there in loue was slaine. (174-75/182-83)	Sonnets 36, 39, 74
40	So betweene them **Loue** did shine, That the *Turtle* saw his right, Flaming in the *Phoenix* sight; Either was the others mine. (175/183)	Sonnet 24
40	Beautie, Truth, and Raritie, … Truth and Beautie buried be … (176/184)	Sonnet 14 (knowledge and art), Sonnet 101 (truth in beauty dyed), Sonnet 60 (the rarities of Nature's truth …) Sonnet 110 (looked on truth askance and strangely)

APPENDIX 2
LOVE'S MARTYR'S POETICAL ESSAYS

This appendix contains a full reproduction of the Poetical Essays. We maintain original line breaks and forms of punctuation, spelling, capitalization, and italicization in this and in the following appendix, which contains *Love's Martyr*'s Dialogues and Cantos. The beginnings and endings of segment numbers have been highlighted in notes. Other notes contain glosses on the material and critical references. Shakespeare's "The Phoenix and Turtle," reproduced in plates 2–3 and modernized in Chapter 3, is not included.

HEREAFTER
FOLLOVV DIVERSE
Poeticall Essaies on the former Sub-
iect; viz: the *Turtle* and *Phoenix*.

Done by the best and chiefest of our
moderne writers, with their names subscribed to their particular workes:
neuer before extant.

And (now first) consecrated by them all generally,
to the loue and merite of the true-noble Knight,
Sir Iohn Salisburie.

Dignum laude virum Musa vetat mori.[1]

[Figure: *Woodcut printer's device of Richard Field, showing an anchor.*]

Anchora Spei.

MDCI.

---

[1] 'The man worthy of praise the Muse forbids to die'. Horace, *Carmina* Book IV (4.8.13ff). Horace was one of Ben Jonson's idols.

Love's Martyr's Poetical Essays

INVOCATIO,
Ad Apollinem & Pierides.[2]

GOod Fate, faire *Thespian Deities*,
   And thou bright God, whose golden Eies,
   Serue as a Mirrour to the siluer Morne,
   When (in the height of Grace) she doth adorne
Her Chrystall presence, and inuites
   The euer-youthfull *Bromius* to delights,[3]
Sprinckling his sute of *Vert* with Pearle,
And (like a loose enamour'd Girle)
   Ingles his cheeke; which (waxing red with shame)[4]
   Instincts the senslesse Grapes to do the same,
Till by his sweete reflection fed,
   They gather spirit, and grow discoloured.

To your high influence we commend
Our following Labours, and sustend[5]
   Our mutuall palmes, prepar'd to gratulate
   An *honorable friend:* then propagate
With your illustrate faculties[6]
   Our mentall powers; Instruct vs how to rise
In weighty Numbers, well pursu'd,
And varied from the Multitude:
   Be lauish once, and plenteously profuse
   Your holy waters, to our thirstie *Muse,*
That we may giue a Round to him
   In a *Castalian* boule, crown'd to the brim.[7]
                   Vatum Chorus.[8]

---

[2] The Pierdes were a group of nine sisters who challenged the muses to a contest of song and lost. Upon defeat, they were turned into magpies.

[3] Bromius = Bacchus, Dionysus.

[4] 'Ingles his cheek' = 'treats his cheek as one does one's ingle or delight, or loved youth playfully pinches and strokes it'. Grosart, *Rosalins Complaint*, 240.

[5] Grosart glosses as 'subtend'; 'suspend' also fits the sense.

[6] 'Illustrate', as an adjective, is a Jonsonian tendency.

[7] See Chapter 2 for a discussion of the stylistic resonances of this poem.

[8] Roughly, 'All poets together'.

Love's Martyr's Poetical Essays

To the worthily honor'd Knight
Sir Iohn Salisburie.

NOblest of minds, here do the Muses *bring*
 Vnto your safer iudgements tast,
Pure iuice that flow'd from the Pierian *springs,*
 Not filch'd, nor borrow'd, but exhaust
 By the flame-hair'd Apollos *hand:*
 And at his well-obseru'd command,
For you infusde in our retentiue braine,
Is now distild thence, through our quilles againe.

Value our verse, as you approue the worth;
 And thinke of what they are create,
No Mercenarie *hope did bring them forth,*
 They tread not in that seruile Gate;
 But a true Zeale, borne in our spirites,
 Responsible to your high Merites,
And an Inuention, *freer then the* Times,[9]
These were the Parents to our seuerall Rimes,
 Wherin Kind, Learned, Enuious, *al may view,*
 That we haue writ worthy our selues and you.
Vatum Chorus.[10]

The first.[11]

The siluer Vault of heauen, hath but one Eie,
And that's the Sunne: the foule-maskt-Ladie, Night
(Which blots the Cloudes, the white Booke of the Skie,)
But one sicke *Phoebe*, feuer-shaking Light[12]:
The heart, one string: so, thus in single turnes,
The world one *Phoenix*, till another burnes.

---

[9] The 'Inuention' is Robert Chester's 'Phoenix-Turtle' conceit.

[10] Stylometric and other data suggest Jonson wrote this poem. See Chapter 2 of this book.

[11] Matchett explains the title of this poem by suggesting whoever wrote it wrote above it, 'the first', as in, 'this poem comes sequentially before the next one'. This is as good an explanation as I think we are likely to get for the title.

[12] 'Phoebe' is either Phoebe, grandmother of Apollo and Artemis, or byname for Artemis, associated with the moon.

Love's Martyr's Poetical Essays

The burning.

Svppose here burnes this wonder of a breath,
In righteous flames, and holy-heated fires:
(Like Musicke which doth rapt it selfe to death,
Sweet'ning the inward roome of mans Desires;)
So she waft's both her wings in piteous strife;
'The flame that eates her, feedes the others life:
Her rare-dead ashes, fill a rare-liue vrne[13]:
'One *Phoenix* borne, another *Phoenix* burne.

Ignoto.[14]

[See plates for original text of 'The Phoenix and Turtle' and Marston's reply. Marston's poem is reproduced again so annotations could be made on it. See Chapter 3 for a modernization of 'The Phoenix and Turtle'.]

A narration and description of a
most exact wondrous creature, arising
out of the Phoenix and Turtle
Doues ashes.

O Twas a mouing *Epicedium!*[15]
Can Fire? can Time? can blackest Fate consume
So rare creation? No; tis thwart to sence,
Corruption quakes to touch such excellence,
Nature exclaimes for Iustice, Iustice Fate,
Ought into nought can neuer remigrate.[16]
Then looke; for see what glorious issue (brighter[17]
Then clearest fire, and beyond faith farre whiter
Then *Dians* tier) now springs from yonder flame?
  Let me stand numb'd with wonder, neuer came

---

[13] See the 'urn' of Shakespeare's poem, 'The Phoenix and Turtle'.

[14] 'Unknown'.

[15] 'Funeral song'. This refers to Shakespeare's preceding poem in the collection.

[16] Matchett glosses the sense as, 'The idea of excellence has been endowed with the properties of matter'. Matchett, *The Phoenix and the Turtle*, 87–8.

[17] '[g]lorious issue' = the new phoenix.

Love's Martyr's Poetical Essays

So strong amazement on astonish'd eie
As this, this measurelesse pure Raritie.
   Lo now; th'xtracture of deuinest *Essence,*
The Soule of heauens labour'd *Quintessence,*
(*Peans* to *Phoebus*) from deare Louer's death,[18]
Takes sweete creation and all blessing breath.
   What strangenesse is't that from the *Turtles* ashes
Assumes such forme? (whose splendor clearer flashes,
Then mounted *Delius*) tell me genuine Muse.[19]
   Now yeeld your aides, you spirites that infuse
A sacred rapture, light my weaker eie:
Raise my inuention on swift Phantasie,
That whilst of this same *Metaphisicall*
God, Man, nor Woman, but elix'd of all
My labouring thoughts, with strained ardor sing,
My Muse may mount with an vncommon wing.

The description of this Perfection.
DAres then thy too audacious sense
Presume, define that boundlesse *Ens,*[20]
                That amplest thought transcendeth?
O yet vouchsafe my *Muse,* to greete
That wondrous rarenesse, in whose sweete
                All praise begins and endeth.
Diuinest Beautie? that was slightest,
That adorn'd this wondrous Brightest,
                Which had nought to be corrupted.
In this, Perfection had no meane
To this, Earths purest was vncleane
                Which vertue euen instructed.
By it all Beings deck'd and stained,
Ideas that are idly fained

---

[18] *Pheobus* = sun, Apollo.
[19] Apollo was said to have been born on Mount Cynthus on the island of Delos.
[20] In Platonic philosophy, 'ens' means 'being'.

Love's Martyr's Poetical Essays

> Onely here subsist inuested.
Dread not to giue strain'd praise at all,
No speech is Hyperbolicall,
> To this perfection blessed.[21]
> Thus close my Rimes, this all that can be sayd,
> This wonder neuer can be flattered.

To Perfection.
A Sonnet.

OFt haue I gazed with astonish'd eye,
  At monstrous issues of ill shaped birth,
  When I haue seene the Midwife to old earth,
Nature produce most strange deformitie.

So haue I marueld to obserue of late,
  Hard fauour'd Feminines so scant of faire,
  That Maskes so choicely, sheltred of the aire,
As if their beauties were not theirs by fate.

But who so weake of obseruation,
  Hath not discern'd long since how vertues wanted,
  How parcimoniously the heauens haue scanted,
Our chiefest part of adornation?

But now I cease to wonder, now I find
  The cause of all our monstrous penny-showes:
  Now I conceit from whence wits scarc'tie growes,
Hard fauourd features, and defects of mind.

---

[21] 'Since no amount of praise is sufficient to the task of honoring this "blessed perfection," no amount of praise can be deemed excessive'. Marston is supplying a rationale for his repeated praise of the Phoenix.
[22] 'Nature has produced so much monstrosity elsewhere because it needed to store up its virtue in order to produce this creature. Everything else is in nature a "[foile]" to this perfection'.

Love's Martyr's Poetical Essays

Nature long time hath stor'd vp vertue, fairenesse,
Shaping the rest as foiles vnto this Rarenesse.[22]

Perfectioni Hymnus.
WHat should I call this creature,
    Which now is growne vnto maturitie?
How should I blase this feature
    As firme and constant as Eternitie?
Call it Perfection? Fie!
    Tis perfecter thē brightest names can light it:
Call it Heauens mirror? I.
    Alas, best attributes can neuer right it.
Beauties resistlesse thunder?
    All nomination is too straight of sence:
Deepe Contemplations wonder?
    That appellation giue this excellence.
Within all best confin'd,
    (Now feebler *Genius* end thy slighter riming)

* *Differentia*   No Suburbes* all is *Mind*,
Deorum & ho-   As farre from spot, as possible
                   defining.

minum (apud
Senecam) sic ha-
bet nostri
melior pars a-
nimus in illis
nulla pars ex-
tra aninum.[23]

Iohn Marston.

Peristeros: or the male Turtle.[24]

---

[23] This quote, taken from Seneca's Preface to *Natural Questions*, may translate as 'the difference between God and human beings is that our better part is mind, but the whole of God's nature is nothing but mind'. Bednarz cites Thomas H. Corcoran's translation in *Questiones Naturales* (Cambridge: Harvard University Press, 1971–1972), Liber 1, Praefatio 13. Bednarz, *Shakespeare and the Truth of Love*, 170, 232.

[24] G. Wilson Knight notes of the title: 'The Greek word for 'dove' is *peristera*, and it is only found in the feminine … Chapman has, deliberately, coined a masculine form of it. His title accordingly serves to remind us, as though with a conscious paradox, that the

163

Love's Martyr's Poetical Essays

NOt like that loose and partie-liuer'd Sect
  Of idle Louers, that (as different Lights,
On colour'd subiects, different hewes reflect;)
  Change their Affections with their Mistris Sights,
That with her Praise, or Dispraise, drowne, or flote,
  And must be fed with fresh Conceits, and Fashions;
Neuer waxe cold, but die: loue not, but dote:
  'Loues fires, staid Iudgem̃ts blow, not humorous Passions,
Whose Loues vpon their Louers pomp depend,
  And quench as fast as her Eyes sparkle twinkles,
  '(Nought lasts that doth to outward worth contend,
  'Al Loue in smooth browes born is tomb'd in wrinkles.)
* *The Turtle*   But like the consecrated *Bird of loue,
* *The Phoenix*   Whose whole lifes hap to his *sole-mate alluded,
  Whome no prowd flockes of other Foules could moue,
  But in her selfe all companie concluded.
She was to him th' *Analisde* World of pleasure,
  Her firmenesse cloth'd him in varietie;
Excesse of all things, he ioyd in her measure,
Mourn'd when she mourn'd, and dieth when she dies.
Like him I bound th' instinct of all my powres,
  In her that bounds the Empire of desert,
And Time nor Change (that all things else deuoures,
  But truth eterniz'd in a constant heart)
Can change me more from her, then her from merit,
That is my forme, and giues my being, spirit.

George Chapman.

Praeludium.[25]

Turtle signifies the female aspect of the male poet's soul'. Matchett responds by calling this interpretation 'nonsense': 'Chapman's title … serves to remind us merely that Greek makes no provision for the Turtle of *Loues Martyr*'. Knight, *The Mutual Flame*, 185; Matchett, *The Phoenix and the Turtle*, 92. Knight's reading is far more compelling in light of modern queer theory, with its emphasis on error and textual play. See Chapter 2 for analysis of this poem.
[25] 'Prelude' or 'preliminary canter'. Parts of this poem appear in a Salusbury manuscript (National Library of Wales MS 5390D) with significant differences under the title 'Proludium'. See Chapter 2 for a discussion of the poem; see also Bednarz, *Shakespeare and the Truth of Love*, 86–7; Brown, *Poems by Sir John Salusbury and Robert Chester*, 5–7; and Matchett, *The Phoenix and the Turtle*, 95–96n.

Love's Martyr's Poetical Essays

WE must sing too? what Subiect *shal we chuse?*
  Or whose great Name *in* Poets Heauen *vse,*
For the more Countenance *to our Actiue* Muse?

Hercules? *alasse his bones are yet sore,*
With his old earthly Labors; *t' exact more*
Of his dull Godhead, *were Sinne: Lets implore*

Phoebus? *No: Tend thy* Cart *still. Enuious Day*
Shall not giue out, that we haue made thee stay,
And foundred thy hote Teame, *to tune our Lay.*

Nor will we beg of thee, Lord of the Vine,
To raise our spirites with thy coniuring Wine,
In the greene circle of thy Iuy twine.

Pallas, *nor thee we call on,* Mankind Maide,[26]
That (at thy birth) mad'st the poore Smith *afraide,*
Who with his Axe thy Fathers *Mid-wife plaide.*

Go, crampe dull Mars, *light* Venus, *when he snorts,*
Or with thy Tribade *Trine, inuent new sports,*
Thou, nor their loosenesse, with our Making *sorts.*[27]

Let the old Boy *your sonne ply his old Taske,*
Turne the stale Prologue *to some painted Maske,*
His Absence in our Verse *is all we aske.*

---

[26] Pallas = Athena.

[27] 'Tribade', or dominant lesbian, is a Jonsonian coinage. 'Tribade trine' refers either to the three Graces or, more likely, the triad of Juno, Venus, and Minerva, whose squabbling brought about the Trojan war. By banishing the goddesses collectively, as tribades, and declaring 'their loosenesse' an impediment to 'our Making', Jonson cleanses his verse of overtones of sexual impropriety. Valerie Traub argues that the 'rejection of their "new sports" implies that tribadism is an illicit form of contact that generates unacceptable forms of literary production'. Traub, *The Renaissance of Lesbianism in Early Modern England* (Cambridge: Cambridge University Press, 2001), 25.

Love's Martyr's Poetical Essays

Hermes *the cheater, cannot mixe with vs,*
Though he would steale his sisters Pegasus,
And rifle him; or pawne his Petasus.

Nor all the Ladies *of the* Thespian Lake,
(Though they were crusht into one forme) could make
A Beauty *of that* Merit, *that should take*

Our Muse *vp by* Commission: *No, we bring*
Our owne true Fire; Now our Thought takes wing
And now an Epode *to deepe eares we sing.*[28]

Epos.

'NOt to know *Vice* at all, and keepe true state,
        Is *Vertue*; and not Fate:
'Next to that *Vertue*, is, to know *Vice* well,
        'And her blacke spight expell.
Which to effect (since no breast is so sure,
        Or safe, but shee'l procure
Some way of entrance) we must plant a guard
        Of *Thoughts,* to watch and ward
At th' *Eye* and *Eare,* (the *Ports* vnto the *Mind;*)
        That no strange or vnkind
Obiect arriue there, but the *Heart* (our spie)
        Giue knowledge instantly.
To wakefull *Reason,* our *Affections* King:
        Who (in th' examining)
Will quickly taste the *Treason,* and commit
        Close, the close cause of it.
"Tis the securest Pollicie we haue,
        "To make our *Sense* our Slaue.
But this faire course is not embrac'd by many;
        By many? scarce by any:
For either our *Affections* do rebell,
        Or else the *Sentinell,*

---

[28] See Chapter 2 for analysis of this and other verse by Jonson.

166

Love's Martyr's Poetical Essays

(That shal ring larum to the *Heart*) doth sleepe,
   Or some great *Thought* doth keepe
Backe the Intelligence, and falsely sweares
   They'r base, and idle Feares,
Whereof the loyall *Conscience* so complaines.
   Thus by these subtill traines,
Do seuerall *Passions* still inuade the *Mind,*
   And strike our *Reason* blind:
Of which vsurping ranke, some haue thought *Loue*
   The first; as prone to moue
Most frequent Tumults, Horrors, and Vnrests,
   In our enflamed brests.
But this doth from their cloud of Error grow,
   Which thus we ouerblow.
The thing they here call *Loue,* is blind *Desire,*
   Arm'd with *Bow, Shafts,* and *Fire;*
Inconstant like the Sea, of whence 'tis borne,
   Rough, swelling, like a Storme:
With whome who sailes, rides on the surge of *Feare,*
   And boiles as if he were
In a continuall Tempest. Now true *Loue*
   No such effects doth proue:
That is an *Essence* most gentile, and fine.
   Pure, perfect; nay diuine:
It is a golden Chaine let downe from Heauen,
   Whose linkes are bright, and euen
That fals like Sleepe on Louers; and combines
   The soft and sweetest *Minds*
In equal knots: This beares no *Brands* nor *Darts*
   To murder different harts,
But in a calme and God-like vnitie,
   Preserues *Communitie.*
O who is he that (in this peace) enioyes
   Th' *Elixir* of all ioyes?
(A Forme more fresh then are the *Eden* bowers,
   And lasting as her flowers:
Richer then *Time,* and as *Times Vertue,* rare,
   Sober, as saddest *Care,*

Love's Martyr's Poetical Essays

A fixed *Thought,* an *Eye* vntaught to glance;)
    Who (blest with such high chance)
Would at suggestion of a steepe *Desire,*
    Cast himselfe from the spire
Of all his Happinesse? But soft: I heare
    Some vicious *Foole* draw neare,
That cries we dreame; and sweares, there's no such thing
    As this chaste *Loue* we sing.
Peace *Luxurie,* thou art like one of those
    Who (being at sea) suppose
Because they moue, the *Continent* doth so:
    No (*Vice*) we let thee know,
Though thy wild Thoughts with *Sparrowes* wings do flie,[29]
    "*Turtles* can chastly die;
And yet (in this t'expresse our selfe more cleare)
    We do not number here
Such Spirites as are onely continent,
    Because *Lusts* meanes are spent:
Or those, who doubt the common mouth of *Fame,*
    And for their *Place,* or *Name,*
Cannot so safely sinne; Their *Chastitie*
    Is meere *Necessitie,*
Nor meane we those, whom *Vowes* and *Conscience*
    Haue fild with *Abstinence:*
(Though we acknowledge who can so abstaine,
    Makes a most blessed gaine:
"He that for loue of goodnesse hateth ill,
    "Is more Crowne-worthy still,
"Then he which for sinnes *Penaltie* forbeares,
    "His *Heart* sinnes, though he feares.)
But we propose a person like our *Doue,*
    Grac'd with a *Phoenix* loue:
A beauty of that cleare and sparkling Light,
    Would make a Day of Night,
And turne the blackest sorrowes to bright ioyes:
    Whose Od'rous breath destroyes

---

[29] Sparrows were thought to be sexually voracious.

Love's Martyr's Poetical Essays

All taste of Bitternesse, and makes the Ayre
  As sweete, as she is faire:
A Bodie so harmoniously composde,
  As if *Nature* disclosde
All her best *Symmetrie* in that one *Feature:*
  O, so diuine a Creature
Who could be false too? chiefly when he knowes
  How onely she bestowes
The wealthy treasure of her Loue in him;
  Making his Fortunes swim
In the full floud of her admir'd perfection?
  What sauage, brute Affection,
Would not be fearefull to offend a *Dame*
  Of this excelling frame?
Much more a noble and right generous *Mind,*
  (To vertuous moodes enclin'd)
That knowes the weight of *Guilt:* He will refraine
  From thoughts of such a straine:
And to his *Sence* obiect this Sentence euer,
  "*Man may securely sinne, but safely neuer.*[30]

Ben Iohnson.[31]

The Phoenix Analysde.

NOw, after all, let no man
  Receiue it for a *Fable,*
If a *Bird* so amiable,
Do turne into a Woman.

Or (by our *Turtles* Augure)
That *Natures* fairest Creature,
Proue of his *Mistris* Feature,
But a bare *Type* and *Figure.*

---

[30] A Senecan aphorism, possibly brought into English by Jonson. Anthea Hume notes that Jonson 'had coined the phrase before he wrote the poem, or a version of the poem already existed in 1600, which he then adapted to meet the requirements of *Love's Martyr* in 1601'. See Hume, '*Love's Martyr*', 68.

[31] In 1601, Jonson had not yet changed the spelling of his last name.

[32] Typically translated as 'Ode Enthusiastic'. An earlier version of this poem was dedicated to 'L.C. of B.', who was almost certainly Lucy, Countess of Bedford.

Love's Martyr's Poetical Essays

Ode 'ἐνθουσιαστική.[32]
SPlendor! O more then mortall,
For other formes come short all
Of her illustrate brightnesse,
As farre as Sinne's from lightnesse.

Her wit as quicke, and sprightfull
As fire; and more delightfull
Then the stolne sports of *Louers,*
When night their meeting couers.

Iudgement (adornd with Learning)
Doth shine in her discerning,
Cleare as a naked vestall
Closde in an orbe of Christall.

Her breath for sweete exceeding
The *Phoenix* place of breeding,
But mixt with sound, transcending
All *Nature* of commending.

Alas: then whither wade I,
In thought to praise this *Ladie,*
When seeking her renowning,
My selfe am so neare drowning?

Retire, and say; Her *Graces*
Are deeper then their Faces:
Yet shee's nor nice to shew them,
Nor takes she pride to know them.

Ben: Iohnson.

FINIS.

APPENDIX 3
LOVE'S MARTYR'S DIALOGUES AND CANTOS

This appendix contains reproductions of segments 4–6, 27–29, and 30–36 of *Love's Martyr* as delineated in the ribbon diagram in Plate 7. These segments correspond to the Prayers (4); parts of the first Dialogue (5–6); the end of Chester's second Dialogue (27–28); Chester's 'Pellican' verse (29); the 'Cantoes Alphabetwise' (30); and the Cantoes 'Verbally Written' (31–36). These areas of text, as shown in the rolling attribution graphs in Plate 9 and the chart of G. Wilson Knight's observations (Table A1.3), suggest that Shakespeare may have assisted Chester in these parts of the book. Emphatically, we do not mean to suggest that these areas were 'authored' by Shakespeare. See Chapter 1 for the theory behind this 'editing' or 'doctoring', to use Knight's term.

An Introduction to the Prayer.

GVide thou great Guider of the Sunne and Moone,[1]
Thou elementall fauourer of the Night,
My vndeserued wit, wit sprong too soone,
To giue thy greatnesse euerie gracious right:
  Let Pen, Hand, Wit and vndeseruing tongue,
  Thy praise and honor sing in euerie song.

In my poore prayer guide my Hand aright,
Guide my dull Wit, guide all my dulled Senses,

---

[1] Segment 4 begins.

Love's Martyr's Dialogues and Cantos

Let thy bright Taper giue me faithfull light,
And from thy Booke of life blot my offences:
      Then arm'd with thy protection and thy loue,
      Ile make my prayer for thy Turtle-doue.[2]

      A Prayer *made for the prosperitie of*
      a siluer coloured Doue, applyed to the
          beauteous Phoenix.

O Thou great maker of the firmament,
That rid'st vpon the winged *Cherubins*,
And on the glorious shining element,
Hear'st the sad praiers of the *Seraphins*,
That vnto thee continually sing Hymnes:
      Bow downe thy listning eares thou God of might,
      To him whose heart will praise thee day and night.

Accept the humble Praiers of that soule,
That now lies wallowing in the myre of Sinne,
Thy mercie Lord doth all my powers controule,
And searcheth reines and heart that are within:
Therefore to thee *Iehouah* Ile begin:
      Lifting my head from my imprisoned graue,
      No mercie but thy mercie me can saue.

The foule vntamed Lion still goes roring,
Old hell-bread *Sathan* enemy to mankind,
To leade me to his iawes that are deuouring,
Wherein no Grace to humane flesh's assign'd,
But thou celestiall Father canst him bind:
Tread on his head, tread Sinne and *Sathan* downe,
And on thy seruants head set Mercies crowne.

Thus in acceptance of thy glorious sight,
I purge my deadly sinne in hope of grace,

---

[2] The introductory stanzas recall Chester's verse in the Christ Church MS addressed to Sir John Salusbury: 'Good-meaning tells me he my friend with stand, / To under-prop my tottering rotten rhyme … / Therefore to thee, sole patron of my good, / I proffer up the proffer of my heart'. See Chapter 1 for a discussion of this poem.

Love's Martyr's Dialogues and Cantos

Thou art the Doore, the Lanthorne and the Light,
To guide my sinfull feete from place to place,
And now O Christ I bow before thy face:
      And for the siluer coloured earthly Doue,
      I make my earnest prayer for thy loue.

Shrowde her ô Lord vnder thy shadowed wings,
From the worlds enuious malice and deceit,
That like the adder-poisoned serpent stings,
And in her way layes a corrupted baite,
Yet raise her God vnto thy mercies height:
      Guide her, ô guide her from pernitious foes,
      That many of thy creatures ouerthrowes.

Wash her O Lord with Hysope and with Thime,
And the white snow she shall excell in whitenesse,
Purge her with mercie from all sinfull crime,
And her soules glorie shall exceed in brightnesse,
O let thy mercie grow vnto such ripenesse:
      Behold her, O behold her gratious King,
      That vnto thee sweet songs of praise will sing.

And as thou leadst through the red coloured waues,
The hoast of thy elected *Israel*,
And from the wrath of *Pharoe* didst them saue,
Appointing them within that land to dwell,
A chosen land, a land what did excell:
      So guide thy siluer Doue vnto that place,
      Where she Temptations enuie may outface.

Increase thy gifts bestowed on thy Creature,
And multiply thy blessings manifold,
And as thou hast adorned her with nature,
So with thy blessed eyes her eyes behold,
That in them doth thy workmanship vnfold,
      Let her not wither Lord without increase,
      But blesse her with ioyes ofspring of sweet peace.
                        Amen. Amen.

Love's Martyr's Dialogues and Cantos

To those of light beleefe.

Y*Ou gentle fauourers of excelling* Muses,
And gracers of all Learning and Desart,
You whose Conceit the deepest worke peruses,
Whose Iudgements still are gouerned by Art:
 Reade gently what you reade, this next conceit
 Fram'd of pure loue, abandoning deceit.
And you whose dull Imagination,
And blind conceited Error hath not knowne,
Of Herbes and Trees true nomination,
But thinke them fabulous that shall be showne:
 Learne more, search much, and surely you shal find,
 Plaine honest Truth and Knowledge comes behind.

Then gently (gentle Reader) do thou fauour,
And with a gracious looke grace what is written,[3]
With smiling cheare peruse my homely labour,
With Enuies poisoned spitefull looke not bitten:
 So shalt thou cause my willing thought to striue,
 To adde more Honey to my new made Hiue.

A meeting Dialogue-wise betweene Na-
ture, the Phoenix, and the Turtle Doue.[4]

Nature.
ALl haile faire *Phoenix,* whither art thou flying?
Why in the hot Sunne dost thou spread thy wings?
More pleasure shouldst thou take in cold shades lying,
And for to bathe thy selfe in wholsome Springs,
Where the woods feathered quier sweetely sings:

---

[3] Again from Chester in Christ Church MS 184: 'O grace them with thy gratious gracing look / That in pure kindness much have undertook'. Whatever meddling may have occurred in other parts of segment 4, it opens and closes on these distinctly Chesterian notes.

[4] Segment 5 begins. From this point on through the end of segment 6, Nature engages in a dialogue with the Phoenix, who is tormented by Envy.

Love's Martyr's Dialogues and Cantos

Thy golden Wings and thy breasts beauteous Eie,
Will fall away in *Phoebus* royaltie.

Phoenix.

O stay me not, I am no *Phoenix* I,
And if I be that bird, I am defaced,
Vpon the *Arabian* mountaines I must die,
And neuer with a poore yong Turtle graced;
Such operation in me is not placed:
 What is my Beautie but a painted wal,
 My golden spreading Feathers quickly fal.

Nature.

Why dost thou shead thy Feathers, kill thy Heart,
Weep out thine Eyes, and staine thy golden Face?
Why dost thou of the worlds woe take a part,
And in relenting teares thy selfe disgrace?
Ioyes mirthful Tower is thy dwelling place;
 All Birdes for vertue and excelling beautie,
 Sing at thy reuerend feet in Loue and Dutie.

Phoenix.

O how thou feed'st me with my Beauties praising!
O how thy Praise sounds from a golden Toung!
O how thy Toung my Vertues would be raising!
And raising me thou dost corrupt thy song;
Thou seest not Honie and Poison mixt among;
 Thou not'st my Beautie with a iealous looke,
 But dost not see how I do bayte my hooke.

Nature.

Tell me, ô tell me, for I am thy friend,
I am Dame *Nature* that first gaue thee breath,
That from *Ioues* glorious rich seate did descend,
To set my Feete vpon this lumpish earth:
What is the cause of thy sad sullen Mirth?
 Hast thou not Beauty, Vertue, Wit and Fauour:
 What other graces would'st thou craue of Nature?

175

Love's Martyr's Dialogues and Cantos

Phoenix.

What is my Beauty but a vading Flower?
Wherein men reade their deep-conceiued Thrall,
Alluring twentie Gallants in an hower,
To be as seruile vassals at my Call?
My Sunne-bred lookes their Senses do exhall:
   But (ô my griefe) where my faire Eyes would loue,
   Foule bleare-eyed Enuie doth my thoughts reprooue.

What is my Vertue but a Tablitorie[5]:
Which if I did bestow would more increase?
What is my Wit but an inhumane glorie:
That to my kind deare friends would proffer peace?
But O vaine Bird, giue ore in silence, cease;
   Malice perchaunce doth hearken to thy words,
   That cuts thy threed of Loue with twentie swords.

Nature.

Tell me (O Mirrour) of our earthly time,
Tell me sweete *Phoenix* glorie of mine age,
Who blots thy Beauty with foule *Enuies* crime,
And locks thee vp in fond *Suspitions* cage?
Can any humane heart beare thee such rage?
   Daunt their proud stomacks with thy piercing Eye,
   Vnchaine Loues sweetnesse at thy libertie.

Phoenix.

What is't to bath me in a wholesome Spring,
Or wash me in a cleere, deepe, running Well,
When I no vertue from the same do bring,
Nor of the balmie water beare a smell?

---

[5] This word is not in the *OED* or any other modern dictionary. For Grosart, 'Tablitorie' is a device 'given by [John] Minsheu as a necklet, necklace, or brooch'. It could refer to 'table', as in a counting device, hence the verb 'increase'. It may also signify 'tablature'; 'Tabletorie' appears in this last sense in the title of a 1598 work of musical notation: Michael Cavendish, *Ayres in Tabletorie to the Lute expressed with two voyces and the base Violl or the voice & Lute only* (London: Printed by Peter Short, on bredstreethill at the signe of the Starre, 1598).

Love's Martyr's Dialogues and Cantos

It better were for me mongst Crowes to dwell,
  Then flocke with Doues, whē Doues sit alwayes billing,
  And [waste] my wings of gold, my Beautie killing.

Nature.
Ile chaine foule *Enuy* to a brazen Gate,
And place deepe *Malice* in a hollow Rocke,
To some blacke desert Wood Ile banish *Hate,*
And fond *Suspition* from thy sight Ile locke:
These shall not stirre, let anie Porter knocke.
  Thou art but yong, fresh, greene, and must not passe,
  But catch the hot Sunne with thy steeled glasse.

Phoenix.
That Sunne shines not within this Continent,
That with his warme rayes can my dead Bloud chearish,
Grosse cloudie Vapours from this Aire is sent,
Not hot reflecting Beames my heart to nourish.
O Beautie, I do feare me thou wilt perish;
  Then gentle *Nature* let me take my flight,
  But ere I passe, set *Enuie* out of sight.

Ile coniure him, and raise him from his graue,
And put vpon his head a punishment:
Nature thy sportiue Pleasure meanes to saue;
Ile send him to perpetuall banishment,
Like to a totterd Furie ragd and rent:
  Ile baffle him, and blind his Iealous eye,
  That in thy actions Secrecie would prye.

Nature.
Ile coniure him, Ile raise him from his Cell,
Ile pull his Eyes from his conspiring head,
Ile locke him in the place where he doth dwell;
Ile starue him there, till the poore slaue be dead,
That on the poisonous Adder oft hath fed:
  These threatnings on the Helhound I will lay,
  But the performance beares the greater sway.

Love's Martyr's Dialogues and Cantos

Nature.
Stand by faire *Phoenix,* spread thy Wings of gold,
And daunt the face of Heauen with thine Eye,
Like *Iunos* bird thy Beautie do vnfold,
And thou shalt triumph ore thine enemie:
Then thou and I in *Phoebus* coach will flie,
      Where thou shalt see and tast a secret Fire,
      That will adde spreading life to thy Desire.

Phoenix.
Arise thou bleare-ey'd *Enuie* from thy bed,
Thy bed of Snakie poison and corruption,
Vnmaske thy big-swolne Cheekes with poyson red,
For with thee I must trie Conclusion,
And plague thee with the Worlds confusion.
      I charge thee by my Power to appeare,
      And by Celestiall warrant to draw neare.

Phoenix.
O what a mistie Dampe breakes from the ground,
Able it selfe to infect this noysome Aire:
As if a caue of Toades themselues did wound,
Or poysoned Dragons fell into dispaire,
Hels damned sent with this may not compare,
      And in this foggie cloud there doth arise
      A damned Feend ore me to tyrannize.

Nature.
He shall not touch a Feather of thy wing,
Or euer haue Authoritie and power,
As he hath had in his dayes secret prying,
Ouer thy calmie Lookes to send a shower:
Ile place thee now in secrecies sweet Bower,
      Where at thy will in sport and dallying,
      Spend out thy time in Amarous discoursing.

Phoenix.
Looke *Nurce,* looke *Nature* how the Villaine sweates,
His big-swolne Eyes will fall vnto the ground,

Love's Martyr's Dialogues and Cantos

With fretting anguish he his blacke breast beates,
As if he would true harted minds confound:
O keepe him backe, his sight my heart doth wound:
>   O *Enuie* it is thou that mad'st me perish,
>   For want of that true Fire my hart should nourish.

Nature.[6]
But I will plague him for his wickednesse,
Enuie go packe thee to some forreine soyle,
To some desertfull plaine or Wildernesse,
Where sauage Monsters and wild beasts do toyle,
And with inhumane Creatures keepe a coyle.
>   Be gone I say, and neuer do returne,
>   Till this round compast world with fire do burne.

Phoenix.
What is he gone? is *Enuie* packt away?
Then one fowle blot is mooued from his Throne,
That my poore honest Thoughts did seeke to slay:
Away fowle griefe, and ouer-heauie Mone,
That do ore charge me with continuall grones.
>   Will you not hence? then with downe-falling teares,
>   Ile drowne my selfe in ripenesse of my Yeares.

Nature.
Fie peeuish Bird, what art thou franticke mad?
Wilt thou confound thy selfe with foolish Griefe?
If there be cause or meanes for to be had,
Thy Nurse and nourisher will find reliefe:
Then tell me all thy Accidents in briefe;
>   Haue I not banisht *Enuy* for thy sake?
>   I greater things for thee ile vndertake.

Phoenix.
Enuie is gone and banisht from my sight,
Banisht for euer comming any more:
But in *Arabia* burnes another Light,
A darke dimme Taper that I must adore,

---

[6] Segment 6 begins.

Love's Martyr's Dialogues and Cantos

This barren Countrey makes me to deplore:
> It is so saplesse that the very Spring,
> Makes tender new-growne Plants be with'ring.

The noisome Aire is growne infectious,
The very Springs for want of Moisture die,
The glorious Sunne is here pestiferous,
No hearbes for *Phisicke* or sweet *Surgerie,*
No balme to cure hearts inward maladie:
> No gift of *Nature,* she is here defaced,
> Heart-curing *Balsamum* here is not placed.

Nature.
Is this the summe and substance of thy woe?
Is this the Anker-hold vnto thy bote?
Is this thy Sea of Griefe doth ouerflow?
Is this the Riuer sets thy ship aflote?
Is this the Lesson thou hast learn'd by rote?
> And is this all? and is this plot of Ground
> The substance of the Theame doth thee confound?

Phoenix.
This is the Anker-hold, the Sea, the Riuer,
The Lesson and the substance of my Song,
This is the Rocke my Ship did seeke to shiuer,
And in this ground with Adders was I stung,
And in a lothsome pit was often flung:
> My Beautie and my Vertues captiuate,
> To Loue, dissembling Loue that I did hate.

Nature.
Cheare vp thy spirit *Phoenix,* prune thy wings,
And double-gild thy Fethers for my newes;
A *Nightingale* and not a *Rauen* sings,
That from all blacke contention will excuse
Thy heauy thoughts, and set them to peruse
> Another Clymat, where thou maist expresse,
> A plot of *Paradice* for worthinesse.

Love's Martyr's Dialogues and Cantos

Ioue in diuine diuinesse of his Soule,
That rides vpon his firie axaltree,
That with his Mace doth humane flesh controule,
When of mans deedes he makes a Registrie,
Louing the good for singularitie:
>   With a vail'd Count'nance and a gracious Smile,
>   Did bid me plant my Bird in *Paphos* Ile.

Phoenix.
What ill diuining Planet did presage,
My timelesse birth so timely brought to light?
What fatal Comet did his wrath engage,
To worke a harmelesse Bird such worlds despight,
Wrapping my dayes blisse in blacke sables night?
>   No Planet nor no Comet did conspire
>   My downefall, but foule *Fortunes* wrathful ire.

What did my Beautie moue her to Disdaine?
Or did my Vertues shadow all her Blisse?
That she should place me in a desart Plaine,
And send forth *Enuie* with a *Iudas* kisse,
To sting me with a Scorpions poisoned hisse?
>   From my first birth-right for to plant me heare,
>   Where I haue alwaies fed on Griefe and Feare.

Nature.
Raile not gainst *Fortunes* sacred Deitie,
In youth thy vertuous patience she hath tyred,
From this base earth shee'le lift thee vp on hie,
Where in Contents rich Chariot thou shalt ride,
And neuer with Impatience to abide:
>   *Fortune* will glorie in thy great renowne,
>   And on thy feathered head will set a crowne.

Phoenix.
T'was time to come, for I was comfortlesse,
And in my Youth haue bene Infortunate:
This Ile of *Paphos* I do hope will blesse,
And alter my halfe-rotten tottering state;

181

Love's Martyr's Dialogues and Cantos

My hearts Delight was almost ruinate.
    In this rich Ile a *Turtle* had his nest,
    And in a Wood of gold tooke vp his rest.

Nature.
Fly in this Chariot, and come sit by me,
And we will leaue this ill corrupted Land,
We'le take our course through the blew Azure skie,
And set our feete on *Paphos* golden sand,
There of that *Turtle Doue* we'le vnderstand:
    And visite him in those delightfull plaines,
    Where Peace conioyn'd with Plenty still remaines.

Phoenix.
I come, I come, and now farewell that strond,
Vpon whose craggie rockes my Ship was rent;
Your ill beseeming follies made me fond,
And in a vastie Cell I vp was pent,
Where my fresh blooming Beauty I haue spent.
    O blame your selues ill nurtred cruell Swaines,
    That fild my scarlet Glorie full of Staines.

Nature.
Welcome immortall Bewtie, we will ride
Ouer the Semi-circle of *Europa,*
And bend our course where we will see the Tide,
That partes the Continent of *Affrica,*
Where the great *Cham* gouernes *Tartaria:*
    And when the starrie Curtaine vales the night,
    In *Paphos* sacred Ile we meane to light.

Phoenix.
How glorious is this Chariot of the day,
Where *Phoebus* in his crystall robes is set,
And to poore passengers directs a way:
O happie time since I with *Nature* met,
My immelodious Discord I vnfret:
    And sing sweet Hymnes, burn Myrrhe &
    Frankensence,
    Honor that Isle that is my sure defence.

182

Love's Martyr's Dialogues and Cantos

Nature.
Looke *Phoenix* ore the world as thou dost ride,
And thou shalt see the pallaces of Kings,
Great huge-built Cities where high States abide,
Temples of Gods, and Altars with rich offrings,
To which the Priests their sacrifices brings:
      Wonders past wonder, strange *Pyramides,*
      And the gold-gathering Strond of *Euphrates.*

Phoenix.
O what rich pleasure dwelleth in this Land!
Greene springing Medowes, high vpreared Hils,
The white-fleest Ewe brought tame vp on the hand,
Faire running Riuers that the Countrie fils,
Sweet flowers that faire balmy Deaw distils,
      Great peopled Cities, whose earth-gracing show,
      Time is asham'd to touch or ouerthrow!

Nature.
Besilent gentle *Phoenix,* Ile repeate,
Some of these Cities names that we descrie,
And of their large foundation Ile intreate,
Their Founder that first rear'd them vp on hie,
Making a glorious Spectacle to each eie:
      Warres wald Defender and the Countries grace,
      Not battred yet with Times controlling Mace.[7]

* * *

The mighty *Macedonian Alexander,*[8]
Marching in louely triumph to his foes,
Being accounted the worlds conquerour,
In *Indie* spies a *Peacocke* as he goes,
      And maruelling to see so rich a sight,
      Charg'd all men not to kill his sweete delight.

---

[7] Segment 6 ends. From here, Nature begins to ruminate at length on British history and legend.

[8] Segment 27 begins near the end of Nature's catalogue of worms and birds. Nature is speaking.

183

Love's Martyr's Dialogues and Cantos

The *Pellican* the wonder of our age,
(As *Ierome* saith) reuiues her tender yong,
And with her purest bloud, she doth asswage
Her yong ones thirst, with poisonous Adder stong,
     And those that were supposed three dayes dead.
     She giues them life once more being nourished.

The vnsatiate *Sparrow* doth prognosticate,
And is held good for diuination,
For flying here and there, from gate to gate,
Foretls true things by animaduertion:
     A flight of *Sparrowes* flying in the day,
     Did prophesie the fall and sacke of *Troy*.

The artificiall nest-composing *Swallow,*
That eates his meate flying along the way,
Whose swiftnesse in our eysight doth allow,
That no imperiall Bird makes her his pray:
     His yong ones being hurt within the eies,
     His helpes them with the herbe *Calcedonies.*

Cecinna and the great *Volateran,*
Being *Pompeis* warlike and approued knights,
Sent letters by these Birds without a man,
To many of their friends and chiefe delights,
     And all their letters to their feete did tie,
     Which with great speed did bring them hastily.

The sweet recording Swanne *Apolloes* ioy,
And firy scorched *Phaetons* delight,
In footed verse sings out his deep annoy,
And to the siluer riuers takes his flight,
     Prognosticates to Sailers on the seas,
     Fortunes prosperitie and perfect ease.
        Cignus in auspicijs semper lætissimus ales,
        Hoc optant nautæ, quia se non mergit in vndis.

Phoenix.
But what sad-mournefull drooping soule is this,
Within whose watry eyes sits Discontent,

Love's Martyr's Dialogues and Cantos

Whose snaile-pac'd gate tels someting is amisse:
From whom is banisht sporting Meriment:
>Whose feathers mowt off, falling as he goes,
>The perfect picture of hart pining woes?

Nature.
This is the carefull bird the *Turtle* Doue,
Whose heauy croking note doth shew his griefe,
And thus he wanders seeking of his loue,
Refusing all things that may yeeld reliefe:
>All motions of good turnes, all Mirth and Ioy,
>Are bad, fled, gone, and falne into decay.

Phoenix.
Is this the true example of the Heart?
Is this the Tutor of faire *Constancy?*
Is this Loues treasure, and Loues pining smart?
Is this the substance of all honesty?
>And comes he thus attir'd, alas poore soule,
>That Destinies foule wrath should thee controule.

See Nourse, he stares and lookes me in the face,
And now he mournes, worse then he did before,
He hath forgot his dull slow heauy pace,
But with swift gate he eyes vs more and more:
>O shall I welcome him, and let me borrow
>Some of his griefe to mingle with my sorrow.

Nature.
Farwell faire bird, Ile leaue you both alone,
This is the *Doue* you long'd so much to see,
And this will proue companion of your mone,
An Vmpire of all true humility:
>Then note my *Phoenix,* what there may ensue,
>And so I kisse my bird. *Adue, Adue.*

Phoenix.
Mother farewell; and now within his eyes,
Sits sorrow clothed in a sea of teares,

185

Love's Martyr's Dialogues and Cantos

And more and more the billowes do arise:
Pale Griefe halfe pin'd vpon his brow appeares,
>His feathers fade away, and make him looke,
>As if his name were writ in Deaths pale booke.

Turtle.
O stay poore *Turtle,* whereat hast thou gazed,
At the eye-dazling Sunne, whose sweete reflection,
The round encompast heauenly world amazed?
O no, a child of Natures true complexion,
>The perfect *Phoenix* of rariety,
>For wit, for vertue, and excelling beauty.

Phoenix.
Haile map of sorrow: *Tur.* Welcome *Cupids* child.
Let me wipe off those teares vpon thy cheekes,
That stain'd thy beauties pride, and haue defil'd
Nature it selfe, that so vsurping seekes
>To sit vpon thy face, for Ile be partener,
>Of thy harts wrapped sorrow more hereafter.

Turtle.
Natures faire darling, let me kneele to thee,
And offer vp my true obedience,
And sacredly in all humility,
Craue pardon for presumptions foule offence:
>Thy lawne-snow-colour'd hand shall not come neare
>My impure face, to wipe away one teare.

My teares are for my *Turtle* that is dead,
My sorrow springs from her want that is gone,
My heauy note sounds for the soule that's fled,
And I will dye for him left all alone:
>I am not liuing, though I seeme to go,
>Already buried in the graue of wo.

Phoenix.
Why I haue left *Arabia* for thy sake,
Because those fires haue no working substance,

Love's Martyr's Dialogues and Cantos

And for to find thee out did vndertake:
Where on the mountaine top we may aduance
     Our fiery alter; let me tell thee this,
     Solamen miseris socios habuisse doloris.

Come poore lamenting soule, come sit by me,
We are all one, thy sorrow shall be mine,
Fall thou a teare, and thou shalt plainly see,
Mine eyes shall answer teare for teare of thine:
     Sigh thou, Ile sigh, and if thou giue a grone,
     I shall be dead in answering of thy mone.

Turtle.
Loues honorable Friend, one grone of yours,
Will rend my sicke-loue-pining hart asunder,
One sigh brings teares from me like *Aprill* showers,
Procur'd by Sommers hote loud cracking thunder:
     Be you as mery as sweet mirth may be,
     Ile grone and sigh, both for your selfe and me.

Phoenix.
Thou shalt not gentle *Turtle,* I will beare
Halfe of the burdenous yoke thou dost sustaine,
Two bodies may with greater ease outweare
A troublesome labour, then Ile brooke some paine,
     But tell me gentle *Turtle,* tell me truly
     The difference betwixt false Loue and true Sinceritie.

Turtle.
That shall I briefly, if youle giue me leaue,
False loue is full of Enuie and Deceit,
With cunning shifts our humours to deceiue,
Laying downe poison for a sugred baite,
     Always inconstant, false, and variable,
     Delighting in fond change and mutable.

True[9] loue, is louing pure, not to be broken,
But with an honest eye, she eyes her louer,

---

[9] Segment 28 begins.

Love's Martyr's Dialogues and Cantos

Not changing variable, nor neuer shoken
With fond Suspition, secrets to discouer,
>True loue will tell no lies, nor ne're dissemble,
>But with a bashfull modest feare will tremble.

False loue puts on a Maske to shade her folly,
True loue goes naked wishing to be seene,
False loue will counterfeite perpetually,
True loue is Troths sweete emperizing Queene:
>This is the difference, true Loue is a iewell,
>False loue, hearts tyrant, inhumane, and cruell.

Phoenix.
What may we wonder at? O where is learning?
Where is all difference twixt the good and bad?
Where is *Apelles* art? where is true cunning?
Nay where is all the vertue may be had?
>Within my *Turtles* bosome, she refines,
>More then some louing perfect true deuines.

Thou shalt not be no more the *Turtle*-Doue,
Thou shalt no more go weeping al alone,
For thou shalt be my selfe, my perfect Loue,
Thy griefe is mine, thy sorrow is my mone,
>Come kisse me sweetest sweete, O I do blesse
>This gracious luckie Sun-shine happinesse.

Turtle.
How may I in all gratefulnesse requite,
This gracious fauor offred to thy seruant?
The time affordeth heauinesse not delight,
And to the times appoint weele be obseruant:
>Command, O do commaund, what ere thou wilt,
>My hearts bloud for thy sake shall straight be spilt.

Phoenix.
Then I command thee on thy tender care,
And chiefe obedience that thou owst to me,
That thou especially (deare Bird) beware

Love's Martyr's Dialogues and Cantos

Of impure thoughts, or vncleane chastity:
>For we must wast together in that fire,
>That will not burne but by true Loues desire.

Turtle.
A spot of that foule monster neare did staine,
These drooping feathers, nor I neuer knew
In what base filthy clymate doth remaine
That spright incarnate; and to tell you true,
>I am as spotlesse as the purest whight,
>Cleare without staine, of enuy, or despight.

Phoenix.
Then to yon next adioyning groue we'le flye,
And gather sweete wood for to make our flame,
And in a manner sacrificingly,
Burne both our bodies to reuiue one name:
>And in all humblenesse we will intreate,
>The hot earth parching Sunne to lend his heate.

Turtle.
Why now my heart is light, this very doome
Hath banisht sorrow from my pensiue breast:
And in my bosome there is left no roome,
To set blacke melancholy, or let him rest;
>Ile fetch sweete mirrhe to burne, and licorice,
>Sweete Iuniper, and straw them ore with spice.

Phoenix.
Pile vp the wood, and let vs inuocate
His great name that doth ride within his chariot,
And guides the dayes bright eye, let's nominate
Some of his blessings, that he well may wot,
>Our faithfull seruice and humility,
>Offer'd vnto his highest Deiety.

Great God *Apollo,* for the tender loue,
Thou once didst beare to wilfull *Phaeton,*
That did desire thy chariots rule aboue,

189

Love's Martyr's Dialogues and Cantos

Which thou didst grieue in hart to thinke vpon:
> Send thy hot kindling light into this wood,
> That shall receiue the Sacrifice of bloud.

Turtle.
For thy sweet *Daphnes* sake thy best beloued,
And for the Harpe receiu'd of *Mercury,*
And for the *Muses* of thee fauored,
Whose gift of wit excels all exellency:
> Send thy hot kindling fire into this wood,
> That shall receiue the Sacrifice of bloud.

Phoenix.
For thy sweet fathers sake great *Iupiter,*
That with his thunder-bolts commands the earth,
And for *Latonas* sake thy gentle mother,
That first gaue *Phoebus* glories liuely breath:
> Send thy hot kindling light into this wood,
> That shall receiue the Sacrifice of bloud.

Stay, stay, poore *Turtle,* ô we are betraid,
Behind yon little bush there sits a spy,
That makes me blush with anger, halfe afraid,
That in our motions secrecly would pry:
> I will go chide with him, and driue him thence,
> And plague him for presumptions foule offence.

Turtle.
Be not affraid, it is the *Pellican,*
Looke how her yong-ones make her brest to bleed,
And drawes the bloud foorth, do the best she can,
And with the same their hungry fancies feede,
> Let her alone to vew our Tragedy,
> And then report our Loue that she did see.

See beauteous *Phoenix* it begins to burne,
O blessed *Phoebus,* happy, happy light,
Now will I recompence thy great good turne,

Love's Martyr's Dialogues and Cantos

And first (deare bird) Ile vanish in thy sight,
      And thou shalt see with what a quicke desire,
      Ile leape into the middle of the fire.

Phoenix.
Stay *Turtle* stay, for I will first prepare;
Of my bones must the Princely *Phoenix* rise,
And ift be possible thy bloud wele spare,
For none but for my sake, dost thou despise
      This frailty of thy life, ô liue thou still,
      And teach the base deceitfull world Loues will.

Turtle.
Haue I come hither drooping through the woods,
And left the springing groues to seeke for thee?
Haue I forsooke to bath me in the flouds,
And pin'd away in carefull misery?
      Do not deny me *Phoenix* I must be
      A partner in this happy Tragedy.

Phoenix.
O holy, sacred, and pure perfect fire,
More pure then that ore which faire *Dido* mones,
More sacred in my louing kind desire,
Then that which burnt old *Esons* aged bones,
      Accept into your euer hallowed flame,
      Two bodies, from the which may spring one name.

Turtle.
O sweet perfumed flame, made of those trees,
Vnder the which the *Muses* nine haue song
The praise of vertuous maids in misteries,
To whom the faire fac'd *Nymphes* did often throng;
      Accept my body as a Sacrifice
      Into your flame, of whom one name may rise.

Phoenix.
O wilfulnesse, see how with smiling cheare,
My poore deare hart hath flong himselfe to thrall,

Love's Martyr's Dialogues and Cantos

Looke what a mirthfull countenance he doth beare,
Spreading his wings abroad, and ioyes withall:
>Learne thou corrupted world, learne, heare, and see,
>Friendships vnspotted true sincerity.

I come sweet *Turtle,* and with my bright wings,
I will embrace thy burnt bones as they lye,
I hope of these another Creature springs,
That shall possesse both our authority:
>I stay to long, ô take me to your glory,
>And thus I end the *Turtle* Doues true story.

Finis. R. C.

>*Pellican.*[10]

VVHat wondrous hart-grieuing spectacle,
Hast thou beheld the worlds true miracle?
With what a spirit did the *Turtle* flye
Into the fire, and chearfully did dye?
He look't more pleasant in his countenance
Within the flame, then when he did aduance,
His pleasant wings vpon the naturall ground,
True perfect loue had so his poore heart bound,
The *Phoenix Natures* deare adopted child,
With a pale heauy count'nance, wan and mild,
Grieu'd for to see him first possesse the place,
That was allotted her, her selfe to grace,
And followes cheerfully her second turne,
And both together in that fire do burne.
O if the rarest creatures of the earth,
Because but one at once did ere take breath
Within the world, should with a second he,[11]
A perfect forme of loue and amitie
Burne both together, what should there arise,
And be presented to our mortall eyes,

---

[10] Segment 29 begins. See Appendix 1 for stylometric information on the 'Pellican' verse.
[11] 'Second he' = mate. See Chapter 2 for discussion of this verse.

192

Love's Martyr's Dialogues and Cantos

Out of the fire, but a more perfect creature?[12]
Because that two in one is put by Nature,
The one hath giuen the child inchaunting beautie,
The other giues it loue and chastitie:
The one hath giuen it wits rarietie,
The other guides the wit most charily:
The one for vertue doth excell the rest,
The other in true constancie is blest.
If that the *Phoenix* had bene separated,
And from the gentle *Turtle* had bene parted,
Loue had bene murdred in the infancie,
Without these two no loue at all can be.
Let the loue wandring wits but learne of these,
To die together, so their griefe to ease:
But louers now adayes do loue to change,
And here and there their wanton eyes do range,
Not pleased with one choise, but seeking many,
And in the end scarce is content with any:
Loue now adayes is like a shadowed sight,
That shewes it selfe in *Phoebus* golden light,
But if in kindnesse you do striue to take it,
Fades cleane away, and you must needs forsake it.
Louers are like the leaues with Winter shoken,
Brittle like glasse, that with one fall is broken.
O fond corrupted age, when birds shall show
The world their dutie, and to let men know
That no sinister chaunce should hinder loue,
Though as these two did, deaths arrest they proue.
I can but mourne with sadnesse and with griefe,
Not able for to yeeld the world reliefe,
To see these two consumed in the fire,
Whom Loue did copulate with true desire:
But in the worlds wide eare I meane to ring
The fame of this dayes wondrous offring,
That they may sing in notes of Chastitie,
The *Turtle* and the *Phoenix* amitie.

---

[12] 'perfect creature' recalls Marston's verse, where the Phoenix is repeatedly referred to as 'perfection'.

Love's Martyr's Dialogues and Cantos

Conclusion.

GEntle conceiuers of true meaning Wit,
Let good Experience iudge what I haue writ,
For the Satyricall fond applauded vaines,
Whose bitter worme-wood spirite in some straines,
Bite like the Curres of *Ægypt* those that loue them,
Let me alone, I will be loth to moue them,
For why, when mightie men their wit do proue,
How shall I least of all expect their loue?
Yet to those men I gratulate some paine,
Because they touch those that in art do faine.
But those that haue the spirit to do good,
Their whips will will neuer draw one drop of bloud:
To all and all in all that view my labour,
Of euery iudging sight I craue some fauour
At least to reade, and if you reading find,
A lame leg'd staffe, tis lamenesse of the mind
That had no better skill: yet let it passe,
For burdnous lodes are set vpon an Asse.
From the sweet fire of perfumed wood,
Another princely *Phoenix* vpright stood:
Whose feathers purified did yeeld more light,
Then her late burned mother out of sight,
And in her heart restes a perpetuall loue,
Sprong from the bosome of the *Turtle-Doue*.
Long may the new vprising bird increase,
Some humors and some motions to release,
And thus to all I offer my deuotion,
Hoping that gentle minds accept my motion.

Finis. R. C.

> *Cantoes Alphabet-wise to faire Phœ-*
> nix made by the Paphian Doue.[13]

A. 1.
A Hill, a hill, a *Phoenix* seekes a Hill;
A promontorie top, a stately Mountaine,

---

[13] Segment 30 begins.

194

Love's Martyr's Dialogues and Cantos

A Riuer, where poore soule she dippes her bill,
And that sweete siluer streame is *Natures* fountaine,
Accomplishing all pleasures at her will:
Ah, be my *Phoenix,* I will be thy *Doue,*
And thou and I in secrecie will loue.

B. 2.
Blaze not my loue, thou Herald of the day,
Blesse not the mountaine tops with my sweet shine,
Beloued more I am then thou canst say,
Blessed and blessed be that Saint of mine,
Balme, honie sweet, and honor of this Clime:
Blotted by things vnseene, belou'd of many,
But Loues true motion dares not giue to any.

C. 3.
Chastnesse farewell, farewell the bed of Glorie,
Constraint adew, thou art loues Enemie,
Come true Report, make of my Loue a Storie,
Cast lots for my poore heart, so thou enioy me,
Come come sweet *Phoenix,* I at length do claime thee,
Chaste bird, too chaste, to hinder what is willing,
Come in mine armes and wele not sit a billing.

D. 4.
Deuout obedience on my knees I profer,
Delight matcht with delight, if thou do craue it,
Denie not gentle *Phoenix* my sweet offer,
Despaire not in my loue, for thou shalt haue it,
Damne not the soule to woe if thou canst saue it:
Doues pray deuoutly, O let me request,
Delicious loue to build within thy nest.

E. 5.
Enuie is banisht, do not thou despaire,
Euill motions tempt thee sooner then the good:
Enrich thy beautie that art fam'd for faire,
Euery thing's silent to conioyne thy blood,
Esteeme the thing that cannot be withstood:

Love's Martyr's Dialogues and Cantos

> Esteeme of me, and I will lend thee fire,
> Euen of mine owne to fit thy sweet desire.

F. 6.

Faint harted soule, why dost thou die thy cheekes,
Fearfull of that which will reuiue thy sence,
Faith and obedience thy sweet mercy seekes,
Friends plighted war with thee I will commence,
Feare not at all, tis but sweet Loues offence,

> Fit to be done, so doing tis not seene,
> Fetcht from the ancient records of a Queene.

G. 7.

Gold beautifying *Phoenix,* I must praise thee,
Granut gracious heauens a delightsome Muse,
Giue me old *Homers* spirit, and Ile raise thee,
Gracious in thought do not my Loue refuse,
Great map of beauty make thou no excuse,

> Gainst my true louing spirit do not carpe,
> Grant me to play my Sonnet on thy Harpe.

H. 8.

Health to thy vertues, health to all thy beauty,
Honour attend thy steps when thou art going,
High heauens force the birds to owe thee duty;
Hart-groning care to thee still stands a woing,
Haue pitty on him *Phoenix* for so doing:

> Helpe his disease, and cure his malady,
> Hide not thy secret glory least he die.

I. 9.

I Loue, ô Loue how thou abusest me,
I see the fire, and warme me with the flame,
I note the errors of thy deity:
In *Vestas* honor, *Venus* lusts to tame,
I in my humors yeeld thee not a name,

> I count thee foolish, fie Adultrous boy,
> I touch the sweete, but cannot tast the ioy.

Love's Martyr's Dialogues and Cantos

K. 10.
Kisses are true loues pledges, kisse thy deare *Turtle,*
Keepe not from him the secrets of thy youth:
Knowledge he'le teach thee vnder a greene spred Mirtle,
Kend shalt thou be of no man, of my truth,
Know first the motion, when the life ensueth:
       Knocke at my harts dore, I will be thy porter,
       So thou wilt let me enter in thy dorter.

L. 11.
Loue is my great Aduotrix, at thy shrine
Loue pleads for me, and from my tongue doth say,
Lie where thou wilt, my hart shall sleepe with thine,
Lamenting of thy beauty fresh as May,
Looke *Phoenix* to thy selfe do not decay:
       Let me but water thy dead saplesse floure,
       Loue giues me hope t'will flourish in an houre.

M. 12.
Make not a Iewell of nice Chastity,
Muster and summon all thy wits in one,
My heart to thee sweares perfect constancy:
Motions of zeale are to be thought vpon,
Marke how thy time is ouerspent, and gone,
       Mis-led by folly, and a kind of feare,
       Marke not thy beauty so my dearest deare.

N. 13.
Note but the fresh bloom'd Rose within her pride,
(No Rose to be compared vnto thee)
Nothing so soone vnto the ground will slide,
Not being gathered in her chiefest beauty,
Neglecting time it dies with infamy:
       Neuer be coy, lest whil'st thy leaues are spred,
       None gather thee, and then thy grace is dead,

O. 14.
O looke vpon me, and within my brow,
Officious motions of my hart appeares,

Love's Martyr's Dialogues and Cantos

Opening the booke of Loue, wherein I vow,
Ouer thy shrine to shed continuall teares:
O no, I see my *Phoenix* hath no Eares,
　　　Or if she haue Eares, yet no Eyes to see,
　　　O all disgraced with continuall follie.

P. 15.
Proud Chastity, why dost thou seeke to wrong
Phoenix my Loue, with lessons too precise?
Pray thou for me, and I will make a song,
Pend in thine honor, none shall equalize,
Possesse not her, whose beauty charmes mine eyes,
　　　Plead, sue, and seeke, or I will banish thee,
　　　Her body is my Castle and my fee.

Q. 16.
Question not *Phoenix* why I do adore thee,
Quite captiuate and prisner at thy call,
Quit me with Loue againe, do not abhor me,
Queld downe with hope as subiugate to thrall,
Quaild will I neuer be despight of all;
　　　Quaking I stand before thee, still expecting
　　　Thine owne consent, our ioyes to be effecting.

R. 17.
Remember how thy beauty is abused,
Ract on the tenter-hookes of foule disgrace,
Riuers are dry, and must be needs refused,
Restore new water in that dead founts place,
Refresh thy feathers, beautifie thy face:
　　　Reade on my booke, and there thou shalt behold
　　　Rich louing letters printed in fine gold.

S. 18.
Shame is ashamed to see thee obstinate,
Smiling at thy womanish conceipt,
Swearing that honor neuer thee begat,
Sucking in poyson for a sugred baite,

Love's Martyr's Dialogues and Cantos

Singing thy pride of beauty in her height:
      Sit by my side, and I will sing to thee
      Sweet ditties of a new fram'd harmony.

T. 19.
Thou art a *Turtle* wanting of thy mate,
Thou crok'st about the groues to find thy Louer,
Thou fly'st to woods, and fertile plaines dost hate:
Thou in obliuion dost true vertue smother,
To thy sweet selfe thou canst not find another:
      Turne vp my bosome, and in my pure hart,
      Thou shalt behold the *Turtle* of thy smart.

V. 20.
Vpon a day I sought to scale a Fort,
Vnited with a Tower of sure defence;
Vncomfortable trees did marre my sport,
Vnlucky Fortune with my woes expence,
Venus with *Mars* would not sweet war commence,
      Vpon an Alter would I offer Loue,
      And Sacrifice my soule poore *Turtle* Doue.

W. 21.
Weepe not my *Phoenix,* though I daily weepe,
Woe is the Herald that declares my tale,
Worthy thou art in *Venus* lap to sleepe,
Wantonly couered with God *Cupids* vale,
With which he doth all mortall sence exhale:
      Wash not thy cheekes, vnlesse I sit by thee,
      To dry them with my sighes immediatly.

X. 22.
Xantha faire Nimph; resemble not in Nature,
Xantippe Loue to patient *Socrates,*
Xantha my Loue is a more milder creature,
And of a Nature better for to please:
Xantippe thought her true Loue to disease,
      But my rare *Phoenix* is at last well pleas'd,
      To cure my passions, passions seldome eas'd.

Love's Martyr's Dialogues and Cantos

Y. 23.

Yf thou haue pitty, pitty my complaining,
Yt is a badge of Vertue in thy sexe,
Yf thou do kill me with thy coy disdaining,
Yt will at length thy selfe-will anguish vexe,
And with continuall sighes thy selfe perplexe:
       Ile helpe to bring thee wood to make thy fire,
       If thou wilt giue me kisses for my hire.

Z. 24.

Zenobia at thy feete I bend my knee,[14]
For thou art Queene and Empresse of my hart,
All blessed hap and true felicity,
All pleasures that the wide world may impart,
Befall thee for thy gracious good desart:
       Accept my meaning as it fits my turne,
       For I with thee to ashes meane to burne.

Finis.

Cantoes Verbally written.[15]

---

[14]Anthea Hume observes, 'Zenobia, Queen of Palmyra in the third century AD who threw off her allegiance to the Roman empire and invaded Egypt, was viewed as a historical forerunner of the English Queen by at least one poet at the end of the Elizabethan period, the anonymous author of "England's Farewell."' See Hume, 'Love's Martyr', 52.

[15]Segment 31 begins. Carleton Brown observes that several of the 'Cantos Verbally written' acrostic titles are borrowed from 'ring posies', preserved in Harl. MS 6910 (1596); Brown, *Poems by Sir John Salusbury and Robert Chester*, lv–lvi. This collection is reprinted in A. H. Bullen, *Some Shorter Elizabethan Poems* (West Minister: Archibald Constable and Co., LTD, 1903), 269–90. Several 'ring posies' reprinted by Bullen are found in *Loues Garlan[d] Or, Posies for Rings, Hand-Ke[r]Chers, and Cloues and such Pretty Tokens that Louers Sent their Loues. Reade, Skanne, then Iudge* (London: Printed by N. Okes for Iohn Spencer, are to be sold at his shop on London Bridge, 1624). Grosart suggests 'The headings of these stanzas seem to be posies out of rings. Cf. *As You Like It*, act iii, sc. 2'; Grosart refers to the exchanges between Touchstone and Rosalind, e.g., 'TOUCHSTONE: … This is the very false gallop of verses. Why do you infect yourself with them? / ROSALIND: Peace, you dull fool, I found them on a tree. / TOUCHSTONE: Truly, the tree yields bad fruit' (3.2.111-13).

Love's Martyr's Dialogues and Cantos

1. *Pittie me that dies for thee.*
PIttie my plainings thou true nurse of pittie,[16]
Me hath thy piercing lookes enioynd to sighing,
That cannot be redressed, for thy beautie
Dies my sad heart, sad heart that's drown'd with weeping[17]:
For what so ere I thinke, or what I doe,
Thee with mine eyes, my thoughts, my heart, I woe.[18]

2. *My life you saue, if you I haue.*
My eyes, my hand, my heart seeke to maintaine
Life for thy loue, therefore be gracious,
You with your kindnesse haue my true heart slaine,
Saue my poore life, and be not tyrannous,
If any grace do in thy breast remaine,
You women haue bene counted amorous;
      I pine in sadnesse, all proceeds from thee,
      Haue me in liking through thy clemencie.

3. *Do thou by me, as I by thee.*
Do not exchange thy loue, lest in exchanging,
Thou beare the burd'nous blot of foule disgrace,
By that bad fault are many faults containing,[19]
Me still assuring nothing is so base,
As in the worlds eye alwayes to be ranging:
I sweare sweete *Phoenix* in this holy case,
      By all the sacred reliques of true loue,
      Thee to adore whom I still constant proue.

4. *Voutsafe to thinke how I do pine,*
In louing thee that art not mine.

---

[16] 'Pity me then, dear friend, and I assure ye, / Even that your pity is enough to cure me' (Shakespeare, Sonnet 111 13–14).

[17] Cf. King Henry's reply to Queen Margaret: 'Ay, Margaret; my heart is drowned with grief, / Whose flood begins to flow within mine eyes, / My body round engirt with misery', *King Henry VI Part II* (3.1.197-200).

[18] Grosart notes '*woe*' = woo (236).

[19] Grosart notes '*containing*' = contained (236).

Love's Martyr's Dialogues and Cantos

Voutsafe with splendor of thy gracious looke,
To grace my passions, passions still increasing:
Thinke with thy selfe how I thy absence brooke,
How day by day, my plaints are neuer ceasing,
I haue for thee all companies forsooke;
       Do thou reioyce, and in reioycing say,
       Pine nere so much Ile take thy griefe away.

In that great gracing word shalt thou be counted
Louing to him, that is thy true sworne louer,
Thee on the stage of honor haue I mounted,
That no base mistie cloud[20] shall euer couer:
Art thou not faire? thy beautie do not smother;
       Not in thy flouring youth, but still suppose
       Mine owne to be, my neuer dying *Rose*.

5. My destinie to thee is knowne,
Cure thou my smart, I am thine owne.

My time in loues blind idlenesse is spent,
Destinie and Fates do will it so,
To *Circes* charming tongue mine eare I lent,
Thee louing that dost wish my ouerthrow:
       Is not this world wrapt in inconstancie,
       Knowne to most men as hels miserie?

Cure of my wound is past all Phisickes skill,
Thou maist be gracious, at thy very looke
My wounds will close, that would my bodie kill,
Smart will be easde that could no plaisters brooke;
I of my *Phoenix* being quite forsooke,
Am like a man that nothing can fulfill:
       Thine euer-piercing eye of force will make me,
       Owne heart, owne loue, that neuer will forsake thee.

6. Ore my heart your eyes do idolatrize.
Ore the wide world my loue-layes Ile be sending,

---

[20] 'To let base clouds o'ertake me in my way' (Sonnet 34).

Love's Martyr's Dialogues and Cantos

My loue-layes in my Loues praise always written,
Heart-comfortable motions still attending,
Your beautie and your vertuous zeale commending,
Eyes that no frosts-cold-rage hath euer bitten:
  Do you then thinke that I in Loues hot fire,
  Idolatrize and surphet[21] in desire.

7. *I had rather loue though in vaine that face,*
Then haue of any other grace.

I being forc'd to carrie *Venus* shield,
Had rather beare a *Phoenix* for my crest,
Rather then any bird within the field,
Loue tels me that her beautie is the best:
  Though some desire faire *Vestas Turtle-doue*,
  In my Birds bosome resteth perfect loue.

Vaine is that blind vnskilfull herauldrie,
That will not cause my bird that is so rare,
Face all the world for her rarietie,
Then who with her for honor may compare?
  Haue we one like her for her pride of beautie,
  Of all the feathered Quier in the aire?

Any but vnto her do owe their dutie:
  Other may blaze, but I will alwaies say,
  Grace whom thou list, she beares the palme away,

8. *What euer fall, I am at call.*

What[22] thunder stormes of enuie shall arise,
Euer to thee my heart is durable,
Fall fortunes wheele on me to tyrannize,
I will be always found inexorable[23]:

---

[21] Grosart notes '*surphet*' = surfeit (236).

[22] Grosart notes '*What*' = whatever (236).

[23] Grosart notes '*inexorable*' = unchangeable (236).

203

Love's Martyr's Dialogues and Cantos

Am I not then to thee most stable?
> At morne, midnight, and at mid-dayes sunne,
> Call when thou wilt, my deare, to thee Ile runne.

9. *I had rather loue, though in vaine that face.*
Then haue of any other grace,

I now do wish my loue should be relieued,
Had I my thoughts in compasse of my will,
Rather then liue and surfeit being grieued,
Loue in my breast doth wondrous things fulfill,
Though loues vnkindnesse many men do kill,
> In her I trust, that is my true sworne louer,
> Vaine he doth write that doth her vertues smother.

That she is faire, *Nature* her selfe alloweth,
Face full of beauty, eyes resembling fire,
Then my pure hart to loue thy hart still voweth,
Haue me in fauour for my good desire,
Of holy loue, Loues Temple to aspire;
Any but thee my thoughts will nere require,
> Other sweet motions now I will conceale
> Grace these rude lines that my hearts thoughts reueale,

10. *Disgrace not me, in louing thee.*
Disgrace be banisht from thy heauenly brow,
Not entertained of thy piercing eie,
Me thy sweete lippes, a sweet touch will allow,
In thy faire bosome would I always lie,
> Louing in such a downe-bed to be placed,
> Thee for to please, my selfe for euer graced.

11.[24] *I had rather loue though in vaine that face,*
Then haue of any other grace.

---

[24] Segment 32 begins.

Love's Martyr's Dialogues and Cantos

I liue enricht with gifts of great content,
Had my desires the guerdon of good will,
Rather then taste of Fortunes fickle bent,
Loue bids me die, and scorne her witlesse skill,
Though Loue command, Despaire doth stil attend,
In hazard proues oft times but doubtfull end.
Vaine is the loue encountred with denayes,[25]
That yeelds but griefe, where grace should rather grow,
Face full of furie, voide of curteous praise:
Then since all loue consists of weale and woe,
Haue still in mind, that loue deserues the best,
Of hearts the touchstone, inward motions louing,
Any that yeelds the fruite of true-loues rest,
Other I loue vnworthie of commending,
Grac'd with bare beautie, beautie most offending.

12. *My selfe and mine, are always thine.*[26]

My care to haue my blooming Rose not wither,
Selfe-louing Enuie shall it not denie,
And that base weed thy growth doth seeke to hinder,
Mine hands shall pull him vp immediatly,
Are they not enuious monsters in thine eie,
       Alwayes with vaine occasions to inclose
       Thine euer growing beautie, like the Rose?

13. *The darting of your eies, may heale or wound,*
Let not empiring lookes my heart confound.

The ey-bals in your head are *Cupids* fire,
Darting such hot sparkles at my brest,
Of force I am enthrald, and do desire
Your gracious loue, to make me happie blest:
Eyes, lippes, and tongue haue caused my vnrest,

---

[25] Grosart notes '*denayes*' = denials (236).
[26] 'Myself and mine are only thine'. Bullen, *Shorter Elizabethan Poems*, 274, col 2; Brown
notes it is also found in Christ Church MS 184, fol 78[b].

Love's Martyr's Dialogues and Cantos

May I vnto the height of grace aspire,
Heale my sicke heart with loues great griefe opprest,
    Or if to fire thou wilt not yeeld such fuell,
    Wound me to death, and so be counted cruell.

Let the wide ope-mouth'd world slaunder the guiltie,
Not my dead *Phoenix,* that doth scorne such shame,
Empiring[27] honor blots such infamie,
Lookes dart away the blemish of that name;
My thoughts prognosticate thy Ladies pittie:
Hearts-ease to thee, this counsell will I giue,
Confound thy foes, but let true louers liue.

14. *You are my ioy, be not so coy.*

You best belou'd, you honor of delight,
Are the bright shining Starre that I adore,
My eyes like Watchmen gaze within the night,
Ioy fils my heart when you do shine before,
Be not disgrasiue[28] to thy friend therefore:
Too glorious are thy lookes to entertaine
Coy thoughts, fell peeuish deeds, our[29] base disdaine.

15. *For you I die, being absent from mine eye.*

For[30] all the holy rites that *Venus* vseth,
You I coniure to true obedience:
I offer faith, which no kind hart refuseth,
Die periur'd Enuie for thy late offence,
Being enamored of rich Beauties pride,
Absent, I freeze in Winters pining cold,
From thee I sit, as if thou hadst denide,

---

[27] Grosart notes '*empiring*' = over-queenly, stately (236).

[28] Grosart notes '*disgrasive*' = disgracing (236).

[29] Grosart notes '*our*' – misprint for 'or' (236).

[30] Grosart notes '*For*' = through (236).

Love's Martyr's Dialogues and Cantos

My loue-sicke passions twentie times retold:
    Eye-dazling Mistris, with a looke of pittie,
    Grace my sad Song, and my hearts pining Dittie.

16. *Send me your heart, to ease my smart.*

Send but a glaunce of amours from thine eie,
Me will it rauish with exceeding pleasure,
Your eye-bals do enwrap my destinie,
Heart sicke with sorrow, sorrow out of measure,
To thinke vpon my loues continuall folly:
Ease thou my paine from pitties golden treasure;
    My griefe proceeds from thee, and I suppose
    Smart of my smart, will my lifes bloud inclose.

17. *Seeing you haue mine, let me haue thine.*

Seeing my passions are so penetrable,
You of all other should be pittifull,
Haue mind of me, and you'le be fauourable,
Mine hart doth tell me you are mercifull,
Let my harts loue be alwayes violable,
Me haue you found in all things dutifull,
    Haue me in fauour, and thy selfe shalt see,
    Thine and none others, will I all wayes be.

18. *Within thy brest, my hart doth rest.*

Within the circuit of a Christall spheare,
Thy eyes are plast, and vnderneath those eyes,
Brest of hard flint, eares that do scorne to heare
My dayes sad gronings, and night waking cries,
Hart sore sicke passions, and Loues agonies,
    Doth it become thy beauty? no, a staine
    Rests on thy bright brow wrinckled with disdaine.[31]

---

[31] Grosart notes 'the wrinkles, not the "disdaine," being the ground of offence' (236).

Love's Martyr's Dialogues and Cantos

19. *O let me heare, from thee my deare.*[32]

O tongue thou hast blasphem'd thy holy Goddesse,
Let me do penance for offending thee,
Me do thou blame for my forgetfulnesse:
Heare my submission, thou wilt succor me:
From thy harts closet commeth gentlenesse,
Thee hath the world admir'd for clemency,
   My hart is sorrie, and Ile bite my tongue,
   Deare that to thee, to thee I offred wrong.[33]

20. *My Phoenix rare, is all my care.*

My life, my hart, my thoughts, I dedicate,
Phoenix to thee, *Phoenix* of all beauty,
Rare things in hart of thee I meditate,
Is it not time, I come to shew my duty?
All fauors vnto thee I consecrate,
My goods, my lands, my selfe, and all is thine,
Care those that list, so thou faire bird be mine.

21. *I would I might, be thy delight.*

I wish for things, would they might take effect,
Would they might end, and we enioy our pleasure,
I vow I would not proffred time neglect,
Might I but gather such vnlook't for treasure,
Be all things enuious I would the[34] respect,
   Thy fauours in my hart I do enroule,
   Delight matcht with delight, doth me controule.

---

[32] 'I would I were / With you, my Dear!'; Bullen, 273, col. 1.
[33] Grosart notes 'Dear [I give] that to thee [to whom] I offered wrong' (236).
[34] Grosart notes '*the*' = thee (236).

Love's Martyr's Dialogues and Cantos

22.[35] *If I you haue, none else I craue.*[36]

If adoration euer were created,
I am a Maister of that holy Art,
You my aduotrix,[37] whom I haue admired,
Haue of my true deuotion bore a part:
None but your selfe may here be nominated,
Else would my tongue my true obedience thwart:
> I cannot flatter, Loue will not allow it,
> Craue thou my hart, on thee I will bestow it.

23. *Be you to me, as I to thee.*[38]

Bee the poore Bee, sucke hony from the flower,
You haue a spacious odoriferous field,
To tast all moysture, where in sweet *Floras* bower,
Me shall you find submissiuely to yeeld,
As a poore Captiue looking for the hower;
I may haue gracious lookes, else am I kild,
> To dye by you were life, and yet thy shame,
> Thee would the wide world hate, my folly blame.

24. *You are the first, in whom I trust.*

You in your bosome hauing plac'd a light,
Are the chiefe admirall vnto my Fleet,
The Lanthorne for to guide me in the night,
First to the shore, where I may set my feet
In safegard, void of Dangers cruell spight,
Whom in disgrace Loue and fel Enuie meet,
> I muster vp my spirits, and they flie;
> Trust of thy faith controules mine enemie.

---

[35] Segment 33 begins.
[36] 'I nought do crave / But you to have.'; Bullen, 275, col. 2.
[37] Grosart notes 'Love is my great Aduotrix, at thy shrine', from Cantos Alphabet-wise (236).
[38] 'Be true to me, / as I to thee.' Bullen, 283, 285. This stanza is also numbered 23 in *Love's Garland* and repeated as number 44.

209

Love's Martyr's Dialogues and Cantos

25. *You are the last my loue shall taste.*

You standing on the tower of hope and feare,
Are timerous of selfe-will foolishnesse,[39]
The onely Viper that doth loue-laies teare,
Last can it not, tis womans peeuishnesse,
My kind affections can it not forbeare,
Loue tels me that tis bred in idlenesse,
  Shall such occasion hinder thee or me?
  Taste first the fruit, and then commend the tree.

26. *If you I had, I should be glad.*[40]

If the Sunne shine, the haruest man is glad,
You are my Sunne, my dayes delightsome Queene,
I am your haruest laborer almost mad,
Had I not my glorious commet seene,
I wish that I might sit within thy shade,
Should I be welcome ere thy beautie fade:
  Be not *Narcissus,* but be alwaies kind,
  Glad to obtain the thing thou neare couldst find.

27. *Though place be far, my heart is nar.*

Though thou my Doue from me be separated,
Place, nor the distance shall not hinder me,
Be constant for a while, thou maist be thwarted,
Far am I not, Ile come to succour thee.
My heart and thine, my sweet shall nere be parted,
Heart made of loue, and true simplicitie:
  Is not Loue lawlesse, full of powerfull might?
  Nar[41] to my heart that still with Loue doth fight.

---

[39] Grosart notes *'selfe-will'* = self-will or foolishness sprung of self-will (236).
[40] 'I would be glad, If you I had.' Bullen, 273 col. 1.
[41] Grosart notes *'Nar'* = near (237).

Love's Martyr's Dialogues and Cantos

28. *My thoughts are dead, cause thou art sped.*

My inward *Muse* can sing of nought but Loue,
Thoughts are his Heralds, flying to my breast
Are entertained, if they thence remoue,
Dead shall their master be, and in vnrest;
Cause[42] all the world thy hatred to reproue,
Thou art that All-in-all that I loue best:
>> Art thou then cruell? no thou canst not be
>> Sped with so foule a fiend as Crueltie.

29. *I send my heart to thee, where gladly I would be.*

I of all other am faire *Venus* thrall,
Send me but pleasant glances of thine eie,
My soule will leape with ioy and dance withall,
Heart of my heart, and soules felicitie:
>> To beauties Queene my heart is sanctified,
>> Thee aboue all things haue I deified.

Where is Affections? fled to Enuies caue?
Gladlie my Thoughts would beare her[43] companie,
I from foule bondage[44] will my *Phoenix* saue,
Would she in loue requite my courtesie,
>> Be louing as thou art faire, else shall I sing,
>> Thy beautie a poisnous bitter thing.

30. *If you me iust haue knowne,*
Then take me for your owne.

If you be faire, why should you be vnkind?
You haue no perfect reason for the same,
Me thinkes it were your glorie for to find

---

[42] Grosart notes '*Cause*' = [Thou are] cause (237).

[43] Affections personified as feminine.

[44] Grosart notes '*foule bondage*' = slavery of 'selfe-will' (237).

211

Love's Martyr's Dialogues and Cantos

Iust measure at my hands, but you to blame,
      Haue from the deepest closet of your heart,
      Knowne my pure thoughts, and yet I pine in smart.

Then in the deepest measure of pure loue,
Take pittie on the sad sicke pining soule,
Me may you count your vnknowne *Turtle-Doue,*
For in my bosomes chamber, I enroule
      Your deepe loue-darting eie, and still will be
      Owne of your owne,[45] despight extremitie.

31. *My heart I send, to be your friend.*

My deare soules comfort, and my hopes true solace,
Heart of my heart, and my liues secret ioy,
I in conceit do thy sweete selfe embrace,
Send cloudie exhalations cleane away
To the blind mistie North, there for to stay:
Be thou my arbour and my dwelling place,
      Your armes the circling folds that shall enclose me,
      Friend me with this, and thou shalt neuer lose me.

32. *I haue no loue, but you my Doue.*

I pine in sadnesse, and in sad songs singing
Haue spent my time, my ditties harsh and ill,
No sight but thy faire sight would I be seeing:
Loue in my bosome keepes his castle still,
But being disseuered I sit alwayes pining,
You do procure me *Niobes* cup[46] to fill,
      My dutie yet remembred I dare proue,
      Doues haue no power for to exchange their Loue,

---

[45] Knight remarks 'Owne of your owne' suggests 'thou mine, I thine' of Sonnet 108 (Knight, *The Mutual Flame*, 172); 'Thou mine, I thine' is found in *Love's Garland*; Bullen, 285.

[46] Grosart notes '*Niobes cup*' = of tears (237).

Love's Martyr's Dialogues and Cantos

34.[47] *I will not change, though some be strange.*

I cannot stir one foote from *Venus* gate,
Will you come sit, and beare me company?
Not one but you can make me fortunate:
Change when thou wilt, it is but cruelty,
Though vnto women it is giuen by fate,
Some gentle minds these ranging thoughts do hate:
> Be thou of that mind, else I will conclude,
> Strange hast thou alter'd Loue, to be so rude.

Thoughts keepe me waking.

Thoughts like the ayrie puffing of the wind,
Keepe a sweet faining in my Loue-sicke brest,
Me still assuring that thou art most kind,
Waking in pleasure, sleeping sure in rest:
> That no sleepes dreamings, nor no waking cries,
> To our sweet louing thoughts, sweet rest denies.

Seeing that my hart made choise of thee,
Then frame thy selfe to comfort me.

Seeing Loue is pleas'd with Loues enamor'd ioyes,
That Fortune cannot crosse sweet *Cupids* will,
My Loues content, not with fond wanton toyes:
Hart of my hart doth Loues vnkindnesse kill,
Made by fond tongues vpbraiding hurtfull skill:
Choise now is fram'd to further all annoyes:
> Of all sweete thoughts, of all sweete happie rest,
> Thee haue I chose, to make me three times blest.

Then let our holy true aspiring loue,
Frame vs the sweetest musicke of Desire:
Thy words shall make true concord, and remoue
Selfe-will it selfe, for *Venus* doth require

---

[47] Segment 34 begins. Note: there is no Canto 33.

Love's Martyr's Dialogues and Cantos

To be acquainted with thy beauties fire:
> Comfort my heart, for comfort tels me this,
> Me hast thou chose of all to be thy blisse.

My heart is bound to fauour thee,
Then yeeld in time to pittie me.

My *Phoenix* hath two starre-resembling Eyes,
Heart full of pittie, and her smiling looke,
Is of the Sunnes complexion, and replies,
Bound for performance by faire *Venus* booke
To faithfulnesse, which from her nurse she tooke:
> Fauour in her doth spring, in vertuous praise,
> Thee Eloquence it selfe shall seeke to raise.

Then in performance of this gracious right,
Yeeld vp that piteous heart to be my Louer,
In recompence how I haue lou'd thy sight,
Time shall from time to time to thee discouer:
To thee is giuen the power of *Cupids* might,
> Pittie is writ in gold vpon thy hart,
> Me promising to cure a curelesse smart.

I ioy to find a constant mind.[48]

I am encompast round about with ioy,
Ioy to enioy my sweete, for she protesteth
To comfort me that languish in annoy,
Find ease if any sorrow me molesteth,
A happie man that such a loue possesseth:
> Constant in words, and alwayes vowes to loue me,
> Mind me she will, but yet she dares not proue me.

My heart by hope doth liue,
Desire no ioy doth giue.

---

[48] 'I joy to find, / A constant mind.' Bullen 274, col. 1.

Love's Martyr's Dialogues and Cantos

My loue and dearest life to thee I consecrate,
Heart of my hearts deare treasure, for I striue
By thy deuinenesse too deuine to nominate,
Hope of approued faith in me must thriue:
> Doth not the God of Loue that's most deuine,
> Liue in thy bosomes closet and in mine?

Desire to that vnspeakable delight,
No sharpe conceited wit can nere set downe,
Ioy in the world to worldly mens ey-sight,
Doth but ignoble thy imperiall crowne:
> Giue thou the onset and the foe will flie,
> Amazed at thy great commanding beautie.

Death shall take my life away,
Before my friendship shall decay.

Death that heart-wounding Lord, sweet louers foe,
Shall lay his Ebone darts at thy faire feete,
Take them into thy hand and worke my woe,
My woe that thy minds anguish will regreet:
> Life, hart, ioy, greeting and all my pleasure,
> Away are gone and fled from my deare treasure.

Before one staine shal blot thy scarlet die,
My bloud shall like a fountaine wash the place,
Friendship it selfe knit with mortality,
Shall thy immortall blemish quite disgrace:
> Decay shall all the world, my Loue in thee
> Shall liue vnstain'd, vntoucht perpetually.

Let truth report what hart I beare,
To her that is my dearest deare.

Let not foule pale-fac'd *Enuy* be my foe,
Truth must declare my spotlesse loyalty,
Report vnto the world shall plainely show

Love's Martyr's Dialogues and Cantos

What hart deare Loue I alwayes bore to thee,
Hart fram'd of perfect Loues sincerity:
     I cannot flatter, this I plainely say,
     Beare with false words, ile beare the blame away.

To change in loue is a base simple thing,
Her name will be orestain'd with periury,
That doth delight in nothing but dissembling?
Is it not shame so for to wrong faire beauty,
My true approued toung must answer I
     Dearest beware of this, and learne of me,
     Deare is that Loue combin'd with Chastity.

Seene hath the eye, chosen hath the hart:
Firme is the faith, and loth to depart.

Seene in all learned arts is my beloued,
Hath anie one so faire a Loue as I?
The stony-hearted sauage hath she moued,
Eye for her eye tempts blushing chastitie,
     Chosen to make their nine a perfect ten,
     Hath the sweet *Muses* honored her agen.

T|he bright-ey'd wandring world doth alwaies seeke,
Heart-curing comfort doth proceed from thee,
Firme trust, pure thoughts, a mind that's always meeke,
Is the true Badge of my loues Soueraigntie:
     The honor of our age, the onely faire,
     Faiths mistris, and Truths deare adopted heire.

And those that do behold thy heauenly beautie,
Loth to forsake thee, spoile themselues with gazing,
To thee all humane knees proffer their dutie,
Depart they will not but with sad amazing:
     To dimme their ey-sight looking gainst the sunne,
     Whose hot reflecting beames will neare be donne.

Love's Martyr's Dialogues and Cantos

No[49] *woe so great in loue, not being heard,*
No plague so great in loue, being long deferd.

No tongue can tell the world my hearts deepe anguish,
Woe, and the minds great perturbation
So trouble me, that day and night I languish,
Great cares in loue seeke my destruction:
　　　In all things gracious, sauing onely this,
　　　Loue is my foe, that I account my blisse.

Not all the world could profer me disgrace,
Being maintained fairest faire by thee,
Hard-fortune shall thy seruant nere outface,
No stormes of Discord[50] should discomfort me:
　　　Plague all the world with frownes my *Turtle-doue,*
　　　So that thou smile on me and be my loue.

Great Mistris, matchlesse in thy soueraigntie,
In lue and recompence of my affection,
Loue me againe, this do I beg of thee,
Being bound by *Cupids* kind direction:
　　　Long haue I su'd for grace, yet stil I find,
　　　Deferd I am by her that's most vnkind.

And if my loue shall be releeu'd by thee,
My heart is thine, and so account of me.

And yet a stedfast hope maintaines my hart,
If anie fauour fauourably proceede
My deare from thee, the curer of my smart,
Loue that easeth minds opprest with neede,
　　　Shall be the true Phisition of my griefe,
　　　Releeu'd alone by thee that yeeld'st reliefe.

---

[49] Segment 35 begins.
[50] Cf. Nestor's reply to Agamemnon, ' … Even so / Doth valour's show and valour's worth divide / In storms of fortune … ' (*Troilus and Cressida* 1.3.45-47).

Love's Martyr's Dialogues and Cantos

By all the holy rites that Loue adoreth,
Thee haue I lou'd aboue the loue of any,
My heart in truth thee alwayes fauoureth,
Heart freed from any one, then freed from many:
      Is it not base to change? yea so they say,
      Thine owne confession loue denies delay.

And by the high imperiall seate of *Ioue,*
So am I forc'd by *Cupid* for to sweare,
Account I must of thee my *Turtle-doue,*
Of thee that Times long memorie shall outweare:
      Me by thy stedfast truth and faith denying,
      To promise any hope on thee relying.

My passions are a hell and death to me,
Vnlesse you feele remorce and pitie me.

My sweetest thoughts sweet loue to thee I send,
Passions deeply ingrafted, vnremouable
Are my affections, and I must commend
A stedfast trust in thee most admirable:
      Hell round enwraps my bodie by disdaine,
      And then a heauen if thou loue againe.

Death haunts me at the heeles, yet is affraid,
To touch my bosome, knowing thou lou'st me,
Me sometimes terrifying by him betraid,
Vnlesse sweete helpfull succour come from thee:
      You well I know, the honor of mine eie,
      Feele some remorcefull helpe in miserie.

Remorce sits on thy brow triumphantly.
And smiles vpon my face with gentle cheere;
Pittie, loues gracious mother dwels in thee,
Me fauouring, abandoning base feare,
      Death is amazed, viewing of thy beautie,
      Thinking thy selfe perfect eternitie.

Love's Martyr's Dialogues and Cantos

My purest loue doth none but thee adore,
My heartie thoughts are thine, I loue no more.

My comfortable sweete approued Mistris,
Purest of all the pure that nature framed,
Loue in the height of all our happinesse,
Doth tell me that thy vertues are not named:
  None can giue forth thy constancie approued,
  But I that tride thy faith, my best beloued.

Thee in the temple of faire *Venus* shrine
Adore I must, and kneele vpon my knee,
My fortunes tell me plaine that thou art mine,
Heartie in kindnesse, yeelding vnto me:
  Thoughts the much-great disturbers of our rest
  Are fled, and lodge in some vnquiet brest.

Thine euer vnremou'd and still kept word,
I pondred oftentimes within my mind:
Loue told me that thou neuer wouldst afford,
None other grace but that which I did find,
  More comfortable did this sound in mine eare,
  Then sweete releasement to a man in feare.

I do resolue to loue no loue but thee,
Therefore be kind, and fauour none but me.

I sometime sitting by my selfe alone,
Do meditate of things that are ensuing,
Resolue I do that thou must end my moue,
To strengthen Loue if loue should be declining.
  Loue in thy bosome dwels, and tels me still,
  No enuious stormes shall thwart affections will.

Loue hath amz'd the world, plac'd in thy brow,
But yet slauish disdaine seekes for to crosse
Thee and my selfe, that haue combin'd our vow,

Love's Martyr's Dialogues and Cantos

Therefore that monster cannot worke our losse:
>   Be all the winds of Anger bent to rage,
>   Kind shalt thou find me, thus my hart I gage.

And from my faith that's vnremoueable,
Fauour be seated in thy maiden eie,
None can receiue it loue more acceptable
But I my selfe, waiting thy pittying mercie:
>   Me hast thou made the substance of delight,
>   By thy faire sunne-resembling heauenly sight.

Ah quoth she, but where is true Loue?
Where quoth he? where you and I loue.
I quoth she, were thine like my loue.
Why quoth he, as you loue I loue.

Ah thou imperious high commaunding Lord,
(Quoth he) to *Cupid* gentle god of Loue,
He that I honor most will not accord,[51]
But striues against thy Iustice from aboue,
Where I haue promist faith, my plighted word
Is quite refused with a base reproue:
>   True louing honour this I onely will thee,
>   Loue thy true loue, or else false loue will kill me.

Where shall I find a heart that's free from guile?
Quoth Faithfulnesse, within my louers brest.
He at these pleasing words began to smile,
Where Anguish wrapt his thoughts in much vnrest:
You did with pretie tales the time beguile,
And made him in conceited pleasure blest,
>   I grac'd the words spoke with so sweet a tong,
>   Loue being the holy burden of your song.

---

[51] Grosart emended the pronoun in line 3 from 'He' to '[S]he', but Knight argues for the original spelling. See Chapter 1 for a discussion of this acrostic.

220

Love's Martyr's Dialogues and Cantos

I grac'd your song of Loue, but by the way,
(Quoth true Experience,) sit and you shall see,
She will enchaunt you with her heauenly lay:
Were you fram'd all of heauenly Pollicie,
Thine eares should drinke the poison of Delay,
Like as I said, so did it proue to be,
      My Mistris beautie grac'd my Mistris song,
      Loue pleasd more with her Eyes then with her Tong.

Why then in deepenesse of sweete Loues delight,
Quoth she, the perfect Mistris of Desire,
He that I honor most bard from my sight,
As a bright Lampe kindles Affections fire:
You Magicke operations worke your spight,
Loue to the mountaine top of will aspires:
      I chalenge all in all, and this I sing,
      Loue is a holy Saint, a Lord, a King.

Ah[52] *Loue, where is thy faith in sweete loue?*
Why loue where hearts conioyne in true loue:
Why then my heart hopes of thy Loues loue,
Else let my heart be plagu'd with false loue.

Why art thou strange to me my Deare?
Not strange when as I loue my deare:
But thou esteem'st not of thy deare.
Yes when I know my dearest deare.

Why is my Loue so false to me?
My loue is thine if thou lou'st me:
Thee I loue, else none contents me.
If thou lou'st me, it not repents me.

Ah quoth he, wher's faith in sweete loue?

---

[52] Segment 36 begins.

Love's Martyr's Dialogues and Cantos

Why quoth she, conioynd in true loue.
Ah quoth he, I hope of thy loue:
Else quoth she, Ile die a false loue.

Ah my Deare, why dost thou kill me?
No my deare, Loue doth not will me.
Then in thine armes thou shalt enfould me.
I, my deare, there thou shalt hold me:
  And holding me betweene thine armes,
  I shall embrace sweete Louers Charmes.

Though death from life my bodie part,
Yet neare the lesse keepe thou my hart.

Though some men are inconstant, fond, and fickle,
Deaths ashie count'nance shall not alter me:
From glasse they take their substance being brittle,
Life, Heart, and Hand shall awaies fauour thee,
My Pen shall write thy vertues registrie,
  Bodie conioyn'd with bodie, free from strife,
  Part not in sunder till we part our life.

Yet my soules life to my deare lifes concluding,
Nere let Absurditie that villaine, theefe,
The monster of our time, mens praise deriding,
Lesse in perseuerance, of small knowledge chiefe,
  Keep the base Gate to things that are excelling,
  Thou by faire vertues praise maist yeeld reliefe,
  My lines are thine, then tell Absurditie,
  Hart of my deare, shall blot his villanie.

Where hearts agree, no strife can be.

Where faithfulnesse vnites it selfe with loue,
Hearts pin'd with sorrow cannot disagree:
Agree they must of force, for from aboue
No wind oppressing mischiefe may we see:
Strife is quite banisht from our companie.
  Can I be sad? no, Pleasure bids me sing,

Love's Martyr's Dialogues and Cantos

Be blessed, for sweete Loue's a happie thing.

Thy vowes my loue and heart hath wonne,
Till thy vntruth hath it vndonne.

Thy true vnspeakable fidelitie.
Vowes made to *Cupid* and his faire-fac'd mother,
My thoughts haue wonne to vertuous chastitie:
Loue thee alone I will, and loue none other,
And if thou find not my loues secrecie,
Heart fauoring thee, then do thou Fancie smother.
       Hath all the world such a true Bird as I,
       Wonne to this fauour by my constancie?

Till that leane fleshles cripple, pale-fac'd Death,
Thy louely Doue shall pierce with his fell dart,
Vntruth in my faire bosome nere takes breath:
Hath any loue such a firme constant heart?
       It is thine owne, vnlesse thou keepe it still
       Vndone shall I be, cleane against my will.

Time shall tell thee, how well I loue thee,[53]

Time the true proportioner of things,
Shall in the end shew my affection,
Tell thee from whence all these my passions spring,
Thee honoring that of loue haue made election:
How often I haue made my offerings,
Well knowne to *Venus* and her louely sonne,
I to the wide world shall my passions runne:
       Loue is a Lord of hearts, a great Commander,
       Thee chalenging to be my chiefe defender.

Most deuine and sacred,
Haue I found your loue vnspotted.

---

[53] 'Time shall tell thee, / How much I love thee!' Bullen 274, col. 2.

Love's Martyr's Dialogues and Cantos

Most reuerend Mistris honor of mine eie,
Deuine, most holy in religious loue,
And Lord it selfe of my hearts emperie,
Sacred in thoughts admitted from aboue,
Haue in remembrance what affection willeth:
I it reuiues the mind, and the mind killeth.
Found haue I written in your skie-like brow,
Your neuer ceasing kind humilitie,
Loue for your sake to me hath made a vow,
Vnspotted shall I find your constancie,
　　　And without staine, to thy pure stainlesse beautie,
　　　Shall my hearts bosome offer vp his dutie.

The want of thee is death to me.[54]

The day shall be all night, and night all day,
Want of the Sunne and Moone to giue vs light,
Of a blacke darknesse, before thy loue will stay
Thee from thy pleasure of thy hearts delight.
Is not Affection nurse to long Delay?
Deaths Messenger, that barres me from thy sight?
　　　To be in absence, is to burne in fire,
　　　Me round enwrapping with hot Loues desire.

I loue to be beloued.[55]

I do acknowledge of all constant pure,
Loue is my true thoughts herrald, and Ile sing
To be of thy thoughts closet, firme and sure,
Be the world still thy vertues deifying:
　　　Beloued of the most, yet most of many,
　　　Affirme my deare, thou art belou'd of any.

I scorne if I be scorned.

---

[54] 'The want of thee, / Is grief to me'. Bullen 276, col. 2.
[55] 'Love to be loved!' Bullen 274, col. 1.

Love's Martyr's Dialogues and Cantos

I being not belou'd by my affection,
Scorne within my thoughts such bad disgrace,
If thou of me do make thy firme election,
I to none other loue will giue my place:
>   Be thou my Saint, my bosomes Lord to proue,
>   Scorned of all, Ile be thy truest loue.
The heart's in paine, that loues in vaine.

The griefe poore louers feele being not beloued,
Hearts anguish, and sad lookes may testifie:
In night they sleepe not, and in day perplexed,
Paine of this sorrow makes them melancholy,
That in disdaine their silly minds are vexed,
Loues terror is so sharpe, so strong, so mightie,
>   In all things vnresistable, being aliue,
>   Vaine he resists that gainst loues force doth striue.

What greater ioy can be then this;
Where loue enioyes each louers wish?

What may we count the world if loue were dead?
Greater in woe, then woe it selfe can be,
Ioy from mans secret bosome being fled,
Cannot but kill the heart immediatly,
Because by ioy the heart is nourished:
>   Then entertaine sweete loue within thy brest,
>   This motion in the end will make thee blest.

Where two harts are vnited all in one,
Loue like a King, a Lord, a Soueraigne,
Enioyes the throne of blisse to sit vpon,
Each sad heart crauing aid, by *Cupid* slaine:
>   Louers be merrie, Loue being dignified,
>   Wish what you will, it shall not be denied.

Finis. quoth R. Chester.

NOTES

Prelims

1   Zeffiro, Andrea, 'Towards a Queer Futurity of Data', *Journal of Cultural Analytics* 1.1 (17 May 2019): 1–17, 16.

Introduction

1   G. Wilson Knight, *The Mutual Flame: On Shakespeare's Sonnets and The Phoenix and Turtle* (London: Methuen, 1955), 54.
2   Robert Chester, *Love's Martyr: Or, Rosalins Complaint: Allegorically Shadowing the Truth of Loue in the Constant Fate of the Phoenix and Turtle* (Imprinted by R. Field for E. Blount, 1601), 153–4.
3   Stanley Wells, *Shakespeare and Co.: Christopher Marlowe, Thomas Dekker, Ben Jonson, Thomas Middleton, John Fletcher and the Other Players in His Story* (New York: Pantheon, 2006), 25–6; Ed Pechter, 'Against Attribution', *Shakespeare Quarterly* 69.4 (2018): 228–55, 234.
4   Pechter, 'Against Attribution', 235–6.
5   Ralph Waldo Emerson, *Parnassus* (Boston: Houghton, Mifflin & Co., 1874), vi.
6   Knight, *The Mutual Flame*, 171.
7   Alexander B. Grosart, *Robert Chester's Love's Martyr or Rosalins Complaint* (London: Trubner, 1878), lxviii.
8   Knight, *The Mutual Flame*, 171.
9   See Stephen Guy-Bray, *Shakespeare and Queer Representation* (London: Routledge, 2021) and Jeffrey Masten, *Queer Philologies: Sex, Language, and Affect in Shakespeare's Time* (Philadelphia: University of Pennsylvania Press, 2016).
10 One copy of the 1601 text is located in the Folger Shakespeare Library; one is in the Huntington Library; another, damaged copy is in The National Library of Wales, Aberystwyth. The 1611 copy, titled 'The Annals of Great Brittaine', is in the British Library.
11 Chester, *Love's Martyr*, 177.

Notes

12 See especially the most recent book-length study of 'The Phoenix and Turtle', James Bednarz's *Shakespeare and the Truth of Love: The Mystery of "The Phoenix and Turtle"* (New York: Palgrave MacMillan, 2012).

13 John Finnis and Patrick H. Martin, 'Another Turn for the Turtle'. *TLS* 18 (April 2003); Clare Asquith, *Shakespeare* Newsletter 50, 2001. For another Jesuit interpretation, see also John Klause, 'The Phoenix and Turtle in Its Time', in *In the Company of Shakespeare: Essays on English Renaissance Literature in Honor of G. Blakemore Evans*, eds. Thomas Moisan, Douglas Bruster, and William H. Bond (Madison, NJ: London, England: Fairleigh Dickinson University Press; Associated University Presses, 2002), 206–30.

14 Ronald Bates, 'Shakespeare's "The Phoenix and Turtle"', *Shakespeare Quarterly* 6.1 (1955): 19–30, 19. Thomas P. Harrison, 'Review of *The Phoenix and the Turtle: Shakespeare's Poem and Chester's Loues Martyr* by William H. Matchett', *Modern Philology* 64.2 (1966): 155–7, 156.

15 See Robert Parry, *Sinetes Passions Vppon His Fortunes Offered for an Incense at the Shrine of the Ladies Which guided His Distempered Thoughtes. The Patrons Patheticall Posies, Sonets, Maddrigals, and Rowndelayes* (London: Printed by T[homas] P[urfoot] for William Holme, to be sould on Ludgate hill at the signe of the holy Lambe, 1597); and Henry Perry, *Egluryn phraethineb. sebh, dosparth ar retoreg, vn o 'r saith gelbhydhyd, yn dysculhuniaith ymadrodh, a 'i pherthynassau* (London: Printiedig gann Ioan Danter yn Lhundain, 1595).

16 William Epsom, *Essays on Shakespeare*, ed. David B. Pirie (Cambridge: Cambridge University Press, 1986), 27. G. Blakemore Evans assigns none of *Sinetes Passions* to Salusbury; see Evans, *The Poems of Robert Parry*, 10–23.

17 Carleton Brown, *Poems by Sir John Salusbury and Robert Chester* (Bryn Mawr: Bryn Mawr College Monographs Series, 1913), liii.

18 See Katherine Duncan-Jones, *Shakespeare: An Ungentle Life* (London: Methuen, The Arden Shakespeare, 2001, 2010), 165.

19 Mark Bland examines this relationship thoroughly in '"As far from all Reuolt": Sir John Salusbury, Christ Church MS 184, and Ben Jonson's First Ode', *English Manuscript Studies, 1100–1700* 8 (2000): 43–78.

20 Bednarz, *Shakespeare and the Truth of Love*, 72; Peter Ackroyd, *Shakespeare: The Biography* (London: Chatto and Windus, 2006), 377.

21 See, for example, Brian Vickers, 'Incomplete Shakespeare: Or, Denying Coauthorship in 1 *Henry VI*', *Shakespeare Quarterly* 58.3 (2007): 311–52.

22 For a discussion of Roderick and other early Shakespeare scholarship, see Vickers, *William Shakespeare: The Critical Heritage, Volume 4, 1753–1765* (London: Routledge, 1976); discussion of Roderick p. 34, reproduction of 'Notes on Shakespeare', p. 337.

Notes

23 I recommend the following studies, many focused on the *More* authorship controversy: John Jowett, ed., *Sir Thomas More. The Arden Shakespeare* (London: Methuen, 2011); MacDonald P. Jackson, "'A Lover's Complaint,' *Cymbeline*, and the Shakespeare Canon: Interpreting Shared Vocabulary', *The Modern Language Review* 103.3 (2008): 621–38; MacDonald P. Jackson, 'Is "Hand D" of *Sir Thomas More* Shakespeare's? Thomas Bayes and the Elliott-Valenza Authorship Tests', *Early Modern Literary Studies* 12.3 (2007): 1–36; T. H. Howard-Hill, *Shakespeare and Sir Thomas More: Essays on the Play and Its Shakespearean Interest* (Cambridge: Cambridge University Press, 1989); and David Scott Kastan, "'To think these trifles some-thing": Shakespearean Playbooks and the Claims of Authorship', *Shakespeare Studies* 36 (2007): 37–48.

24 Jowett, *More*, 19.

25 Ibid., 437–53. In the text's appendix, Jowett takes a more objective stance, establishing criteria by which 'the hand' of Shakespeare might be identifiable; to paraphrase, these factors include handwriting, spelling, vocabulary, collocations and idioms.

26 Despite the growing body of serious work in the field of early modern stylometric analysis, scholars engaging in attribution studies of early modern works – particularly if Shakespeare is involved – may face scepticism or accusations of bardolatry or be perceived to be doing 'fringe scholarship'. Referring to ongoing controversies over *More*, T. H. Howard-Hill notes, 'The discrepancy of the results of stylistic studies and critical judgment tends to bring only the first into disrepute, for whereas critical evaluations of the merits of a composition depend ultimately on critical taste and experience, the "scientific" methods of stylometrics are discredited when stylometrists disagree on particular issues or their methods are not understood by critics'. See T. H. Howard-Hill, *Shakespeare and Sir Thomas More: Essays on the Play and Its Shakespearean Interest* (Cambridge: Cambridge University Press, 1989), 4.

27 Nan Z. Da, 'The Computational Case against Computational Literary Studies', *Critical Inquiry* 45.3 (2019): 601–39.

28 See Da's essay 'The Digital Humanities Debacle' in *The Chronicle of Higher Education*, 27 March 2019. https://www.chronicle.com/article/The-Digital-Humanities-Debacle/245986.

29 Jack Halberstam, *The Queer Art of Failure* (Durham: Duke University Press, 2011), 88.

30 Halberstam, *Failure*, 88.

31 Richard Halpern, *Shakespeare's Perfume: Sodomy and Sublimity in the Sonnets, Wilde, Freud, and Lacan* (Philadelphia: University of Pennsylvania Press, 2002), 21.

Notes

32 Stockton's review of Madhavi Menon's *Shakesqueer* – 'Shakespeare and Queer Theory', *Shakespeare Quarterly* 63.2 (2012): 224–35 – charts and critiques this history, as does Valerie Traub's erudite essay on un/historicizing queerness: 'The New Unhistoricism in Queer Studies', *PMLA* 128.1 (2013): 21–39.

33 David Halperin, *Saint Foucault: Towards a Gay Hagiography* (Oxford: Oxford University Press, 1997), 62; Lee Edelman, *No Future: Queer Theory and the Death Drive* (Durham: Duke University Press, 2004), 17.

34 To engage in a sound computationally queer analysis of something like a title page, one might, for example, gather a large number of title pages by numerous authors and across periods and then, after comparing like to like, making a determination as to which data segments behave differently from the rest or that disrupt a pattern in the larger data. I would consider that kind of analysis 'queer' in the sense used in this study.

35 Hoyt Long and Richard Jean So, 'Literary Pattern Recognition: Modernism between Close Reading and Machine Learning', *Critical Inquiry* 42.2 (2016): 235–67, 236.

36 Ibid., 237.

37 Adam Isaiah Green, 'Queer Theory and Sociology: Locating the Subject and the Self in Sexuality Studies', *Sociological Theory* 25.1 (2007): 26–45, 37.

38 Jack Halberstam, David L. Eng, and José Esteban Muñoz, 'What's Queer About Queer Studies Now?' *Social Text* 23.3–4 (2005): 1–17.

39 Large-scale statistical analysis indicates real-world implications for these kinds of readings. See Eve Kraicer and Andrew Piper, 'Social Characters: The Hierarchy of Gender in Contemporary English-Language Fiction', *Journal of Cultural Analytics* 1.1 (2019): 1–28.

40 Ted Underwood, 'Dear Humanists: Fear Not the Digital Revolution', *The Chronicle of Higher Education*, 27 March 2019. https://www.chronicle.com/article/Dear-Humanists-Fear-Not-the/245987.

41 'Queer', adj. *OED*.

42 Seth Lerer, *Error and the Academic Self: The Scholarly Imagination, Medieval to Modern* (New York: Columbia University Press, 2002), 140.

43 Michael D.C. Drout, Michael Kahn, Mark D. LeBlanc, and C. Nelson. 'Of Dendrogrammatology: Lexomic Methods for Analyzing the Relationships among Old English Poems', *Journal of English and Germanic Philology* 110.3 (2011): 301–36, 301.

44 Until recently, the vast majority of research involving cladistic analysis has focused on biological taxonomies; to this day, the *OED* defines 'cladistics' as the 'systematic classification of groups of organisms on the basis of shared characteristics thought to derive from a common ancestor. Also, the study of the branching of evolutionary lines of descent and the

Notes

relationship between branches'. Contemporary cladistic analysis originates principally from German entomologist Willi Henning's work on phylogenic systematics; other important studies making use of cladistics include Cavalli-Sforza's decades-long work on population structures (1974–1994), which yielded his controversial dendrogram of population dispersals. See Cavalli-Sforza (et al), *The History and Geography of Human Genes* (Princeton: Princeton University Press, 1994).

45 See Appendix 1 for more on this rationale. Also, see Maciej Eder, Jan Rybicki, and Mike Kestemont, '"Stylo": A Package for Stylometric Analyses', *Computational Stylistics Group* (2018): 16.

46 We use larger sample sizes later in the study by combining segments that tended to group together in these earlier tests, such as: Segments 2–3, 5–6, 7–17, 18–26, 27–28, 30, 31–32, 33–34, 35–36. This grouping made each group ~2,000 words or more, the size Maciej Eder recommends for reliable authorship attribution, although some known texts in benchmark studies resist attribution and need larger sample sizes. Eder, 'Short Samples in Authorship Attribution: A New Approach', *DH* (2017); for studies on short sample size attributions, see Graeme Hirst and O. Feiguina, 'Bigrams of Syntactic Labels for Authorship Discrimination of Short Texts', *Literary and Linguistic Computing* 22.4 (2007): 405–17; and Kim Luyckx and Walter Daelemans, 'The Effect of Author Set Size and Data Size in Authorship Attribution', *Literary and Linguistic Computing* 26.1 (2011): 35–55.

47 See Appendix 1 for explanation of culling rates.

48 'Intimacy', noun, *OED*.

49 Jacob Gaboury, 'Critical Unmaking: Toward a Queer Computation', in *The Routledge Companion to Media Studies and Digital Humanities* (Berkeley: University of California Press, 2018), 484, 490.

50 Bednarz, *Shakespeare and the Truth of Love*, 10.

51 Drout et al notes, 'In contrast to corpus linguistics and some computational stylometry (and also contra Franco Moretti's call for "distant reading"), lexomic methods include a regular use of traditional close reading, philological analysis, source study and interpretation'. See Michael C. Drout, Yvette Kisor, Leah Smith, Natasha Piirainen, and Allison Dennet, *Beowulf Unlocked: New Evidence from Lexomic Analysis* (New York: Palgrave Macmillan, 2016), 5–6.

52 For an excellent study on early modern intimacy and homoeroticism, see James M. Bromley, *Intimacy and Sexuality in the Age of Shakespeare* (Cambridge: Cambridge University Press, 2011), 6, 28.

53 Masten, *Queer Philologies: Sex, Language, and Affect in Shakespeare's Time* (Philadelphia: University of Pennsylvania Press, 2016), 33.

54 Vickers, 'Incomplete Shakespeare', 312.

55 Chester, *Love's Martyr*, A3–A4.

Notes

56 Knight, *The Mutual Flame*, 176.

57 The 1611 version is a reissue, not a reprint, since it adds a new title page to Richard Field's 1601 sheets. Duncan-Jones and Woudhuysen note that the University of Wales copy, lacking a title page and the Poetical Essays section, was owned by Frances Wolfreston, who also owned the only surviving copy of Q1 *Venus and Adonis* (also a Field text). See Duncan-Jones and Woudhuysen, *The Arden Shakespeare: Shakespeare's Poems* (London: The Arden Shakespeare, 2007, 2020), 500.

Chapter 1

Parts of this chapter have been heavily modified from the essay 'Can Conversation Be Quantified? A Cladistic Approach to Shakespeare's and Jonson's Influences in *Love's Martyr*', in Kristen-Abbot Bennett's *Conversational Exchanges in Early Modern England: 1549-1640* (Newcastle upon Tyne: Cambridge Scholars, 2015).

1 The entirety of Martial's epigram reads: 'You are mistaken, insatiable thief of my writings, who think a poet can be made for the mere expense which copying, and a cheap volume cost. The applause of the world is not acquired for six or even ten sesterces. Seek out for this purpose verses treasured up, and unpublished efforts, known only to one person, and which the father himself of the virgin sheet, that has not been worn and scrubbed by bushy chins, keeps sealed up in his desk. A well-known book cannot change its master. But if there is one to be found yet unpolished by the pumice-stone, yet unadorned with bosses and cover, buy it: I have such by me, and no one shall know it. Whoever recites another's compositions, and seeks for fame, must buy, not a book, but the author's silence.' See translation by Henry G. Bohn in *The Epigrams of Martial* (London: Bel and Daldy, 1865), 59.

2 Adam Fitzgerald. 'An Interview with Fred Moten: In Praise of Harold Bloom, Collaboration and Book Fetishes', *Litbub*. 5 August 2015. https://lithub.com/an-interview-with-fred-moten-pt-i. (accessed 5 April 2021).

3 Emphasis in original.

4 Ibid.

5 Niccolò Machiavelli, 'Letter to Francesco Vettori', in *The Prince* (Cambridge: Hackett, 1995), 3.

6 Ibid.

7 See Eve Sedgwick's theory of "nonce taxonomies" in *Epistemology of the Closet* (Berkeley: University of California Press, 1990), 23–24.

8 See Drout (et al), 'Of Dendrogrammatology'.

9 Walter Ong, *Ramus, Method, and the Decay of Dialogue* (Chicago: University of Chicago Press, [1958], 2004), xvi.

231

Notes

10 John Guillim, *A Display of Heraldrie* (London: Printed by William Hall for Raphe Mab, 1611).

11 While biological taxonomists refer to these objects as 'cladograms', most scholars in the computational humanities use 'dendrograms', a term that will be used in this study.

12 Hierarchical cluster analysis is a dimension reduction technique. For example, one could just compare one's texts on the basis of the frequencies of two words – 'the' and 'and'. This information could then be plotted easily on an x/y graph ('the' on one axis, 'and' on the other), and then one can measure the distances between the texts, which are points fixed by the two frequency values. However, it is usually better to use more than two words – either all the words in a set of texts, or all the most frequent ones. If you count more than two words, you may produce a multi-dimensional graph rather than the two-dimensional one you get with just 'the' and 'and'. If you count 150 words, each text is a point fixed by 150 values – a point in 150-dimensional space. That is hard to draw, but not hard to model mathematically, so you can work out the distances between points in that space. Hierarchical clustering generally works by looking for the closest two points, pairing them, then looking for the next two closest. See Downey, Drout, Khan and Leblanc., "Books Tell Us: Lexomic and Traditional Evidence for the Sources of Guthlac A', *Modern Philology* 110.2 (2012): 153–81.

13 Much of what is presented here has been paraphrased from the lexomics tutorials available on Wheaton College's website (https://wheatoncollege.edu/academics/special-projects-initiatives/lexomics/). Downey (et al) provides a technical overview of lexomic methods, included here for the sake of completeness: '[Lexomic analysts] use the free implementation of hierarchical, agglomerative cluster analysis ... to group the texts and create branching diagrams, or dendrograms, of their relationships ... This clustering method uses a dissimilarity (or distance) metric for the grouping of texts without prespecifying the number of groups .... [Lexomic analysts] use the most commonly used distance metric, Euclidean distance, a multidimensional extension of Pythagoras's theorem for right triangles. This metric makes use of all n words in a collection of texts to measure the dissimilarity between two texts. The distance measure is computed for each pair of texts among T texts, resulting in $T \times (T-1)/2$ distances, which are then used to create groupings, or clades, of texts by clustering texts that are most similar ... The dissimilarity between two clades (i.e., two collections of texts) is the average of all Euclidean distances between two texts, one from clade 1, the other from clade 2'. See appendix 1 for rationale behind using the similar Delta method, adopted in this study ("'Books Tell Us,'" 157–9).

Notes

14 To clarify: 'clades' are merely gatherings or 'clusterings' of text that are of greatest similarity to one another; each clade consists of 'leaves', which represent chunks of text of a certain size prespecified by the analyst.

15 Downey (et al), "Books Tell Us", 159–60.

16 See Carla Freccero, *Queer / Early / Modern* (Durham: Duke University Press, 2005).

17 Adam Fitzgerald (2015), 'An Interview with Fred Moten, Part 1', *Literary Hub*, 5 August 2015. Available online: https://lithub.com/an-interview-with-fred-moten-pt-i/ (accessed 1 June 2020).

18 Indeed, as Jonathan Hope has pointed out, dendrograms default to dichotomous relationships and appear to be very clear, but in fact are mere representations of data that is not dichotomous. When hierarchical analysis pairs two points, they are removed from the pool of potential pairs, so some points get paired with things that were not their closest neighbours (because that neighbour has already been taken). Similarly, dendrograms imply that differences are absolute – branch A versus branch B – when they are relative. This is true in biology too, where dendrograms are often used for evolution/species differentiation, so a continuous process of shift is represented as a series of abrupt, dichotomous changes. The concept of 'species' is a construct that frequently breaks down when you try to identify species in the wild – just as the concept of 'authorship' can be said to break down as you look more closely at *Love's Martyr*. For use of dendrograms in biology, see Cavalli-Sforza (et al), *The History and Geography of Human Genes* (Princeton: Princeton University Press, 1994).

19 See Brian Vickers' *Shakespeare, Co-Author* for a representative study.

20 I am inclined to agree with James Bednarz that the editor of the Poetical Essays might have been Edward Blount.

21 Knight, *The Mutual Flame*, 171.

22 A partial reproduction can be found in the enigmatic Latham Davis, *Shake-speare England's Ulysses, The Masque of Love's Labor's Won or The Enacted Will* (Seaford, DE: M. N. Willey, 1905).

23 Grosart, *Rosalins Complaint*, lxviii.

24 Ibid., lxiii.

25 Ibid.

26 Knight, *The Mutual Flame*, 171, 174.

27 Ibid., 24.

28 Ibid.

29 Ibid., 30.

30 Ibid.

31 Fitzgerald, 'An Interview'.

32 See 'A Brief History of Singular "They"' (2018). *Oxford English Dictionary Online* (accessed 1 June 2021).

Notes

33 Wyndham Lewis, *The Lion and the Fox: The Role of the Hero in the Plays of Shakespeare* (London: Methuen, [1927], 1966), 149. Knight cites Lewis and clearly draws inspiration from his claims.

34 Knight, *The Mutual Flame*, 31.

35 Ibid.

36 Ibid.

37 Ibid., 171–2.

38 Knight, *The Mutual Flame*, 173; Chester, *Love's Martyr*, 145.

39 Knight, *The Mutual Flame*, 174.

40 Ibid.

41 Ibid.

42 Ibid., 167. To maintain consistency with Knight's reading of these lines, I have included his modernizations of the text in this section.

43 Knight, 168; Chester, 144.

44 For a detailed and still-unrivalled account of Salusbury's personal affairs, see Brown's juicy introductory material in *Poems of Sir John Salusbury and Robert Chester* (London: Kegan Paul, 1914), xxxviii–xxxix.

45 Brown, *Poems by Sir John Salusbury and Robert Chester*, 13–18, 36–8, 47–52 and 54–6; also, see G. Blakemore Evans, *The Poems of Robert Parry* (Tempe: Arizona Center for Medieval and Renaissance Studies, 2005), 17–18.

46 Chester, *Love's Martyr*, 161.

47 Both facsimile copies available on *EEBO* (1601 and 1611) have 'He' on seventh line. The work of 'unediting the Renaissance', to use Leah S. Marcus's phrase, has direct links with early modern queer theory. See Jeffrey Maten's *Textual Intercourse: Collaboration, Authorship, and Sexualities in Renaissance Drama* (Cambridge: Cambridge University Press, 1997) and Leah S. Marcus's *Unediting the Renaissance: Shakespeare, Marlow, and Milton* (New York: Routledge, 1996).

48 Chester, *Love's Martyr*, 132.

49 Ibid., 125.

50 Matchett, *The Phoenix and the Turtle*, 128–32.

51 Knight, *The Mutual Flame*, 171.

52 Ibid., 160.

53 Throughout this chapter, I modulate between first person singular and plural to account for computational research produced by and with Jonathan Hicks, the lead research assistant of this project.

54 For more on text size in attribution studies, see Maciej Eder, 'Does Size Matter? Small Samples, Big Problems', *Digital Humanities 2010* (Conference Abstracts. King's College London, 2010).

55 For advanced work using the R package, see studies in bibliography by Maciej Eder and Patrick Juola; for an introduction to R, see Matthew Jockers and Rosamond Thalken, *Text Analysis with R: For Students of Literature*. Second Edition (Cham, Switzerland: Springer, 2020).

Notes

56 Figure 1.3, 77 MFFW by rank: the, and, to, of, in, that, a, my, his, i, with, is, thy, for, this, her, be, he, all, me, not, doth, but, did, by, thou, their, from, it, will, do, as, you, haue, at, she, being, shall, was, him, then, are, no, our, they, so, if, on, hath, where, when, or, which, what, whose, some, them, most, there, had, selfe, we, vnto, may, would, such, within, these, vpon, now, can, should, neuer, an, many, away, vp.

57 Since the poems of the Poetical Essays are, with the exception of Jonson's, very short in length, they present difficulty for macro-level analysis of the type attempted here. Further inquiry into all supplementary verse therefore requires a more focused analysis, the data and implications of which will be assessed in chapter two.

58 Of course, it is possible that someone not credited at all in *Love's Martyr* might also have made these edits; on this we can only speculate.

59 Vickers, 'Co-Author', 58.

60 Texts were selected based on appropriateness to the project's goals and accessibility to works containing original spellings. Most texts were extracted through *EEBO*; in certain cases, textual gaps were filled based on archival material accessed directly at the Folger Shakespeare Library and through the LUNA database. Folio versions of Shakespeare's plays were used. For Chester and Salusbury's work, we consulted Carleton Brown's study of the Christ Church MS 184 at Oxford, excluding poems speculated by G. Blakemore Evans not to have been authored by Salusbury. See Evans, 10–23.

61 Segment 16 of *Romeo and Juliet*, clustering with segment 5 of *Love's Martyr*, starts with 'Going to find a barefoot brother out' (5.2.5); Segment 17 of the play, clustering with segments 6 and 27–28, starts with 'Lady come from that nest / Of death, contagion, and unnatural sleep' (5.3.151-2).

62 Only segment 29, the 'Pellican' verse, moves drastically, clustering here with Jonson's poetry. See Appendix 1 for a more focused analysis of 'Pellican'.

63 Scholars have tended to attribute these poems to Salusbury in an offhand sort of way, noting the formal similarities between Salusbury's known verse and the verse of the Cantos. See studies by Grosart, Matchett, Epsom and Knight.

64 Brown, *Poems by Sir John Salusbury and Robert Chester*, 15; Knight, *The Mutual Flame*, 174–5.

65 Knight, *The Mutual Flame*, 175.

66 Ibid., 174.

67 The differences between Figures 1.10 and 1.11 begin at rank 37, 'your' and 'do', respectively. Up to rank 37, the function words are identical. In Figure 1.9, most notably missing is the pronoun 'thee'.

235

Notes

68   Brown, *Poems by Sir John Salusbury and Robert Chester*, 36.

69   Chester, *Love's Martyr*, 163–4.

70   Knight, *The Mutual Flame*, 176. Moreover, Chester seems to have borrowed directly from these lines in his dedication to Salusbury, which includes the conditional warning, 'if Absurdutie like a theefe haue crept into any part of these Poems' (3–4). Or, perhaps, might Chester's dedication, too, have been written in collaboration?

71   Joel Fineman, *Shakespeare's Perjured Eye: The Invention of Poetic Subjectivity in the Sonnets* (Berkeley: University of California Press, 1986).

72   See Eve Sedgwick, *Between Men: English Literature and Male Homosocial Desire* (New York: Columbia University Press, 2015).

73   In these tests, we followed the stylometric method 'Rolling Stylometry' from Maciej Eder's study that combined supervised machine-learning classification with sequential analysis. According to Eder, this combined methodology is more reliable than Delta method, for the visualizations are enhanced in SVM and NSC classifications due to class assignment based on normalized decision values. See Eder, 'Rolling Stylometry', 461–2. The training set of texts, or 'reference set' are the same as the ones used throughout. For more reliable results, a sample size of 5000 words is recommended. To achieve this, our reference set for Chester includes both his poetical works from Christ Church MS 184 and segments 7–8, 16–22 of *Love's Martyr*, since his manuscript poems are only 2158 words in length. Including only four segments of the King Arthur section and Dialogue 2 of *Love's Martyr* ensures the model is not over-fitted; tests performed with Salusbury's poems in the training set used a sample size of 2,000 words, since his manuscript poems are only 2,336 words in length; twenty-fold cross-validation protocols were also followed in classification tests to curb over-fitting.

74   For a detailed investigation into the personal relationship between Jonson and Salusbury, and also a comprehensive investigation into the contents of the Christ Church MS 184, see Bland, 'As far from all Reuolt'.

75   Chester, *Love's Martyr*, A3.

76   The sub-stylistic traces revealed in computation recall Roland Barthes' 'scriptor' and Michel Foucault's 'author-function'. See Barthes, 'The Death of the Author', in *Image / Music / Text*, trans. Stephen Heath (New York: Hill and Wang, 1977) and Foucault, 'What Is an Author?' in *Language, Counter-Memory, Practice: Selected Essays and Interviews by Michel Foucault* ed. Donald Bouchard and trans. Sherry Simon (Ithaca: Cornell University Press, 1977).

77   Foucault, 'What Is an Author?', 129.

78   Ibid.

Notes

Chapter 2

1   Jennie Livingston, *Paris is Burning*. United States: Off White Productions, 1990.

2   *Paris is Burning*.

3   See Bednarz, *Shakespeare and the Poets' War* (New York: Columbia University Press, 2001), 56–7, 99–100.

4   David Riggs, *Ben Jonson: A Life* (Cambridge: Harvard University Press, 1989), 79.

5   For representative work on early modern friendship, see studies Masten, *Textual Intercourse*; Alan Bray's *The Friend* (Chicago: University of Chicago Press, 2003); John S. Garrison's *Friendship and Queer Theory in the Renaissance: Gender and Sexuality in Early Modern England* (London: Routledge, 2014); Allan Bloom's *Shakespeare on Love and Friendship* (Chicago: University of Chicago Press, 2000); Laurie Shannon's *Sovereign Amity: Figures of Friendship in Shakespearean Contexts* (Chicago: University of Chicago Press, 2002); Tom MacFaul's *Male Friendship in Shakespeare and His Contemporaries* (Cambridge: Cambridge University Press, 2007); and James M. Bromley's *Intimacy and Sexuality in the Age of Shakespeare* (Cambridge: Cambridge University Press, 2012).

6   Suzanne Gossett admits that the poets' war may be 'viewed generously as creating a kind of intertextual rivalry', but sees strife and antagonism at the centre of it all; she claims of Marston, for example, '[his joking pseudonym, Kinsayder (that is, Mar-stone, or "castrator's song") significantly rejects male homosocial bonding for implied bodily damage'. Gossett, "Marston, Collaboration, and Eastward Ho!" *Renaissance Drama* 33 (2004): 181–200, 196. On debates over collaboration and competition within the poets' war, see Bednarz; Charles Cathcart's *Marston, Rivalry, Rapprochement, and Jonson* (London: Routledge, 2008); Heather Anne Hirschfeld's *Joint Enterprises: Collaborative Drama and the Institutionalization of the English Renaissance Theater* (Massachusetts: University of Massachusetts Press, 2004); James Shapiro's *Rival Playwrights: Marlow, Jonson, Shakespeare* (New York: Columbia University Press, 1991); Michelle O'Callaghan's *The English Wits: Literature and Sociability in Early Modern England* (Cambridge: Cambridge University Press, 2007); and Matthew Steggle's *Wars of the Theatres: The Poetics of Personation in the Age of Jonson* (Victoria: University of Victoria Press, 1998).

7   Herford and Simpson, *Ben Jonson*, Vol. 1, 140.

8   Techniques called Support Vector Machine (SVM) and Nearest Shrunken Centroids (NSC): see Appendix 1 for discussion of these methods.

Notes

9 Matchett, *The Phoenix and the Turtle*, 80.

10 For an overview of this general view see Bednarz, 'Contextualizing "The Phoenix and Turtle": Shakespeare, Edward Blount and the *Poetical Essays* Group of *Love's Martyr*', *Shakespeare Survey* 67 (2014): 131–49.

11 See Appendix 2 for a textual reproduction of the Poetical Essays' title page.

12 Further publication details are discussed in the introduction.

13 Grosart glosses the word as meaning our modern 'subtend', though 'suspend' also fits the context.

14 In classical mythology, the Castalian springs flow in a ravine between the Phaedriades, a pair of cliffs that overlook the sacred Oracle at Delphi. Here, the sun god Apollo slayed the monstrous Python, a female serpent said to guard a stone that sits at the exact centre of the Earth. In Roman times and beyond, the Castalian waters were considered a source of divine or poetic inspiration, so its appearance at the outset of the Poetical Essays is unsurprising and conventional. It also appears in the epigraph to Shakespeare's *Venus and Adonis* and in work by Chapman, as I later discuss.

15 See Shapiro's *Rival Playwrights: Marlow, Jonson, Shakespeare* (New York: Columbia University Press, 1991), 14. Similarly, Bednarz describes the poets' conflict as 'a vehicle for aggressively expressing differences .... in literary theory', and as a 'basic philosophical debate on the status of literary and dramatic authorship. See Bednarz, 'Representing Jonson: *Histriomastix* and the Origin of the Poets' War', *Huntington Library Quarterly* 54.1 (1991): 1–30, 23. Heather Anne Hirschfeld considers the conflict in light of economic pressures in late Elizabethan theatre: 'So, rather than measuring the work of collaborating dramatists solely in terms of "gentlemanly" interaction at court, I suggest that joint work would have been, and should be now, understood at least in terms of guild relations', and more generally in economic, and therefore competitive, terms'. See Hirschfeld, *Joint Enterprises*, 10.

16 Masten, *Textual Intercourse*, 35.

17 Ibid., 91, 36.

18 In the sonnets, too, we witness an eroticized love between the speaking poet and a 'fair youth', a gentleman (whoever he may be) of higher social standing than the poet, contrasted sharply with the poet's tumultuous relationship with a dark-haired mistress. According to most critical accounts, the poet-youth relationship is elevated in part because it is supposedly 'pure' and non-sexual, or at least non-sodomitical: sexual intensity becomes submerged, yielding a type of idealized platonic love. The idea that such love therefore does not constitute a 'homosexual' relationship has been the subject of endless and, I believe,

Notes

largely meaningless debate. It is laughable to consider the intellectual gymnastics that critics have performed in order either to heterosexualize the poet's desires or to write them off as merely platonic – ask any college freshman first encountering these poems in an introductory literature course to set the record straight (or 'gay', as they are incorrectly wont to conclude). In an important essay, Magreta De Grazia argues that the poet's relationship with the dark-haired mistress would have been far more scandalous than his affair with the fair youth; see 'The Scandal of Shakespeare's sonnets', *Shakespeare Survey* 46 (1993): 35–50. See also Robert Matz's rebuttal, 'The Scandals of Shakespeare's Sonnets', *ELH* 77.2 (2010): 477–508.

19 See Douglas Lanier, 'Masculine Silence: *Epicoene* and Jonsonian Stylistics', *College Literature* 21.2 (1994): 1–18.

20 Herford and Simpson, *Ben Jonson*, Vol. 1, 143.

21 Lorna Hutson, 'Liking Men: Ben Jonson's Closet Opened', *ELH* 71.4 (2004): 1065–96, 1077.

22 See Hutson, 'Liking Men' and 'Civility and Virility in Ben Jonson', *Representations* 78.1 (2002): 1–27.

23 Huston, 'Liking Men', 1077.

24 For studies that address this group directly, see Joe Lee Davis, *The Sons of Ben: Jonsonian Comedy in Caroline England* (Detroit: Wayne State University Press, 1967) and Hugh MacLean, ed., *Ben Jonson and the Cavalier Poets* (New York: Norton, 1974).

25 David Riggs, *Ben Jonson: A Life* (Cambridge: Harvard University Press, 1989), 79. See also George E. Rowe, who claims that 'the intensity of competition' between these poet-playwrights 'increases the more closely they are linked (hence, for example, Jonson's focus on Marston in the War of the Theaters)', *Distinguishing Jonson: Imitation, Rivalry, and the Direction of a Dramatic Career* (Lincoln: University of Nebraska Press, 1988), 20; see also Rebecca Yearling, *Ben Jonson, John Marston, and Early Modern Drama: Satire and the Audience* (London: Palgrave Macmillan, 2016).

26 Francis Meres, *Palladas Tamia, Wit's Treasury, Being the Second Part of Wit's Commonwealth* (London: Printed by P. Short for Cuthbert Burbie, 1598), 277.

27 Wayne Koestanbaum, *The Queen's Throat: Opera, Homosexuality, and the Mystery of Desire* (New York: Poseidon Press, 1993), 39.

28 On flyting, see Michelle O'Callaghan, *The English Wits*; Ward Parks, 'Flyting, Sounding, Debate: Three Verbal Contest Genres', *Poetics Today* 7.3 (1986): 439–58; and Margaret Galway's much earlier 'Flyting in Shakespeare's Comedies', *The Shakespeare Association Bulletin* 10 (1935): 183–91.

29 O'Callaghan, *The English Wits*, 6.

30 Masten, *Textual Intercourse*, 4.

Notes

31 Joseph Lowenstein, *Ben Jonson and Possessive Authorship* (Cambridge: Cambridge University Press, 2002), 2.

32 See Charles Cathcart, *Marston, Rivalry, Rapprochement, and Jonson* (Aldershot: Ashgate Publishing, 2008) and MacDonald P. Jackson and Neil, Michael, eds., *The Selected Plays of John Marston* (Cambridge: Cambridge University Press, 1986).

33 Cathcart, *Marston*, 28.

34 Ibid.

35 There is credible speculation that *What You Will* was actually staged before *Love's Martyr's* was published. However, Marston's play was not published until 1607, giving him ample time to incorporate the unmistakable reference to *Love's Martyr* in the quarto of this work. Other changes were made to the play as well; see Bednarz, *Shakespeare and the Truth of Love*, n. 204, and James Doelman, 'Charles Fitz-Geffry and the "War of the Theatres"', *English Theatre* 11.1 (2008): 99–106.

36 Chester, *Love's Martyr*, 180.

37 Cathcart, *Marston*, 21.

38 See Tom Cain, ed., *Poetaster* (Manchester: Manchester University Press, 1996), 24.

39 Jackson and Neill, eds., *Selected Plays*, xiv.

40 The scholarly tendency is to claim that three of Jonson's four poems in the Poetical Essays were adapted from earlier works. However, only the last few lines of 'Praeludium' appear earlier, in a poem titled 'Proludium' in a Salusbury family manuscript held at the National Library of Wales (MS 5390 D), and in another manuscript (the Thorn-Drury MS) at the Folger Shakespeare Library. In both, 'Epos' immediately follows 'Proludium', and in both, 'Epos' is the clearly identified title of the second poem (see Bednarz, *Shakespeare and the Truth of Love*, 216, note 50, for a different understanding). For reasons that will become clearer, it is worth noting that the first-person pronouns 'my' and 'me' appear alongside 'our' within the lines of this 'Proludium'. Jonson's fourth poem in the Poetical Essays appeared first in the Rawl-poet 31 MS (from the library of Richard Rawlinson) at the Bodleian. This poem was addressed 'To: L: C: off: B:', very likely Lucy, Countess of Bedford; see B. H. Newdigate's study, *The Poems of Ben Jonson*, 365–6.

41 Chester, *Love's Martyr*, 190.

42 Cathcart, *Marston*, 24.

43 Ibid., 16–34.

44 Ibid., 28.

45 Matthew L. Jockers and Daniela M. Witten, 'A Comparative Study of Machine Learning Methods for Authorship Attribution', *Literary and Linguistic Computing* 25.2 (2010): 215–24. See also Jockers, 'Testing

Notes

Authorship in the Personal Writings of Joseph Smith Using NSC Classification', *Literary and Linguistic Computing* 28.3 (2013): 371–81. The NSC technique is often used in DNA analysis; see Robert Tibshirani, Trevor Hastie, Balasubramanian Narasimhan, and Gilbert Chu, 'Class Prediction by Nearest Shrunken Centroids, with Applications to DNA Microarrays', *Statistical Science* 18.1: 104–17.

46 The training set included Chester's poems found in Christ Church Oxford MS 184 and segments 7–26 of *Love's Martyr*; Shakespeare's sonnets, *Lucrece*, and *Venus and Adonis*; Marston's *Pygmalion, Satires, and Scourge of Villainy*; Chapman's *Achilles Shield, Ovid's Banquet of Sense, Euthymiae Raptus, The Shadow of Night*; and Jonson's *Epigrams, The Forest*, and *Underwoods*.

47 Bootstrap Consensus Tree includes segments 7–26 and 38 (only 'Invocatio') of *Love's Martyr* and the following poetical works: George Chapman's *Achilles Shield* (1598); *Evthymiae Raptvs; Or Teares of Peace* (1609); *Ouids Banquet of Sence* (1595) [includes *A Coronet for His Mistresse Philosophie, The Amorous Zodiack*, and *The Amorous Contention of Phillis and Flora*]; *The Shadovv of Night* (1594); Robert Chester's poems in Christ Church MS 184 (1597–8?); Ben Jonson's *Epigrammes* (1616); *The Forrest* (1616) [excludes *Praeludium* and *Epode*]; *Vnder-Vvoods* (1640); John Marston's *The Metamorphosis of Pigmalions Image* (1598); *Scovrge of Villanie* (1599); and William Shakespeare's *Lucrece* (1594); *Sonnets* (1609) [excludes 'A Lover's Complaint']; and *Venus and Adonis* (1593).

48 Using a different computational method – a Delta cluster analysis of most frequent words – I first posited this theory in Kristen Abbot-Bennett's collection, *Conversational Exchanges in Early Modern England*. See 'Can Conversation Be Quantified? A Cladistic Approach to Shakespeare's and Jonson's Influences in *Love's Martyr*', in *Conversational Exchanges in Early Modern England: 1549–1640* (Newcastle-upon-Tyne: Cambridge Scholars Publishing, 2015). Here, I also suggested that the 'Ignoto' verse was by Ben Jonson, a result obtained by lumping it with the other unattributed verse in the Poetical Essays – altogether this verse signifies as 'more like Jonson' than any other poet involved with *Love's Martyr*. I have come to question this aspect of this earlier study because we have no reason to believe that all the unattributed verse was composed by the same person, and 'Ignoto' is too small for statistical analysis on its own.

49 Ben Jonson, *Sejanus, His Fall* in Herford and Simpson, *Ben Jonson*, Vol. 4 (Oxford: Oxford UP, 1947), 351.

50 See Bednarz, 'Contextualizing'. Bednarz cites as incorrect Margaret Healy's claim that '"the poets intermittently claim to be speaking

241

Notes

as a 'vatum chorus', as one" *after* the invocation and dedication', but Matchett claims there is no other way to read Jonson's momentary but important shift to the first-person in 'Epos': 'As "Epos" stands, the one singular pronoun ["But soft: I heare, / Some vicious *Foole* draw near" (2A4ᵛ)] forces the realization that the others are true plurals, that Jonson with them is speaking for all the poets in a manner similar to that in the "Vatum Chorus" poems'. See Healy, *Shakespeare, Alchemy, and the Creative Imagination: The Sonnets and 'A Lovers Complaint'* (Cambridge: Cambridge University Press, 2011), 205 and Matchett, *The Phoenix and the Turtle*, 95–96n.

51 Chester, *Love's Martyr*, 172.

52 Allott's *England's Parnassus: Or, The Choysest Flowers of our Moderne Poets with Their Poeticall Comparisons* (London, for N. L., C. B., and T. H., 1600) contains the final line of 'Praeludium', the Senecan aphorism '*Man may securely sinne, but safely neuer*'. For Anthea Hume, this is evidence that Jonson 'had coined the phrase before he wrote the poem, or a version of the poem already existed in 1600, which he then adapted to meet the requirements of *Love's Martyr* in 1601'. See Hume, '*Love's Martyr*, "The Phoenix and the Turtle", and the Aftermath of the Essex Rebellion', *The Review of English Studies, New Series* 40.157 (1989): 48–71, 68.

53 See earlier fn. 40; 'Proludium' contains a mix of the first-person plural and singular. For a detailed discussion of Jonson's pronominal changes, see again Matchett, *The Phoenix and the Turtle*, 95–96n. See also Knight, *The Mutual Flame*, 186–8. I concur with Knight that the fact that this poem had existed in another form prior to *Love's Martyr* 'can have little bearing on our interpretation, except to remind us that the kind of work we are discussing was, like Shakespeare's "sugred Sonnets," *coterie* poetry, with its own freemasonry of allusion and intent' (emphasis in original). *The Mutual Flame*, 188.

54 Hugh Craig, 'The Weight of Numbers: Common Words and Jonson's Dramatic Style', *Ben Jonson Journal* 6.1 (2016): 243–59, 254.

55 As, for example, in *Epiocene*, when Morose asks, 'you have fastened on a thicke quilt, or flockbed, on the out-side of the dore; that if they knocke with their daggers, or with brickbats, they can make no noise?' Craig, 'The Weight of Numbers', 254.

56 Craig, 'The Weight of Numbers', 258 (my emphasis).

57 Jonson wrote freely about his disdain for the gentlemen of his time as well as their writing style, which he deemed not 'manly' enough and womanish. See studies by Lorna Hutson already cited.

58 These tests use various feature sets and frequencies, as well as randomized groups of training and test sets. For more information, see Appendix 1.

Notes

59 Chester, *Love's Martyr*, 171.

60 Ibid., 133.

61 In Jonson's final poem, his 'Ode Enthusiastic', he describes 'Iudgement', personified female, as 'Cleare as a naked vestal / Closde in an orbe of Christall'; however, in the 'Invocatio' signed 'Vatum Chorus', the 'silver Morne', also personified female, is described as having a 'Chrystall presence'. An *EEBO* search on Jonson and all variants of the word 'christall' show that only once in his career did he, or someone on his behalf, choose the spelling that appears in the Invocation. (In 1616 folio 'crystall' appears in *Part of the King's Entertainment in passing to his Cornonation*. However, it was originally spelled 'cristall' in the 1604 printing of *B. Ion: his part of King Iames his royall and magnificent entertainement through his honorable cittie of London, Thurseday the 15. of March. 1603*). Likewise, a search for Marston and the term returned no results. Yet, throughout *Love's Martyr*, variants of the word 'Christall', 'Cristall', 'Chrystall' or 'Crystal' appear twelve times, and of these, seven times the 'y' form is chosen. We performed a search on *EEBO* of the term in all texts from 1595 to 1623 (so as to include the first folio) to see if any meaningful patterns would emerge. Overwhelmingly, 'y'-spellings were contained to sermons, religious tracts, related moralistic texts, histories and translations; a small minority of such spellings were associated with original dramatic or poetic works. Over the same period, a search for 'i'-spellings returned not only a significantly larger number of hits and records (1322 hits versus 515; 818 records versus 287) but also a significantly greater number of results in categories of original prose and poetry. As in queer theory, so sometimes in computational studies: the tiniest units of language may convey fundamental meanings that are too easily lost or overlooked. See John Jowett's *Sir Thomas More*, where he notes that Shakespeare (and other early modern authors) tended to favour peculiar spellings for certain words, and that such idiosyncrasies must be regarded as part of a whole when assessing stylistic (and, therefore, authorial) patterns, even when it comes down to a single word.

62 Grosart, *Rosalins Complaint*, 240.

63 George Chapman, *The Poems of George Chapman*, ed. Phyllis Brooks Bartlett (New York: Modern Language Association of America, 1941), 34. The lines are from the second part of the poem 'Hymnvs in Cynthiam', ll. 162–9. Originally in Chapman, *The Shaddovv of Night Containing Two Poeticall Hymnes, Deuised by G.C. Gent*. STC 4990 (London: Printed by R[ichard] F[ield] for William Ponsonby, 1594), D2^r.

243

Notes

64 John Marston, *The Scourge of Villanie*. STC 17485 (London: Printed by I[ames] R[oberts] and are to be sold by Iohn Buzbie, in Paules Church-yard, at the signe of the Crane, 1598), C8^r. I thank Jonathan Hicks for drawing attention to this passage.

65 Bednarz convincingly argues that Edward Blount organized the Poetical Essays supplement in 'Contextualizing "The Phoenix and Turtle"'.

66 Katherine Duncan-Jones, *Ungentle Shakespeare: Scenes from His Life* (London: The Arden Shakespeare, 2000), 144.

67 Chester, *Love's Martyr*, 177.

68 For discussions of the phoenix myth in European literature, see John Spencer Hill, 'The Phoenix', *Religion and Literature* 16 (1984): 61–6; Thomas P. Harrison, *They Tell of Birds: Chaucer, Spenser, Milton, Drayton* (Austin: University of Texas Press, 1956); A. H. R. Fairchild, '"The Phoenix and Turtle": A Critical and Historical Interpretation', *Englische Studien* 33 (1904): 337–84; and Bednarz, *Shakespeare and the Truth of Love*.

69 Matchett paraphrases the line, 'The idea of excellence has been endowed with the properties of matter'. Matchett, *The Phoenix and the Turtle*, 87–8.

70 Chester, *Love's Martyr*, 180.

71 Ibid., 180.

72 Ibid., 182.

73 Ibid., 132.

74 Ibid.

75 Knight, *The Mutual Flame*, 202.

Chapter 3

1 Joannis Naperi, *De Arte Logistica* (Edinburgh: Edinburgh Press, [<1617], 1839), 3.

2 'The Canonization', in *The Songs and Sonnets of John Donne*, ed. Theodore Redpath. Second Edition (Harvard: Harvard University Press, 2009), 237–8.

3 Though terms such as 'transgender' and 'non-binary' are contemporary, early modern people theorized notions of gender instability in a number of ways, particular though the figure of the hermaphrodite. Unlike talk of early modern 'homosexuality', then, it is not quite anachronistic to speak of non-binary gender in an early modern sense. For additional studies on early modern hermaphroditism, see Jenny C. Mann, 'How to Look at a Hermaphrodite in Early Modern England', *Studies in English Literature, 1500–1900* 46.1 (2006): 67–91; Thomas Laqueur, *Making Sex: Body and Gender from the Greeks to Freud* (Cambridge,

Notes

MA: Harvard University Press, 1990), 135–42; Ann Rosalind Jones and Peter Stallybrass, 'Fetishizing Gender: Constructing the Hermaphrodite in Renaissance Europe', in *Body Guards: The Cultural Politics of Gender Ambiguity*, ed. Julia Epstein and Kristina Straub (New York and London: Routledge, 1991), 80–111; Lorraine Daston and Katherine Park, 'The Hermaphrodite and the Orders of Nature: Sexual Ambiguity in Early Modern France', *GLQ* 1.4 (1995): 419–38; and Gilbert, *Early Modern Hermaphrodites: Sex and Other Stories* (New York: Palgrave, 2002).

4   Critics agree that the poem is both difficulty and unusual. Ralph Waldo Emerson, often credited with rescuing this poem from obscurity, opines in *Parnassus* that 'this poem, if published for the first time, and without a known author's name, would find no general reception. Only the poets would save it' (vi). I. A. Richards says more or less the same thing: 'Is it not fitting that the greatest English poet should have written the most mysterious poem in English?' (86). Hallet Smith notes, simply, 'there is nothing else like it' (1889), and B. H. Newdigate claims that 'the lines on the Phoenix and Turtle … present one of the most difficult problems to be found in [Shakespeare's] works' (xvi). Ranjee G. Shahani, making perhaps the most comprehensive assessment, concludes that '[a]s a composition "The Phoenix and Turtle" is unique in European literature' (99). Appraisals like these might be expected to cast an imaginative pall over critical possibility, yet few works written in English have engendered so many ingenious interpretations. See Richards, I. A. 'The Sense of Poetry: Shakespeare's "The Phoenix and the Turtle"', *Daedalus* 87 (1958): 86–94; Emerson, *Parnassus*; Hallet Smith, 'The Phoenix and Turtle', in *The Riverside Shakespeare: Second Edition* ed. G. Blakemore Evans (New York: Houghton Mifflin Company, 1997); and Ranji Shahani, 'The Phoenix and the Turtle', *Notes and Queries* CX (1946): 99–101.

5   For an expressly queer-oriented reflection on the poem, see Karl Steel's essay 'Number There in Love Was Slain', in Madhavi's Menon's *Shakesqueer: A Queer Companion to the Complete Works of Shakespeare* (Durham: Duke University Press, 2011), 271–7.

6   As he puts it in *No Future*, 'The Child has come to embody for us the telos of the social order and come to be seen as the one for whom that order is held in perpetual trust'. Edelman, 11.

7   See *Cruising Utopia: The Then and There of Queer Futurity* (New York: NYU Press, 2009), 1. Muñoz gets us to reconsider Walter Ong's claim that 'possibilities are kept in agitation within this poem in a way such possibilities seldom enough are'. See Walter Ong, 'Metaphor and Twinned Vision' (*The Phoenix and the Turtle*)', *The Sewanee Review* 63.2 (1955): 193–201, 200.

245

Notes

8   Munoz, *Cruising Utopia*, 9.

9   For an excellent study on Shakespearean metaphysics, see Michael Witmore's *Shakespearean Metaphysics* (London: Continuum, 2008), where he shows how Shakespeare 'favored a view of the world in which order and change are seen to emerge holistically from things themselves (immanence) rather than being localized in certain metaphysically isolated pockets (punctualism)'. Witmore, 1.

10   'Phoenix' derives its force from a collection of borrowed ideas. Drawing on the avian bestiary motif of Chaucer's *Parliament of Fowles*, it uses birds to stage an allegory about human matters, focusing most obviously on the Platonic tradition of the merging of souls. In its idealization of 'married chastity', it recalls the chivalric romance tradition from Mallory to Spenser, and in its deployment of the phoenix, it hails a long history of literature preoccupied with the bird's regenerative powers, especially treatments of it in Ovid and Lactantius. Hyder Rollins notes 'the mythical bird of Arabia has been more of less of a commonplace in English poetry since the eighth or ninth century, when an anonymous Anglo-Saxon poet translated Lactantius's *Phoenix* as an allegory of Christ'. See Hyder Rollins, ed., *The Phoenix Nest, 1593* (Cambridge: Harvard University Press, 1931), x. Ovid's *Amores* 2.6 mourns the death of a parrot, a likely source for Shakespeare's treatment of the phoenix in a funerary setting, though Ovid's tone is largely comical. More immediately, of course, the poem draws upon Chester's erotic revitalization of the phoenix myth. The popular 1593 miscellany *The Phoenix Nest,* containing elegies on Philip Sidney, certainly influenced all the volume's contributors. Bednarz locates two additional sites of influence for Shakespeare's poem in John Skelton's *Phyllyp Sparowe*, a satirical poem lamenting the death of a pet, and Matthew Roydon's 'An Elegy or Friend's Passion for his Astrophil', which also mourns Sidney. For more on Shakespeare's widely drawn phoenix-lore, see Douglas McMillan's 'The Phoenix in the Western World from Herodotus to Shakespeare', *The D.H. Lawrence Review* 5.3 (1972): 238–67.

11   Chester, *Love's Martyr*, 177–8, 182, 133.

12   Michel Foucault, 'What is Critique?' (1978) in *The Politics of Truth* (Los Angeles: Semiotext(e), 2007), 44–5. This is a decidedly queer take on critique in that it signifies refusal of nonsense, definitions, taxonomies, limits and estimations of worth imposed from without. To be queer is, arguably, to reject the Aristotelian conception of the good life, focused as it is on the idea that one's life ought to be structured in terms of a communal telos that leads to *eudaimonia*, or human flourishing – a heteronormative if not actually heterosexual sense of flourishing, and all that this entails. In his 1978 lecture on virtue, Foucault claims that '[t]here

246

Notes

is something in critique which is akin to virtue. And in a certain way, what I wanted to speak to you about is this critical attitude as virtue in general'. Judith Butler, reading Foucault, similarly describes virtue as 'established through its difference from an uncritical obedience to authority'. See Foucault, 'What is Critique?', 25, and Judith Butler, 'What is Critique? An Essay on Foucault's Virtue', in *The Political: Readings in Continental Philosophy*, ed. David Ingram (London: Basil Blackwell, 2002), 311.

13 Walter Ong paraphrased the alleged claim as 'All the things that Aristotle has said are inconsistent because they are poorly systematized and can be called to mind only by the use of arbitrary mnemonic devices'. See Ong's discussion in *Ramus, Method, and the Decay of Dialogue: From the Art of Discourse to the Art of Reason* (Chicago: University of Chicago Press, [1958], 2004), 46–7.

14 Having succumbed to Phyllis, the beautiful (and sometimes Indian) wife of Alexander the Great, Aristotle is observed by Alexander and a friend as she mounts the philosopher with a bridle and forces him to carry her on his back through a garden. The moral of the story is straightforward: beware, men, of feminine power, because if it can fool Alexander and humiliate the great Aristotle, it can destroy you as well. The misogynist overtones, however, are only part of the story. Like Richard Brathwaite's well-known figure of 'Acquaintance' in *The English Gentleman* (1630), the image is also a commentary on the status of early modern friendship between men. It establishes a pattern that follows Eve Sedgwick's theory of triangulated homosocial desire almost exactly, with a critical twist: erotic desire is mediated not just by the presence of a woman, but by a non-Western hierarch, a queen herself, subordinating and scolding a man of famed intellectual power. The viewer, presupposed of course to be a man, identifies not with Aristotle or Alexander, nor even his friend, but rather enters the scene as yet another spectator, watching on in voyeuristic awe at the sadomasochistic spectacle. Since Aristotle was Alexander's tutor, overtones of Greek pederasty also become an instant subtext; the viewer is effectively seduced, even interpellated, into an all-male circuit of spectatorial wantonness. Far from merely depicting a generic anxiety over the sexual power of women, the image floods the viewer with a constellation of themes and concerns around male friendship and how it is mediated by differences in class, education, and proximity to feminine, and non-Western, influence.

15 See Rosemond Tuve, 'Ramus and Metaphysical Poetics', in *Renaissance Essays*. eds. Paul Oskar Kristeller (et al) (Rochester: University of Rochester Press, 1992), 272, 281. In other words, one need not prove that Shakespeare and his peers read logical treatises or were in any way Ramists in order to examine their work within this pervasive, possibly even inescapable,

247

Notes

intellectual atmosphere. Even so, in a copy of Abraham Fraunce's *The Lawyers Logicke* (1588) held at the Folger Shakespeare Library, an unattributed handwritten note indicates: 'Shakespeare is generally credited with having derived his legal knowledge from [this book]'. It is entirely possible that Shakespeare did happen upon this book or another such popular Ramist text. Fraunce's volume is filled with Ramist diagrams of legal cases and includes diagrammatic analysis of poems by Philip Sidney and Edmund Spenser. See *The Lavviers Logike, Exemplifying the Pracepts of Logike by the Practise of the Common Lawe, by Abraham Fraunce* (London: Imprinted by William How, for Thomas Gubbin, and T. Newman, 1588).

16 On this basis, some have argued that the 'The Phoenix and Turtle' is two works, 'Threnos' its own, though highly dependent, piece of poetry – a claim that makes little sense to expound upon unless one is willing to argue that the two works ought to be understood independently or that Shakespeare might not have been the author of the first thirteen quatrains of 'Phoenix'. I join most critics in rejecting these views, though I do believe its separation from the rest of the poem warrants some attention; I return to this question in my analysis of 'Threnos'.

17 I make several minor editorial adjustments from this transcription. Katherine Duncan-Jones and H.R. Woudhuysen, *The Arden Shakespeare: Shakespeare's Poems*. Third Series (London: Bloomsbury, 2007, 2020).

18 I recognize that in a post-Barthesian and Foucauldian critical milieu, it may be controversial or outmoded to consider issues of authorial intent. However, this poem's rhetorical and logical partitions seemingly require one to acknowledge a type of authorial agency in these opening lines.

19 I agree with Matchett's claim that the voice 'modifies what is said by revealing the speaker's attitude toward it', imparting an awareness of the poet or the 'speaker of these words'. I disagree about the intent of these words, which, he argues, is that the poem '*necessarily made a statement about Essex and the Queen*' (Matchett's emphasis). Matchett, *The Phoenix and the Turtle*, 36, 187. Matchett's 'close reading in context' joins a long history of studies that seek to historicize by engaging in reductive interpretations that see historical figures – above all the Queen and Robert Deveraux, Earl of Essex – in its characters.

20 See Appendix 1 for a table of the phoenix and the word 'Arabian' in *Love's Martyr*. No other bird is associated so insistently with this imagery, both inside the book and elsewhere.

21 See Ronald Bates' 'Shakespeare's "The Phoenix and Turtle"' *Shakespeare Quarterly* 6 (1955): 19–30, and G. Bonnard's 'Shakespeare's Contribution to R. Chester's *Loves Martyr*', *English Studies* 19 (1937): 66–9.

Notes

22 As discussed in chapter 2, Marston's first poem responds directly to the poem, and Chester's 'Pellican' verse draws significant inspiration from it as well. See Appendix 1 for more on the authorship of 'Pellican'.

23 H. Neville Davies cites many lines of Biblical verse to argue that the crow performs the function of a 'mourner' in a typical Christian burial. This argument strikes me as unnecessary; the crow is stated to be a 'mourner', and if a funeral is being enacted in this poem, as one surely is, it must be based loosely on Elizabethan Christian burial rites. Regarding the use of the word 'right' in stanza four, Davies argues that 'rite' imparts 'a truer indication of the primary sense of the line'. Based on this claim, and on the observation that stanzas four and five are 'roughly parallel' – to my mind, stanzas two and five are more alike – Davies offers his explanation of 'treble-dated': it 'calls attention to the venerability and endurance of a bird whose experience comprehends, in Yeats' words, "What is past, passing, or to come" … presumably a mourner at many funerals'. See 'The Phoenix and Turtle: Requiem and Rite', *The Review of English Studies, New Series* 46.184 (1995): 525–30, 525, 528.

24 Cited in Emma Phipson's spectacular bestiary, *Animal Lore in Shakespeare's Time* (London: Kegan Paul, Trench, 1886), 253.

25 Cunningham, J. V. '"Essence" and the Phoenix and Turtle'. *ELH* 19 (1952): 265–76.

26 Bednarz, *Shakespeare and the Truth of Love*, 104.

27 Ibid., 109.

28 Ibid.

29 My non-religious reading of the poem has precedent in Bednarz, whose subtle reading of Trinitarian doctrine leads to a theorizing of 'poetic theology' that does not capitulate to religious interpretation (as does J. V. Cunningham's), and in Lynn Enterline's '"The Phoenix and the Turtle", Renaissance Elegies, and the Language of Grief' in *Early Modern English Poetry: A Critical Companion*, ed. Patrick Cheney and Garrett A. Sullivan, Jr. (New York: Oxford University Press, 2007).

30 The word 'perfection' appears in the titles of three out of his four poems in *Love's Martyr*. See Appendix 2 for reproductions of this verse.

31 Scholars cannot decide if scholastics actually had such a debate or if this was made up by anti-scholastics to characterize scholastic pedantry. We see several examples of this or a similar image in early modern texts. For example, WIlliam Sclater claims that scholastics argued over whether angels 'did occupie a place; and so, whether many might be in one place at one time; and how many might sit on a Needles point; and six hundred such like needlesse points'. See Sclater's *An Exposition with Notes Upon the First and Second Epistles to the Thessalonians* (London: Printed by John Haviland and sold by Richard Thrale at the Cross Keyes at Paul's Gate, 1630), 385.

Notes

32 Ramus sought to develop a logical method that would simulate 'natural' reasoning as opposed to the 'artificial' reasoning he perceived in the works of Aristotle and his disciples. In *Animadversiones*, Ramus describes the Aristotelian problem as one involving 'two logics', where only one universal method can approximately natural reason: 'Aristotle wished to make two logics, one for science, and the other for opinion; in which. … he has very greatly erred. For although articles of knowledge are on the one hand necessary and scientific, and on the other contingent and matters of opinion, so it is nevertheless that as sight is common in viewing all colors, whether permanent or changeable, so the art of knowing, that is to say, dialectic or logic, is one and the same doctrine in respect to perceiving all things, as will be seen by its very parts.' This statement had enormous implications for the reshaping of Aristotelian logic, which is traditionally divided into dialectic – the logic 'for science' – and rhetoric, 'for opinion'. While Aristotelian rhetoric may draw upon dialectic, the two remain distinct, as persuasive claims cannot be held to the same quasi-mathematical standards explicated in dialectical proofs. By collapsing the logic of 'science' with that of 'opinion', Ramus opens logical analysis up to a full range of discourses, including poetry, which becomes one of the primary methods Ramists use to understand logical laws. In doing so, as Tamara Goeglin notes, the 'Ramists … violated the scholastic boundary between the figurative and the literal by effectively equalizing the status of dialectical and poetic languages'. Under Ramism, a poem may explain logical laws, just as a logical treatise may profitably use poetical examples to make its case. This was achieved, by Ramus and his followers, through the use of poetic examples in widely circulated pamphlets and textbooks on logic and rhetoric. These pamphlets demystified scholastic theories by exposing them to the literate public, which explains some of the outrage over Ramus's reforms. See Ramus translated and cited by Wilbur Samuel Howell's indispensable in *Logic and Rhetoric in England* (New York: Russell and Russell, [1956], 1961), 154, and Goeglin, '"Wherein Hath Ramus Been so Offensive?": Poetic Examples in the English Ramist Logic Manuals (1574–1672)', *Rhetorica* 14.1 (1996): 73–101, 77.

33 Knight, *The Mutual Flame*, 153. Maurice Evans makes a similar claim when he claims, 'Shakespeare's lovers cannot, at least symbolically, exist on earth'. See G. Blakemore Evans, ed., *Narrative Poems* (New York: Penguin, 1989), 53.

34 Book IV of Aristotle's *Metaphysics* in *The Complete Works of Aristotle*, ed. Jonathan Barnes (Princeton: Princeton University Press, 1984), 1588.

35 This principle is not to be confused with bivalence, which stipulates that every proposition is either true or false. For full and technical

Notes

definitions of these laws and related terms see Irving Copi's chapter on syllogism in *Symbolic Logic*. Fifth Edition (New York: Pearson, 1979).

36   See Bart Kosko, *Fuzzy Thinking: The New Science of Fuzzy Logic* (New York: Hyperion, 1994). Kosko cites a thought experiment in Descartes' *Meditations,* which demonstrates how one may imagine a shift from Aristotelian or binary logic to multivalued logic. Observing a plug of wax before an open flame, Descartes notes that the object loses its original sensate properties – its size expands, its smell alters, its surface temperature changes, and so on. At which point does it finally cease to be a plug of wax and become something else, say, a vapour or a puddle on the ground? There are many variations on this logical puzzle, including the 'sorites' paradox involving a heap of sand that becomes, eventually, a non-heap, though the precise point at which this happens is seemingly impossible to determine. Useful as Aristotelian laws of identity may be, they lack subtlety: for Aristotle, there is either 'wax' or 'not-wax', no shades of grey between the extremes. This observation formed the basis of mounting early modern hostility towards Aristotelian schemas, as evidenced by scathing critiques from Pico, Valla, Ramus, and Bacon, among others. Despite these critiques, it will take hundreds of years for logicians John Stuart Mill and Bertrand Russell to pave a path to the post or anti-Aristotelian formulas of multivalued or fuzzy logic, a late-twentieth-century emendation of Aristotle. By the 1970s, the term 'multivalued' formally enters logical discourse as opposed to binary, bivalent or Boolean forms of logic, the many progeny of Aristotelian syllogism. For a technical applied treatment of fuzzy logic, see Timothy Ross, *Fuzzy Logic with Engineering Applications*. Fourth Edition (New York: Wiley, 2016); for a computational study applying the principles of fuzzy logic to gender identity, see V. Sanz and S. Guadarrama, 'Applying a Fuzzy Model Approach to the Classification of Sexual Differences: Beyond the Male/Female Binary', *Annual Meeting of the North American Fuzzy Information Processing Society* (2012): 1–6.

37   See Ann Rosalind Jones and Peter Stallybrass, 'Fetishizing Gender: Constructing the Hermaphrodite in Renaissance Europe', in *Body Guards: The Cultural Politics of Gender Ambiguity*, ed. Julia Epstein and Kristina Straub (New York: Routledge, 1991), 80. See also studies cited in fn. 3 of this chapter.

38   Edward Wilson-Lee, 'Shakespeare by Numbers: Mathematical Crisis in *Troilus and Cressida*', *Shakespeare Quarterly* 64.4 (2013): 449–72, 469.

39   For an excellent introduction to non-binary philosophy, see Robin Dembroff's 'Beyond Binary: Genderqueer as Critical Gender Kind', *Philosophers Imprint* 20.9 (2020): 1–23.

Notes

40 I should qualify my earlier claim that the poem shirks metaphysics or logic-as-metaphysics insofar as such an interpretation would seem to contradict the idea that a notational reading of the poem is how one may best understand the non-binary 'nature' of the Phoenix-Turtle. To say that the kind of rational practice articulated above is something the speaker of this poem would not be interested in pursuing (as I believe to be the case) is not to say that it does not want us, the reader, to do this work, and thereby to learn a kind of lesson by parsing the poem's many layers of logical tension. Put differently, in terms of a trans or nonbinary philosophical perspective, we might think of the problem as axiological, residing in the value one places on such rational assessments. Simply because a thing does not conform to a given rational ruleset does not mean that it must be rejected as impossible; instead, we might imagine a new taxonomical rationality altogether, as trans activists have been successful in doing through (for example) the implementation of the singular 'they'. But one cannot effectively arrive at such a place without, first, critique of that which imposes and oppresses.

41 The number three, never mentioned but often suggested in this poem (the 'treble-dated Crow' is granted access to funerary proceedings by the speaker; 'threne' and 'Threnos' might be overlooked puns), may be Aristotle's excluded middle, the betweenness of 'property' that his laws of identity negate.

42 Ronald Bates, 'Shakespeare's "The Phoenix and Turtle"', *Shakespeare Quarterly* 6 (1955): 19–30, 28.

43 G. Wilson Knight, *Christian Renaissance: With Interpretations of Dante, Shakespeare and Goethe* (London: Methuen, 1933), 236–7.

44 Not for a moment confused by his burst of love for Helena, Lysander then chooses to invoke reason to justify his obviously (and multiply) irrational feelings: "Things growing are not ripe until their season / So I, being young, till now ripe not to reason; / And touching now the point of human skill, / Reason becomes the marshal to my will". (2.2.117-20). Far from deploring reason, Lysander 'marshals' it to his will; it is the tool, ironically and comically, that he adopts to reconstruct his imaginary love affair with Helena.

45 I first argued this point in my 2011 MA thesis, 'The Phoenix and Turtle: Shakespeare's Fuzzy Apocalypse'. Matthew Zarnowieki arrived at this reading independently in 'Reading Shakespeare Miscellaneously: Ben Jonson, Robert Chester, and the Vatum Chorus of *Loves Martyr*'. See *Formal Matters: Reading the Materials of English Renaissance Literature*, ed. Allison K. Deutermann and András Kiséry (Manchester: Manchester University Press, 2013).

46 Chester, *Love's Martyr*, 16.

Notes

Afterword

1 Kim Hall, *Things of Darkness: Economies of Race and Gender in Early Modern England* (Ithaca: Cornell University Press, 1995), 254.
2 Happily, such work is already being done, in a sense, by Stephen Guy-Bray in his forthcoming book on Renaissance line endings.
3 Jacob Gaboury, 'Critical Unmaking', 485.
4 Zeffiro, 'Towards a Queer Futurity of Data', 5.
5 Ibid., 12.

BIBLIOGRAPHY

Ackroyd, Peter. *Shakespeare: The Biography*. London: Chatto and Windus, 2006.

Ahmed, Sara. *Queer Phenomenology: Orientations, Objects, Others*. Duke: Duke University Press, 2006.

Allot, Robert. *England's Parnassus; or the Choycest Flowers of Our Modern Poets, with Their Poeticall Comparisons, Descriptions of Bewties, Personages, Castles, Pallaces, Mountaines, Groves, Seas, Springs, Rivers, &c. Whereunto Are Annexed Other Various Discourses, Both Pleasant and Profitable*. London: for N. L., C. B., and T. H., 1600.

Andrews, Meghan C. 'Shakespeare the Formalist: Reading and Rewriting John Marston in the Poets' War'. *Texas Studies in Literature and Language* 63.1 (2021): 1–27.

Asquith, Clare. 'A Phoenix for Palm Sunday: Was Shakespeare's Poem a Requiem for Catholic Martyrs?' *TLS* 13 (2001): 14–15.

Barnes, Jonathan, ed. *The Complete Works of Aristotle*. Princeton: Princeton University Press, 1984.

Bastian, Mathieu, Sebastien Heymann, and Mathieu Jacomy. 'Gephi: An Open Source Software for Exploring and Manipulating Networks'. *International AAAI Conference on Web and Social Media* (2009).

Barthes, Roland. 'The Death of the Author'. In *Image/Music/Text*. Stephen Heath, trans. New York: Hill and Wang, 1977.

Bates, Ronald. 'Shakespeare's "The Phoenix and Turtle"'. *Shakespeare Quarterly* 6 (1955): 19–30.

Bednarz, James. 'Representing Jonson: *Histriomastix* and the Origin of the Poets' War'. *Huntington Library Quarterly* 54.1 (1991): 1–30.

Bednarz, James. 'Marston's Subversion of Shakespeare and Jonson: *Histriomastix* and the War of the Theaters'. *Medieval and Renaissance Drama in England* 6 (1993): 103–28.

Bednarz, James. *Shakespeare and the Poets' War*. New York: Columbia University Press, 2001.

Bednarz, James. *Shakespeare and the Truth of Love: The Mystery of "The Phoenix and Turtle"*. New York: Palgrave MacMillan, 2012.

Bednarz, James. 'Contextualizing "The Phoenix and Turtle": Shakespeare, Edward Blount and the *Poetical Essays* Group of *Love's Martyr*'. *Shakespeare Survey* 67 (2014): 131–49.

Bibliography

Bland, Mark. '"As far from all Reuolt": Sir John Salusbury, Christ Church MS 184, and Ben Jonson's First Ode'. *English Manuscript Studies, 1100–1700* 8 (2000): 43–78.

Blome, Richard. *The Gentlemans Recreation. In Two Parts*. London: Printed by S. Roycroft for Richard Blome, dwelling at the upper end of Dutchy-Lane, near Somerset-House in the Strand, 1686.

Bloom, Allan. *Shakespeare on Love and Friendship*. Chicago: University of Chicago Press, 2000.

Bly, Mary. *Queer Virgins and Virgin Queans on the Early Modern Stage*. Oxford: Oxford University Press, 2000.

Bohn, Henry G. *The Epigrams of Martial*. London: Bel and Daldy, 1865.

Bonnard, G. 'Shakespeare's Contribution to R. Chester's *Loves Martyr*'. *English Studies* 19 (1937): 66–9.

Borukhov, Boris. 'A More Precise Date for Shakespeare's "The Phoenix and the Turtle"'. *Notes and Queries* 260 (2015): 567–8.

Bradbrook, M. C. 'The Phoenix and the Turtle'. *Shakespeare Quarterly* 6.3 (1955): 356–8.

Braithwaite, Richard. *The English Gentleman Containing Sundry Excellent Rules or Exquisite Observations, Tending to Direction of Every Gentleman, of Selecter Ranke and Qualitie; How to Demeane or Accommodate Himself in the Manage of Publicke or Private Affaires*. London: Printed by Iohn Haviland, and are to be sold by Robert Bostock at his shop at the signe of the Kings head in Pauls Church-yard, 1630.

Bray, Alan. 'Homosexuality and the Signs of Male Friendship in Elizabethan England'. *History Workshop* 29 (1990): 1–19.

Bray, Alan. *The Friend*. Chicago: University of Chicago Press, 2003.

Bromley, James M. *Intimacy and Sexuality in the Age of Shakespeare*. Cambridge: Cambridge University Press, 2012.

Bromley, James M. 'Cruisy Historicism: Sartorial Extravagance and Public Sexual Culture in Ben Jonson's *Every Man Out of His Humour*'. *JEMCS* 16.2 (2016): 21: 58.

Brooks, Harold F., ed. *The Arden Shakespeare: A Midsummer Night's Dream*. 1979. London: Bloomsbury, 2006.

Brown, Carleton. *Poems by Sir John Salusbury and Robert Chester*. Bryn Mawr: Bryn Mawr College Monographs Series, 1913.

Burdick, Anne and Johanna Drucker, Peter Lunefeld, Todd Presner, and Jeffrey Schnapp. *Digital_Humanities*. Cambridge: MIT Press, 2012.

Burrow, Colin, ed. *The Oxford Shakespeare: The Complete Sonnets and Poems*. Oxford: Oxford University Press, 2002.

Burrows, J. 'All the Way Through: Testing for Authorship in Different Frequency Strata'. *Literary and Linguistic Computing* 22.1 (2007): 27–47.

Bibliography

Burrows, J. 'Never Aay Always Again: Reflections on the Numbers Game'. *Text and Genre in Reconstruction*. McCarty, W., ed. London: OpenBook Publishers, 2010. 23–35.

Burrows, J. and Hugh Craig, "A Collaboration about a Collaboration: The Authorship of *King Henry VI, Part Three*. *Collaborative Research in the Digital Humanities*. M. Deegan and W. McCarty, eds. Farnham: Ashgate, 2012.

Butler, Judith. 'What is Critique? An Essay on Foucault's Virtue'. *The Political: Readings in Continental Philosophy*. David Ingram, ed. London: Basil Blackwell, 2002.

Cain, Tom. ed. *Poetaster*. Manchester: Manchester University Press, 1996.

Cathcart, Charles. *Marston, Rivalry, Rapprochement, and Jonson*. London: Routledge, 2008.

Cavalli-Sforza, Luigi Luca, Paolo Menozzi, and Alberto Piazza. *The History and Geography of Human Genes*. Princeton: Princeton University Press, 1994.

Cavendish, Michael. *Ayres in Tabletorie to the Lute expressed with two voyces and the base Violl or the voice & Lute only*. London: Printed by *Peter Short*, on bredstreethill at the signe of the Starre, 1598.

Chambers, R. W. 'Some Sequences of Thought in Shakespeare and in the 147 Lines of Sir Thomas More'. *Modern Language Review* 26 (1931): 251–80.

Chapman, George. *The Shaddovv of Night Containing Two Poeticall Hymnes, Deuised by G.C. Gent*. STC 4990. London: Printed by R[ichard] F[ield] for William Ponsonby, 1594.

Chapman, George. *The Poems of George Chapman*. Phyllis Brooks Bartlett, ed. New York: Modern Language Association of America, 1941.

Chester, Robert. *Love's Martyr*: Loves martyr: Or, Rosalins complaint. Allegorically shadowing the truth of loue, in the constant fate of the phœnix and turtle. A poeme enterlaced with much varietie and raritie; now first translated out of the venerable Italian Torquato Cæliano, by Robert Chester. With the true legend of famous King Arthur, the last of the nine worthies, being the first essay of a new Brytish poet: collected out of diuerse authenticall records. To these are added some new compositions, of seuerall moderne writers whose names are subscribed to their seuerall workes, vpon the first subiect: viz. the phœnix and turtle. STC 5119. London: Imprinted by R. Field for E. Blount, 1601.

Cirillo, A. R. 'The Fair Hermaphrodite: Love-Union in the Poetry of Donne and Spenser'. *SEL, 1500–1900* 9 (1969): 87.

'Cladistics, *n*'. *The Oxford English Dictionary*. Second Edition. *OED Online*. Oxford University Press. 3 August 2020.

Copi, Irving. *Symbolic Logic*. Fifth Edition. New York: Pearson, 1979.

Craig, Hugh. 'Is the Author Really Dead? An Empirical Study of Authorship in English Renaissance Drama'. *Empirical Studies of the Arts* 18.2 (2000): 119–34.

Bibliography

Craig, Hugh. 'Shakespeare's Vocabulary: Myth and Reality'. *Shakespeare Quarterly* 62.1 (2011): 53–74.

Craig, Hugh. 'The Weight of Numbers: Common Words and Jonson's Dramatic Style'. *Ben Jonson Journal* 6.1 (2016): 243–59.

Craig, Hugh. Intelligent Archive (Rosella IA 3.0). Newcastle: Centre for Literary and Linguistic Computing. 2019. https://www.newcastle.edu.au/research-and-innovation/centre/education-arts/cllc/intelligent-archive (accessed 1 June 2020).

Craig, Hugh and Arthur Kinney. *Shakespeare, Computers, and the Mystery of Authorship*. Cambridge: Cambridge University Press, 2013.

Crewe, Jonathan. 'Disorderly Love: Sodomy Revisited in Marlowe's Edward II'. *Criticism* 51.3 (2009): 385–99.

Cunningham, J. V. '"Essence" and the Phoenix and Turtle'. *ELH* 19 (1952): 265–76.

Da, Nan Z. 'The Computational Case against Computational Literary Studies'. *Critical Inquiry* 45.3 (2019): 601–39.

Da, Nan Z. 'The Digital Humanities Debacle'. *The Chronicle of Higher Education*. 27 March 2019. https://www.chronicle.com/article/The-Digital-Humanities-Debacle/245986.

Daston, Lorraine and Katherine Park, 'The Hermaphrodite and the Orders of Nature: Sexual Ambiguity in Early Modern France'. *GLQ* 1.4 (1995): 419–38.

Davies, H. Neville. 'The Phoenix and Turtle: Requiem and Rite'. *The Review of English Studies, New Series* 46.184 (1995): 525–30.

Davis, Joe Lee. *The Sons of Ben: Jonsonian Comedy in Caroline England*. Detroit: Wayne State University Press, 1967.

Dembroff, Robin. 'Beyond Binary: Genderqueer as Critical Gender Kind'. *Philosophers Imprint* 20.9 (2020): 1–23.

DiGangi, Mario. *The Homoerotics of Early Modern Drama*. Cambridge: Cambridge University Press, 1997.

Donne, John. *The Songs and Sonnets of John Donne*. Second Edition. Theodore Redpath, ed. Harvard: Harvard University Press, 2009.

Evans, Mel and Alan Hogarth. 'Stylistic Palimpsests: Computational Stylistic Perspectives on Precursory Authorship in Aphra Behn's Drama'. *Digital Scholarship in the Humanities* 36.1 (2021): 64–86.

Doelman, James. 'Charles Fitz-Geffry and the "War of the Theatres."' *English Theatre* 11.1 (2008): 99–106.

Downey, Sarah, Michael Drout, Michael J. Khan, and Mark D. Leblanc. "Books Tell Us: Lexomic and Traditional Evidence for the Sources of Guthlac A'. *Modern Philology* 110.2 (2012): 153–81.

Droeshout, Martin, and Stephen Jerome. *The Arraignment of the Whole Creature Att the Barre of Religion, Reason, and Experience*. STC 13069. London: Printed by B. Alsop and Tho: Favvcet, 1631.

Bibliography

Drout, Michael D. C., Michael Kahn, Mark D. LeBlanc, and C. Nelson. 'Of Dendrogrammatology: Lexomic Methods for Analyzing the Relationships among Old English Poems'. *Journal of English and Germanic Philology* 110.3 (2011): 301–36.

Drout, Michael C., Yvette Kisor, Leah Smith, Natasha Piirainen, and Allison Dennet. *Beowulf Unlocked: New Evidence from Lexomic Analysis*. New York: Palgrave Macmillan, 2016.

Duncan-Jones, Katherine. *Ungentle Shakespeare: Scenes from His Life*. London: The Arden Shakespeare, 2000.

Duncan-Jones, Katherine. 'Playing Fields or Killing Fields: Shakespeare's Poems and "Sonnets"'. *Shakespeare Quarterly* 54.2 (2003): 127–41.

Duncan-Jones, Katherine and H. R. Woudhuysen. *The Arden Shakespeare: Shakespeare's Poems*. Third Series. 2007. London: The Arden Shakespeare, 2020.

Edelman, Lee. *No Future: Queer Theory and the Death Drive*. Durham: Duke University Press, 2004.

Eder, Maciej. 'Does Size Matter? Small Samples, Big Problems'. *Digital Humanities 2010*. Conference Abstracts. King's College London, 2010.

Eder, Maciej. 'Rolling Stylometry'. *Digital Scholarship in the Humanities* 31.3 (2016): 457–69.

Eder, Maciej., J. Rybicki, and M. Kestemont. 'Stylometry with R: A Package for Computational Text Analysis'. *The R Journal* 8.1 (2016): 107–21.

Eder, Maciej, J. Rybicki, and M. Kestemont. '"Stylo": A Package for Stylometric Analyses'. *Computational Stylistics Group* (2018).

Elliott, Ward E. Y. 'And Then There Were None: Winnowing the Shakespeare Claimants'. *Computers and the Humanities* 30 (1996): 191–245.

Elliott, Ward E. Y. 'The Professor Doth Protest Too Much Methinks: Problems with the Foster "Response"'. *Computers and the Humanities* 32 (1999): 420–90.

Elliott, Ward E. Y. and Robert Valenza. '*A Lover's Complaint* to Shakespeare'. *Shakespeare Quarterly* 48 (1997): 177–207.

Emerson, Ralph Waldo. *Parnassus*. Boston: Houghton Mifflin, 1875.

Enterline, Lynn. 'The Phoenix and the Turtle', Renaissance Elegies, and the Language of Grief'. *Early Modern English Poetry: A Critical Companion*. Patrick Cheney and Garrett A. Sullivan, Jr., eds. New York: Oxford University Press, 2007.

Epsom, William. *Essays on Shakespeare*. David B. Pirie, ed. Cambridge: Cambridge University Press, 1986.

Erne, Lukas. 'Reconsidering Shakespearean Authorship'. *Shakespeare Studies* 36 (2007): 26–36.

Erne, Lucas. *Shakespeare as Literary Dramatist*. Second Edition. Cambridge: Cambridge University Press, 2013.

Bibliography

Evans, Maurice, ed. *Narrative Poems*. New York: Penguin, 1989.

Fairchild, A. H. R. '"The Phoenix and Turtle": A Critical and Historical Interpretation'. *Englische Studien* 33 (1904): 337–84.

Ferguson, Roderick A. *Aberrations in Black: Toward a Queer of Color Critique*. Minneapolis: University of Minnesota Press, 2004.

Fineman, Joel. *Shakespeare's Perjured Eye: The Invention of Poetic Subjectivity in the Sonnets*. Berkeley: University of California Press, 1986.

Finnis, John and Patrick H. Martin. 'Another Turn for the Turtle'. *TLS* 18 (2003): 12–14.

Fitzgerald, Adam (2015). 'An Interview with Fred Moten, Part 1'. *Literary Hub*. 5 August 2015. Available online: https://lithub.com/an-interview-with-fred-moten-pt-i/ (accessed 1 June 2020).

Foucault, Michel. 'What Is an Author?' *Language, Counter-Memory, Practice: Selected Essays and Interviews by Michel Foucault*. Donald Bouchard and Sherry Simon, trans. Donald Bouchard, ed. Ithaca: Cornell University Press, 1977.

Foucault, Michel. 'What is Critique?' 1977. *The Politics of Truth*. Los Angeles: Semiotext(e), 2007.

Frauce, Abraham. *The Lavviers Logike, Exemplifying the Pracepts of Logike by the Practise of the Common Lawe, by Abraham Fraunce*. London: Imprinted by William How for Thomas Gubbin and T. Newman, 1588.

Freebury-Jones, D. 'Kyd and Shakespeare: Authorship versus Influence'. *Authorship* 6.1 (2017): 1–24.

Freccero, Carla. *Queer/Early/Modern*. Durham: Duke University Press, 2005.

Gaboury, Jacob. 'Critical Unmaking: Toward a Queer Computation'. *The Routledge Companion to Media Studies and Digital Humanities*. Berkeley: University of California Press, 2018.

Galway, Margaret. 'Flyting in Shakespeare's Comedies'. *The Shakespeare Association Bulletin* 10 (1935): 183–91.

Garrison, John S. *Friendship and Queer Theory in the Renaissance: Gender and Sexuality in Early Modern England*. London: Routledge, 2014.

Gilbert, Ruth. *Early Modern Hermaphrodites: Sex and Other Stories*. New York: Palgrave, 2002.

Gilman Sherman, Anita. 'Fantasies of Private Language in "The Phoenix and Turtle" and "The Ecstasy"'. *Shakespeare and Donne: Generic Hybrids and the Cultural Imaginary*. Judith H. Anderson and Jennifer C. Vaught, eds. New York: Fordham University Press, 2013.

Glimp, David. *Increase and Multiply: Governing Cultural Reproduction in Early Modern England*. Minneapolis: University of Minnesota Press, 2003.

Goeglein, Tamara A. '"Wherein Hath Ramus Been so Offensious?": Poetic Examples in the English Ramist Logic Manuals (1574–1672)'. *Rhetorica* 14.1 (1996) 73–101.

Bibliography

Goldberg, Jonathan. *Shakespeare's Hand*. Minneapolis: University of Minnesota Press, 2020.

Goldberg, Jonathan and Medhavi Menon. 'Queering History'. *PMLA* 120.5 (2005): 1608–17.

Gossett, 'Marston, Collaboration, and Eastward Ho!' *Renaissance Drama* 33 (2004): 181–200, 196.

Grady, Hugh. *Shakespeare and Impure Aesthetics*. Cambridge: Cambridge University Press, 2009.

de Grazia, Magreta. 'The Scandal of Shakespeare's Sonnets'. *Shakespeare Survey* 46 (1993): 35–50.

De Grazia, Magreta and Peter Stallybrass. 'The Materiality of the Shakespearean Text'. *Shakespeare Quarterly* 44.3 (1993): 255–83.

Green, Adam Isaiah. 'Queer Theory and Sociology: Locating the Subject and the Self in Sexuality Studies'. *Sociological Theory* 25.1 (2007): 26–45.

Grosart, Alexander B. *Robert Chester's Love's Martyr or Rosalins Complaint*. London: Trubner, 1878.

Groves, Beatrice. '"One Man at One Time May Be in Two Placys": Jack Juggler, Proverbial Wisdom, and Eucharistic Satire'. *Medieval and Renaissance Drama in England* 27 (2014): 40–56.

Guillim, John. *A Display of Heraldrie: Manifesting a More Easie Accesse to the Knowledge Thereof then Hath Beene Hitherto Published by Any, through the Benefit of Method, Whereinto It Is Now Reduced by the Industry of Joh. Gwillim Pursuiuant of Armes*. STC 12501. London: Printed by William Hall for Raphe Mab, 1611.

Guy-Bray, Stephen, *Against Reproduction: Where Renaissance Texts Come From*. Toronto: University of Toronto Press, 2009.

Guy-Bray, Stephen. *Shakespeare and Queer Representation*. London: Routledge, 2021.

Halberstam, Jack, David L. Eng, and José Esteban Muñoz. 'What's Queer about Queer Studies Now?' *Social Text* 23.3–4 (2005): 1–17.

Halberstam, Jack. *The Queer Art of Failure*. Durham: Duke University Press, 2011.

Halberstam, Jack. *Wild Things: The Disorder of Desire*. Duke: Duke University Press, 2020.

Hall, Kim. *Things of Darkness: Economies of Race and Gender in Early Modern England*. Ithaca: Cornell University Press, 1995.

Halperin, David. *Saint Foucault: Towards a Gay Hagiography*. Oxford: Oxford University Press, 1997.

Halpern, Richard. *Shakespeare's Perfume: Sodomy and Sublimity in the Sonnets, Wilde, Freud, and Lacan*. Philadelphia: University of Pennsylvania Press, 2002.

Hammerschmidt-Hummel, Hildegard. 'The Phoenix and the Turtle: Notate zur Entstehung des Werks und zur Entschlüsselung seiner Figuren als

Bibliography

historische Persönlichkeiten'. *Anglistik: Mitteilungen des Deutschen Anglistenverbandes* 14.2 (2003): 71–4.

Harper, Sally. 'Elizabethan Tune List from Lleweni Hall, North Wales'. *Royal Musical Association Research Chronicle* 38 (2005): 45–98.

Harrison, Thomas P. 'Love's Martyr,' by Robert Chester: A New Interpretation'. *The University of Texas Studies in English* 30 (1951): 66–85.

Harrison, Thomas P. *They Tell of Birds: Chaucer, Spenser, Milton, Drayton*. Austin: University of Texas Press, 1956.

Harrison, Thomas P. 'Review of *The Phoenix and the Turtle: Shakespeare's Poem and Chester's Loues Martyr* by William H. Matchett'. *Modern Philology* 64.2 (1966): 155–7.

Healy. *Shakespeare, Alchemy, and the Creative Imagination: The Sonnets and 'A Lovers Complaint'*. Cambridge: Cambridge UP, 2011.

Herford, C. H., Evelyn Simpson, and Perry Simpson. *Ben Jonson*. 11 Vols. Oxford: Oxford University Press, 1925–1952.

Hill, John Spencer. 'The Phoenix'. *Religion and Literature* 16 (1984): 61–6.

Hirschfeld, Heather Anne. *Joint Enterprises: Collaborative Drama and the Institutionalization of the English Renaissance Theater*. Amherst: University of Massachusetts Press, 2004.

Honigmann, E. A. J. *Shakespeare: The 'Lost Years'*. 1985. Manchester: Manchester University Press, 1999.

Hoover, D. L. (2019). *The Delta Spreadsheets*. https://wp.nyu.edu/exceltextanalysis/deltaspreadsheets/ (accessed 18 September 2019).

Hope, Jonathan. *Shakespeare and Language: Reason, Eloquence and Artifice in the Renaissance*. London: The Arden Shakespeare, 2010.

Howard-Hill, T. H. *Shakespeare and Sir Thomas More: Essays on the Play and its Shakespearean Interest*. Cambridge: Cambridge University Press, 1989.

Howell, Samuel. *Logic and Rhetoric in England*. 1956. New York: Russell and Russell, 1961.

Hume, Anthea. '*Love's Martyr*, "The Phoenix and the Turtle", and the Aftermath of the Essex Rebellion'. *The Review of English Studies, New Series* 40.157 (1989): 48–71.

Hutson, Lorna. 'Civility and Virility in Ben Jonson'. *Representations* 78.1 (2002): 1–27.

Hutson, Lorna. 'Liking Men: Ben Jonson's Closet Opened'. *ELH* 71.4 (2004): 1065–96.

Jackson, MacDonald P. 'Is "Hand D" of *Sir Thomas More* Shakespeare's? Thomas Bayes and the Elliott-Valenza Authorship Tests'. *Early Modern Literary Studies* 12.3 (2007). <http://purl.oclc.org/emls/12-3/jackbaye.htm>. Web. 6 August 2019.

Bibliography

Jackson, MacDonald P. "'A Lover's Complaint,' *Cymbeline*, and the Shakespeare Canon: Interpreting Shared Vocabulary'. *The Modern Language Review* 103.3 (2008): 621–38.

Jockers, Matthew L. and Rosamond Thalken. *Text Analysis with R: For Students of Literature*. Second Edition. Cham, Switzerland: Springer, 2020.

Jackson, Macdonald P. and Michael Neill, eds. *The Selected Plays of John Marston*. Cambridge: Cambridge University Press, 1986.

Jockers, Matthew L. and Daniela M. Witten. 'A Comparative Study of Machine Learning Methods for Authorship Attribution'. *Literary and Linguistic Computing* 25.2 (2010): 215–24.

Jockers, Matthew L. *Macroanalysis: Digital Methods and Literary History*. Urbana, IL: University of Illinois Press, 2013.

Jockers, Mathew. 'Testing Authorship in the Personal Writings of Joseph Smith Using NSC Classification'. *Literary and Linguistic Computing* 28.3 (2013): 371–81.

Johnson, E. Patrick and Mae G. Henderson, eds. *Black Queer Studies: A Critical Anthology*. Durham: Duke University Press, 2005.

Jones, Ann Rosalind and Peter Stallybrass. 'Fetishizing Gender: Constructing the Hermaphrodite in Renaissance Europe'. *Body Guards: The Cultural Politics of Gender Ambiguity*. Julia Epstein and Kristina Straub, eds. New York and London: Routledge, 1991.

Jonson, Ben. *Ben Jonson's Conversations with William Drummond of Hawthorden*. R.F. Patterson, ed. London: Blackie and Son Limited, 1923.

Jowett, John, ed. *Sir Thomas More*. Third Edition. London: Methuen, The Arden Shakespeare, 2011.

Juola, Patrick. *Authorship Attribution: Foundations and Trends in Information Retrieval*. Boston: Now Publishers, 2008.

Kahan, Jeffrey. "'I Tell You What Mine Author Says": A Brief History of Stylometrics'. *ELH* 82.3 (2015): 815–44.

Kastan, David Scott. "'To Think These Trifles Some-thing": Shakespearean Playbooks and the Claims of Authorship'. *Shakespeare Studies* 36 (2007): 37–48.

Kincaid, Jamaica. *A Small Place*. 1988. New York: Farrar, Straus and Giroux, 2001.

Klause, John. 'The Phoenix and Turtle in Its Time'. *In the Company of Shakespeare: Essays on English Renaissance Literature in Honor of G. Blakemore Evans*. Thomas Moisan, Douglas Bruster, and William H. Bond, eds. London, England: Associated University Presses, 2002.

Knapp, Jeffrey. 'What Is a Co-Author?' *Representations* 89.1 (2005): 1–29.

Knapp, Jeffrey. 'Shakespeare as Coauthor'. *Shakespeare Studies* 36 (2007): 49–59.

Knight, G. Wilson. *Christian Renaissance: With Interpretations of Dante, Shakespeare and Goethe*. London: Methuen, 1933.

Bibliography

Knight, G. Wilson. *The Mutual Flame: On Shakespeare's Sonnets and The Phoenix and Turtle*. London: Methuen, 1955.

Knight, Jeffrey Todd. 'Making Shakespeare's Books: Assembly and Intertexuality in the Archives'. *Shakespeare Quarterly* 60.3 (2009): 304–40.

Koestanbaum, Wayne. *The Queen's Throat: Opera, Homosexuality, and the Mystery of Desire*. New York: Poseidon Press, 1993.

Kosko, Bart. *Fuzzy Thinking: The New Science of Fuzzy Logic*. New York: Hyperion, 1994.

Kraicer, Eve and Andrew Piper. 'Social Characters: The Hierarchy of Gender in Contemporary English-Language Fiction'. *Journal of Cultural Analytics* 1.1 (2019): 1–28.

Labreche, Ben. 'Patronage, Friendship, and Sincerity in Bacon and Spenser'. *Studies in English Literature, 1500–1900*. 50.1 (2010): 83–108.

Laqueur, Thomas. *Making Sex: Body and Gender from the Greeks to Freud*. Cambridge: Harvard University Press, 1990.

Lanier, Douglas. 'Masculine Silence: *Epicoene* and Jonsonian Stylistics'. *College Literature* 21.2 (1994): 1–18.

Lerer, Seth. *Error and the Academic Self: The Scholarly Imagination, Medieval to Modern*. New York: Columbia University Press, 2002.

Lesser, Zachary and Benedict Robinson, eds. *Textual Conversations in the Renaissance: Ethics, Authors, Technologies*. Aldershot: Ashgate Publishing, 2006.

Lewis, Wyndham. *The Lion and the Fox: The Role of the Hero in the Plays of Shakespeare*. 1927. London: Methuen, 1966.

Livingston, Jennie. *Paris is Burning*. United States: Off White Productions, 1990.

Lloyd-Roberts, Tom. 'Bard of Lleweni? Shakespeare's Welsh Connection'. *New Welsh Review* 23 (1993–4): 11–18.

Long, Hoyt and Richard Jean So. 'Literary Pattern Recognition: Modernism between Close Reading and Machine Learning'. *Critical Inquiry* 42.2 (2016): 235–67.

Long, Kathleen. *Hermaphrodites in Renaissance Europe*. London: Routledge, 2006.

Lorde, Audre. 'The Master's Tools Will Never Dismantle the Master's House'. 1984. *Sister Outsider: Essays and Speeches*. Berkeley: Crossing Press, 2007.

Love, Harold. *Attributing Authorship: An Introduction*. Cambridge: Cambridge University Press, 2002.

Lowenstein, Joseph. *Ben Jonson and Possessive Authorship*. Cambridge: Cambridge University Press, 2002.

Machiavelli, Niccolò. *The Prince*. 1532. Cambridge: Hackett, 1995.

MacFaul, Tom. *Male Friendship in Shakespeare and His Contemporaries*. Cambridge, Cambridge University Press, 2007.

Bibliography

MacFaul, Tom. *Poetry and Paternity in Renaissance England: Sidney, Spenser, Shakespeare*. Cambridge: Cambridge University Press, 2010.

MacLean, Hugh, ed. *Ben Jonson and the Cavalier Poets*. New York: Norton, 1974.

Macpherson, C. B. *The Political Theory of Possessive Individualism: Hobbes to Locke*. Oxford: Oxford University Press, 2011.

Magnusson, Lynne and David Schalkwyk, eds. *The Cambridge Companion to Shakespeare's Language*. Cambridge: Cambridge University Press, 2019.

Mann, Jenny C. 'How to Look at a Hermaphrodite in Early Modern England'. *Studies in English* Literature, *1500-1900* 46.1 (2006): 67–91.

Marcus, Leah S. *Unediting the Renaissance: Shakespeare, Marlow, and Milton*. New York: Routledge, 1996.

Marcus, Leah S. 'The Author and/or the Critic'. *Shakespeare Studies* 36 (2007): 90–100.

Marotti, Arthur F. 'Christ Church, Oxford, and beyond: Folger MS V.a.345 and Its Manuscript and Print Sources'. *Studies in Philology* 113.4 (2016): 850–78.

Marston, John. *The Scourge of Villanie Three Bookes of Satyres*. STC 17485. London: Printed by I[ames] R[oberts] and are to be sold by Iohn Buzbie, in Paules Church-yard, at the signe of the Crane, 1598.

Masten, Jeffrey. *Textual Intercourse: Collaboration, Authorship, and Sexualities in Renaissance Drama*. Cambridge: Cambridge University Press, 1997.

Masten, Jeffrey. *Queer Philologies: Sex, Language, and Affect in Shakespeare's Time*. Philadelphia: University of Pennsylvania Press, 2016.

Matchett, William. *The Phoenix and the Turtle: Shakespeare's Poem and Chester's Loues Martyr*. The Hague: Mouton & Co., 1965.

Matz, Robert. 'The Scandals of Shakespeare's Sonnets'. *ELH* 77.2 (2010): 477–508.

McMillan, Douglas. 'The Phoenix in the Western World from Herodotus to Shakespeare'. *The D.H. Lawrence Review* 5.3 (1972): 238–67.

Melfi, Theodore. *Hidden Figures*. United States: Fox 2000 Productions, 2016.

Menon, Madhavi. *Shakesqueer: A Queer Companion to the Complete Works of Shakespeare*. Durham: Duke University Press, 2011.

Menon, Madhavi. 'HexaSexuality'. *Shakespeare in Our Time: A Shakespeare Association of America Collection*. Dympna Callaghan and Suzanne Gossett, eds. London: The Arden Shakespeare, 2016.

Meres, Francis. *Palladas Tamia, Wit's Treasury, Being the Second Part of Wit's Commonwealth*. London, 1598.

Moss, Daniel. '"The Second Master of Love": George Chapman and the Shadow of Ovid'. *Modern Philology* 111.3 (2014): 457–84.

Moten, Fred. *The Universal Machine*. Durham: Duke University Press, 2018.

Bibliography

Muñoz, Jose Esteban. *Cruising Utopia: The Then and There of Queer Futurity*. New York: New York University Press, 2009.

Newdigate, B. H. *The Phoenix and Turtle*. Oxford: Oxford University Press, 1937.

Noble, William S. 'What Is a Support Vector Machine?' *Computational Biology* 24.12 (2006): 1565–7.

O'Callaghan, Michelle. *The English Wits: Literature and Sociability in Early Modern England*. Cambridge: Cambridge University Press, 2007.

Ong, Walter. 'Metaphor and Twinned Vision' (*The Phoenix and the Turtle*)'. *The Sewanee Review* 63.2 (1955): 193–201.

Ong, Walter. *Ramus, Method, and the Decay of Dialogue*. 1958. Chicago: University of Chicago Press, 2004.

OED. 'A Brief History of Singular "They"' (2018). *Oxford English Dictionary Online*. Available online: https://public.oed.com/blog/a-brief-history-of-singular-they/ (accessed 1 June 2021).

Parks, Ward. 'Flyting, Sounding, Debate: Three Verbal Contest Genres'. *Poetics Today* 7.3 (1986): 439–58.

Parry, Robert. *Sinetes Passions Vppon His Fortunes Offered for an Incense at the Shrine of the Ladies Which Guided His Distempered Thoughtes. The Patrons Patheticall Posies, Sonets, Maddrigals, and Rowndelayes. Together with Sinetes Dompe*. STC 19338. London: Printed by T[homas] P[urfoot] for William Holme, to be sould on Ludgate hill at the signe of the holy Lambe, 1597.

Pechter, Ed. 'Against Attribution'. *Shakespeare Quarterly* 69.4 (2018): 228–55.

Perry, Henry. *Egluryn phraethineb. sebh, dosparth ar retoreg, vn o 'r saith gelbhydhyd, yn dysculhuniaith ymadrodh, a 'i pherthynassau*. STC 19775. London: Printiedig gann Ioan Danter yn Lhundain, 1595.

Philip, M. NourBese. *She Tries Her Tongue, Her Silence Softly Breaks*. 1989. Middletown: Wesleyan University Press, 2015.

Phipson, Emma. *Animal Lore in Shakespeare's Time*. London: Kegan Paul, 1886.

Prince, F. T. *Shakespeare: The Poems*. London: Methuen, 1960.

Plecháč, Petr. 'Relative contributions of Shakespeare and Fletcher in Henry VIII: An Analysis Based on Most Frequent Words and Most Frequent Rhythmic Patterns'. *Digital Scholarship in the Humanities* (2020). https://doi.org/10.1093/llc/fqaa032.

Rhodes, Neil and Jonathan Sawday, eds. *The Renaissance Computer: Knowledge Technology in the First Age of Print*. London: Routledge, 2000.

Reiss, Timothy J. 'From Trivium to Quadrivium: Ramus, Method and Mathematical Technology'. *The Renaissance Computer: Knowledge Technology in the First Age of Print*. Neil Rhodes and Jonathan Sawday, eds. London: Routledge, 2000.

Bibliography

Richards, I. A. 'The Sense of Poetry: Shakespeare's "The Phoenix and the Turtle"'. *Daedalus* 87 (1958): 86–94.

Riggs, David. *Ben Jonson: A Life*. Cambridge: Harvard University Press, 1989.

Rodrigues, Don. 'Can Conversation Be Quantified? A Cladistic Approach to Shakespeare's and Jonson's Influences in *Love's Martyr*'. *Conversational Exchanges in Early Modern England: 1549–1640*. Kristen-Abbot Bennett, ed. Newcastle upon Tyne: Cambridge Scholars Press, 2015.

Rollins, Hyder Edward, ed. *The Phoenix Nest, 1593*. Cambridge: Harvard University Press, 1931.

Ross, Timothy. *Fuzzy Logic with Engineering Applications*. Fourth Edition. New York: Wiley, 2016.

Rowe, George E. *Distinguishing Jonson: Imitation, Rivalry, and the Direction of a Dramatic Career*. Lincoln: University of Nebraska Press, 1988.

Russell, Legacy. *Glitch Feminism: A Manifesto*. London: Verso, 2020.

Rybicki, J. and M. Heydel. 'The Stylistics and Stylometry of Collaborative Translation: Woolf's *Night and Day* in Polish'. *Literary and Linguistic Computing* 28.4: 708–17, 2013.

Rybicki, J. 'Vive La Diffe´rence: Tracing the (Authorial) Gender Signal by Multivariate Analysis of Word Frequencies'. *Digital Scholarship in the Humanities* 31.4 (2016): 746–61.

Rybicki, J., D. Hoover, and M. Kestemont. 'Collaborative Authorship: Conrad, Ford and Rolling Delta'. *Literary and Linguistic Computing* 29.3: 422–31, 2014.

Sanchez, Melissa E. *Queer Faith: Reading Promiscuity and Race in the Secular Love Tradition*. New York: New York University Press, 2019.

Sanchez, Melissa E. *Shakespeare and Queer Theory*. London: The Arden Shakespeare, 2020.

Sanz, V. and S. Guadarrama. 'Applying a Fuzzy Model Approach to the Classification of Sexual Differences: Beyond the Male/Female Binary'. *2012 Annual Meeting of the North American Fuzzy Information Processing Society* (2012): 1–6.

Schwarz, Kathryn. *What You Will: Gender, Contract, and Shakespearean Social Space*. Philadelphia: University of Pennsylvania Press, 2011.

Schoenfeldt, Michael. *The Cambridge Introduction to Shakespeare's Poetry*. Cambridge: Cambridge University Press, 2010.

Sclater, William. *An Exposition with Notes Upon the First and Second Epistles to the Thessalonians*. STC 21835. London: Printed by John Haviland and sold by Richard Thrale at the Cross Keyes at Paul's Gate, 1630.

Sedgwick, Eve. *Between Men: English Literature and Male Homosocial Desire*. 1985. New York: Columbia University Press, 2015.

Sedgwick, Eve. *Epistemology of the Closet*. Berkeley: University of California Press, 1990.

Bibliography

Seltzer, Daniel. "'Their Tragic Scene": "The Phoenix and Turtle" and Shakespeare's Love Tragedies'. *Shakespeare Quarterly* 12.2 (1961): 91–101.

Shahani, Ranjee G. 'The Phoenix and the Turtle'. *Notes and Queries* CX (1946): 99–101.

Shannon, Laurie. *Sovereign Amity: Figures of Friendship in Shakespearean Contexts*. Chicago: University of Chicago Press, 2002.

Shapiro, James. *Rival Playwrights: Marlow, Jonson, Shakespeare*. New York: Columbia University Press, 1991.

Silberman, Lauren. 'Hermaphrodite'. *The Spenser Encyclopedia*. A. C. Hamilton, ed. Toronto: University of Toronto Press, 1990.

Sinfield, Alan. *Shakespeare, Authority, Sexuality: Unfinished Business in Cultural Materialism*. London: Routledge, 2006.

Smith, Hallet. 'The Phoenix and Turtle'. *The Riverside Shakespeare: Second Edition*. G. Blakemore Evans, ed. New York: Houghton Mifflin Company, 1997.

Stanivukovic, Goran, ed. *Queer Shakespeare: Desire and Sexuality*. London: The Arden Shakespeare, 2017.

Steel, Karl. 'Number There in Love Was Slain'. *Shakesqueer: A Queer Companion to the Complete Works of Shakespeare*. Madhavi Menon, ed. Durham: Duke University Press, 2011.

Stein, Gertrude. *Three Lives*. 1909. New York: Penguin Classics, 1990.

Steggle, Matthew. *Wars of the Theatres: The Poetics of Personation in the Age of Jonson*. Victoria: University of Victoria Press, 1998.

Stockton, Will. 'Shakespeare and Queer Theory'. *Shakespeare Quarterly* 63.2 (2012): 224–35.

Taylor, Gary. 'Text and Authorship'. *Shakespeare in Our Time: A Shakespeare Association of America Collection*. Dympna Callaghan and Suzanne Gossett, eds. London: The Arden Shakespeare, 2016.

Tibshirani, Robert and Trevor Hastie, Balasubramanian Narasimhan, and Gilbert Chu. 'Class Prediction by Nearest Shrunken Centroids, with Applications to DNA Microarrays'. *Statistical Science* 18.1 (2003): 104–17.

Tiffany, Grace. *Erotic Beasts and Social Monsters: Shakespeare, Jonson, and Comic Androgyny*. Newark: University of Delaware Press, 1995.

Tipton, Alzada. 'The Transformation of the Earl of Essex: Post-Execution Ballads and "The Phoenix and the Turtle."' *Studies in Philology* 99.1 (2002): 57–80.

Tonstad, Linn Marie. *Queer Theology: Beyond Apologetics*. Eugene, OR: Cascade Press, 2019.

Traub, Valerie. *Thinking Sex with the Early Moderns*. Philadelphia: University of Pennsylvania Press, 2016.

Traub, Valerie. *The Renaissance of Lesbianism in Early Modern England*. Cambridge: Cambridge University Press, 2001.

Bibliography

Traub, Valerie. 'The New Unhistoricism in Queer Studies'. *PMLA* 128.1 (2013): 21–39.

Trinkhaus, Charles. 'Lorenzo Valla's Anti-Aristotelian Natural Philosophy'. *I Tatti Studies: Essays in the Renaissance* 5 (1993): 279–325.

Tubbs, Robert, Alice Jenkins, and Nina Engelhardt, eds. *The Palgrave Handbook of Literature and Mathematics*. Cham, Switzerland: Palgrave, 2021.

Tuve, Rosemond. *Elizabethan and Metaphysical Poetry: Renaissance Poetic and Twentieth Century Critics*. Chicago: University of Chicago Press, 1947.

Tuve, Rosemond. 'Ramus and Metaphysical Poetics'. *Renaissance Essays*. Paul Oskar Kristeller, Philip Paul Wiener, William J. Connell, eds. Rochester: University of Rochester Press, 1992.

Tyldum, Morten. *The Imitation Game*. United States: Black Bear Pictures, 2014.

Underwood, Ted. 'Dear Humanists: Fear Not the Digital Revolution'. *The Chronicle of Higher Education*. 27 March 2019. https://www.chronicle.com/article/Dear-Humanists-Fear-Not-the/245987.

Underwood, Ted. *Distant Horizons: Digital Evidence and Literary Change*. Chicago: University of Chicago Press, 2019.

Van Halteren, H., H. Baayen, F. Tweedie, M. Haverkort, and A. Neijt 'New machine learning methods demonstrate the existence of a human stylome'. *Journal of Quantitative Linguistics* 12.1 (2005): 65–7.

Vickers, Brian. *William Shakespeare: The Critical Heritage, Volume 4, 1753–1765*. London: Routledge, 1976.

Vickers, Brian. *Shakespeare, Co-Author: A Historical Study of Five Collaborative Plays*. Oxford: Oxford University Press, 2004.

Vickers, Brian. 'Coauthors and Closed Minds'. *Shakespeare Studies* 36 (2007): 26–36.

Vickers, Brian. 'Incomplete Shakespeare: Or, Denying Coauthorship in 1 Henry VI'. *Shakespeare Quarterly* 58.3 (2007): 311–52.

Waite, Alice Vinton. 'Ben Jonson's Grammar'. *Modern Language Notes* 24.5 (1909): 137–40.

Watson, Robert N. 'Lord Capulet's Lost Compromise: A Tragic Emendation and the Binary Dynamics of *Romero and Juliet*'. *Renaissance Drama* 43.1 (2015): 53–84.

Wells, Stanley. *Shakespeare and Co.: Christopher Marlowe, Thomas Dekker, Ben Jonson, Thomas Middleton, John Fletcher and the Other Players in His Story*. New York: Pantheon, 2006.

Wilson-Lee, Edward. 'Shakespeare by Numbers: Mathematical Crisis' in *Troilus and Cressida*. *Shakespeare Quarterly* 64.4 (2013): 449–72.

Witmore, Michael. *Shakespearean Metaphysics*. London: Continuum, 2008.

Bibliography

Witmore, Michael and Jonathan Hope. 'Shakespeare by the Numbers: On the Linguistic Texture of the Late Plays'. *Early Modern Tragicomedy*. Subha Mukherji and Raphael Lynne, eds. Cambridge: D. S. Brewer, 2007.

Wittgenstein, Ludwig. *Tractatus Logico-Philosophicus*. 1922. London: Routledge, 2001.

Woolf, Virginia. *To the Lighthouse*. 1927. London: Vintage Classics, 2004.

Woolf, Virginia. *The Waves*. 1931. London: Vintage Classics, 2004.

Wright, D. 'Using Word N-grams to Identify Authors and Idiolects: A Corpus Approach to a Forensic Linguistic Problem'. *International Journal of Corpus Linguistics* 22.2 (2017): 212–41.

Underwood, Richard Allan. *Shakespeare's 'The Phoenix and Turtle': A Survey of Scholarship*. Salzburg: University of Salzburg, 1974.

Yearling, Rebecca. *Ben Jonson, John Marston, and Early Modern Drama: Satire and the Audience*. London: Palgrave Macmillan, 2016.

Zarnowieki, Matthew. 'Reading Shakespeare Miscellaneously: Ben Jonson, Robert Chester, and the Vatum Chorus of *Loves Martyr*'. *Formal Matters: Reading the Materials of English Renaissance Literature*. Allison K. Deutermann and András Kiséry, eds. Manchester: Manchester University Press, 2013.

Zeffiro, Andrea, 'Towards a Queer Futurity of Data'. *Journal of Cultural Analytics* 1.1 (2019): 1–17.

INDEX

aberrant data and queerness 13–16
Agamben, Giorgio 103
Amores (Ovid) 90, 103 n. 10
Animadversiones (Ramus) 117 n. 31
anonyms in *Love's Martyr* 80–92
anti-Aristotelianism 104–6, 117 n. 31
anti-normativity 13
'Arabian bird' 110–11, 142–43
   see also phoenix myth
Aristotelianism 101–6, 114, 115–23
   see also logic; Reason/reason
Asquith, Clare 7
attribution studies 9–11, 67, 80–92
author / collaborator dyad 37
author concept 31, 73, 80, 81
   as analytical category 36–7, 67
   distinct from authorial practices 22
   and Jonson 86–7
   and Marston 91–2
   queer critique 33, 36, 66
authorial singularity 31–3, 55
authorial voice 5, 109–12, 114–15
authorship, collaborative 36–7, 67
   and analytical precision 37

Bates, Ronald 7, 124
Bednarz, James 6 n. 12, 21, 76 n. 15, 103
   n. 10, 116
bias in machine learning 16
bioinformatics 17
'bird of loudest lay' 110–12
birds, allegorical 103 n. 10, 112–15
Blount, Edward 5, 24
Bodleian Library 82 n. 40
bootstrap consensus trees (BCT) 55,
   84–5, 137
Brown, Carleton 8, 42 n. 44, 51 n. 60,
   56, 58, 60, 135 n. 2

burial rites, Elizabethan 113 n. 23
Butler, Judith 104 n. 12

Castalian waters 75, 75 n. 14, 90
Cathcart, Charles 80–2, 83
Chambers, R.W. 10
Chapman, George 93–6
   contributor to 'Invocatio' 90–1
   poetry comparted to *Love's Martyr*
   141
Chester, Robert 8, 24, 81, 88–2
   negative assessments 38, 57–8
   poetry in MS compared to *Love's*
   Martyr 57
Christ Church 184 (manuscript) 8,
   51 n. 60, 56, 60, 135 n. 2
cladistic analysis *See* hierarchical
   agglomerative clustering
close reading 11
   as intimacy 21
collaboration 23, 24, 75–9
   among social equals 60–2
   and 'radical singularity' 31–2, 36–7,
   141
   scholarship on 76–7
collaborative network of *Love's Martyr*
   74–9
   see also coterie dynamics; Vatum
   Chorus
competition, queer 69–9, 92–8
computational literary study 9–12,
   14–16
   'distance' in 19–22
   positivist aura 15
   queer critique of 20
   value of 27
computational methodology 16–19,
   34–6, 45, 64, 135–38

Index

computational stylistics 33
   see also stylometry
'Conclusion' (Chester) 138–42
Corey, Dorian 69, 78
coterie dynamics 74–9, 92–6
counter-narrative 12, 13
Craig, Hugh 87
'culling' percentage 135–6
Cunningham, J.V. 115–16

Da, Nan Z. 11
data visualization 33–5, 45–5
Davies, H. Neville 113 n. 23
De Anima (Aristotle) 103
dendrograms 17, 33–6
   queerness in 23, 36–7
Dialogues and Cantos (in *Love's Martyr*)
   38–45, 56, 59–61
Display of heraldry, A (Guillim) 34, 35
'distance' in computational analysis
   19–24
distance metrics 17, 36, 136
'distant reading' 20–2
Donne, John 99
drag 69–71
Drout, Michael 17, 33, 35–6
Duncan-Jones, Katherine 8, 92

Early English Books Online (EEBO)
   43 n. 47, 51 n. 60, 135
Edelman, Lee 13, 102
Eder, Maciej 64, 135, 136, 137
editor role 37
editorial distortion 43–4
   and queer theory 43 n. 47
Egluryn Ffraethineb (Perry) 7
'Elegy' (Roydon) 103 n. 10
Elizabeth I 6–7
Emerson, Ralph Waldo 2, 38, 102 n. 4
Empson, William 7–8
encoded language 42, 44
Eng, David L. 15
England's Parnassus (Allott) 87
English Gentleman, The (Brathwaite)
   105 n. 14
Epigrams (Martial) 31
epistemological paradigm 15

errant gestures 11–12
Essex rebellion (1601) 6, 8–9, 66
Evans, G. Blakemore 51 n. 60, 135 n. 2

familial similarity 17
Field, Richard 5, 24
Fineman, Joel 63
Finnis, John 7
Fitzgerald, Adam 31
flyting 79
Folger Shakespeare Library 5, 27,
   51 n. 60, 107
     Thorn-Drury MS 82 n. 40
Foucault, Michel 67, 104, 104 n. 12
friendship among men 76, 105 n. 14
futurity 102–3, 129–30

Gaboury, Jacob 20, 23
genomics 17
Gephi (visualization tool) 136, 137
glitches 15, 42–4
Goeglin, Tamara 117 n. 32
Gossett, Suzanne 72 n. 6
Green, Adam Isaiah 15
Grosart, Alexander B. 2, 8, 38, 43
Guy-Bray, Stephen 4, 6

Halberstam, Jack 11, 15
Hall, Kim 131
Halperin, David 13
Halpern, Richard 11
Harrison, Thomas P. 7
hermaphrodite, figure of 101 n. 3, 119
heteronormativity 11–12
Hicks, Jonathan 45 n. 53, 91 n. 64
hierarchical agglomerative clustering
   (HAC) 16–17
hierarchical cluster analysis (CA) 34, 136
Hirschfeld, Heather Anne 76 n. 15
Howard-Hill, T.H. 11 n. 26
Huntington Library 5 n. 10
Hutson, Lorna 77

Ignoto 80, 90
interiority/exteriority 63
intimacy 4, 19–24, 77
   and stylometry 19

271

Index

Jackson, MacDonald P. 82
Jonson, Ben 73, 77
    caricatured by Marston 81–2
    poetry compared to *Love's Martyr* 53
    relationship with co-authors 86–7,
        95–6
    and Vatum Chorus 82
Jowett, John 10

'King Arthur' (Chester) 56
Klause, John 7 n. 13
Knight, G. Wilson 2–4, 5, 24, 25, 37,
        117, 124
    reading of *Love's Martyr* 38–45,
        144–55
    Shakespearean 'doctoring' theory
        51, 55, 56–68
Koestenbaum, Wayne 78–9
Kosko, Bart 118–19

Lawyers Logicke, The (Fraunce) 106 n. 15
Lerer, Seth 17
Lewis, Wyndham 40
lexomic analysis *See* hierarchical ag-
        glomerative clustering
Lexos suite and Lexomics 17, 35, 55
Line, Anne and Roger 7
logic, Aristotelian 101, 118, 125
    as computational schema 120–1
    and nonsense 124
    refuted in 'Phoenix and Turtle'
        120–1
    see also Reason/reason
logic, deviant 16, 79, 103, 114–15, 119
logic, fuzzy 118–19, 118 n. 36
Long, Hoyt 14
Lord Chamberlain's Men 8
love 115–16
    corporality 117–18
    and reason 106–15, 125
Love's Martyr
    collaboration in 8, 23–4, 67, 74–9
    computational analysis 45–55, 64–5
    critical reception 38
    dedicatee 7–8
    dedication (Vatum Chorus) 81–2,
        84, 88

gender ambiguity in 43–4, 97
heteronormative readings 43–4
homoeroticism, female 64
intertextual relationships 49–55
intratextual relationships 45–9
'Invocatio' (Vatum Chorus) 84–5,
    88–92
narrative and computational
    segments 46–9
as political allegory 6–7, 110 n. 19
publication history 5–9
summary 6
*see also individually signed poems
    and sections*
Lowenstein, Joseph 80

Machiavelli 32–3
machine learning methods 64, 137–38
    as queer 15–16
'married chastity' 103 n. 10, 123–4
Marston, John 81–2
    and 'Invocatio' 89
    poetry compared to *Love's Martyr* 52
    'read' of Shakespeare's 'Phoenix and
        Turtle' 92–3
Martial on authorship 31
Martin, Patrick H. 7
Masten, Jeffrey 4, 22, 76
Matchett, William 44, 90, 110 n. 19,
    138–39
Meditations (Descartes) 118 n. 36
Meres, Francis 78
Metaphysics (Aristotle) 118
methodology 34–6, 135–38
mistakes, epistemology of 44
Montaigne (Michel de) 76
Moretti, Franco 20, 21
Moten, Fred 31–3, 36–7, 39, 55, 141
Muñoz, Jose Esteban 15, 102–3, 133
Mutual Flame, The (Knight) 38–45

Napier, John (*De Arte Logistica*) 99
National Library of Wales, Aberystwyth
    5 n. 10
    MS 5390D 82 n. 40
nearest shrunken centroids (NSC)
    73 n. 8, 83, 137–38

Index

Neil, Michael 82
Neoplatonism in 'Phoenix and Turtle'
 115–16
Network Analysis 137
non-binary identity 101 n. 3, 117–18,
 119, 121, 121 n. 39
normativity/anti-normativity 12–19

O'Callaghan, Michelle 79
Ong, Walter 34, 105 n. 13, 117
ontologies 14–15
orthography 89 n. 61, 126

Parliament of Fowles (Chaucer) 103 n. 10
Pechter, Ed 1
'Pellican' (Chester) 89, 96–7, 138–42
'Peristeros' (Chapman) 93–5, 96
'Phoenix and Turtle' (Shakespeare)
 97–8, 101–30
 'Anthem' 115–23
 birds in 112–14
 critique of Ramism 122–3
 death of Phoenix 102, 111–12
 deviant logic 103–4, 119–23
 form 106–7, 109, 123–4, 127
 'Invocation' 109–15
 recursion 129–30
 temporality 102, 127–28
 thematic sources 103 n. 10
 'Threnos' 106, 107, 107 n. 16, 123–4
 transcribed text of 107–9
 typography and layout 126, 128
 see also Reason/reason
phoenix myth 5–6, 103 n. 10, 110–11
 association with Elizabeth I 7
Phoenix Nest, The (1593) 103 n. 10
Phoenix-Turtle conceit 5–7, 66, 71, 72,
 94–5, 103
 gender ambiguity 43–4
 Platonism 97
Phyllis and Aristotle 105–6, 105 n. 14
Poetaster (Jonson), shade in 69
Poetical Essays (in *Love's Martyr*) 69–98
 authorial interactivity 2, 92–7
 Chester as contributor 88–92
 metaphysical themes 103–4

organization of 73–5
 title page and 'Invocatio' 74–5
poetics 117 n. 32
Poetomachia see poets' war
poets' war 70–3, 76–9
positivist aura of computation 15
potentiality 101–3, 122, 129
'Praeludium' (Jonson) 82–3, 86–7, 95
principal component analysis (PCA)
 55, 136
pronouns
 confusion in *Love's Martyr* 12,
  42–4, 97
 signaling authorship 86–7
 singular 'they' 39–40
Property 115, 118–20, 122
 see also Aristotelianism

QAnon 14
queer (category) 12–14
queer analysis 11–12, 79, 104, 126
 for contradictory evidence 91
queer analytics 1–28, 33
 decentering ontologies 14–15, 22,
  36–7
 mapping processes and networks 22
queer studies 11, 131–3
queer theory 3–4
 and computation 4, 9–12, 37, 101
Queen Elizabeth I *See* Elizabeth I

R (programming suite) 45, 136
Ramism 33–4, 104, 106, 116–17, 117
 n. 32
 critique of 122–3
 logic trees and dendograms 33–4,
  106 n. 15
Ramus, Petrus 104–6
Rawlinson, Richard 82 n. 40
Reason/reason 101–30
 and desire 98, 104, 106–15, 125
 in 'Phoenix and Turtle' 123–8
recursion xiii, 26, 102, 103, 129–30
resistance 104
Riggs, David 78
Roderick, Richard 10

273

Index

rolling attribution 64–5
Rollins, Hyder 103 n. 10
Rowe, George E. 78 n. 25
RuPaul's Drag Race 72

Salusbury, John 7, 23–4, 37
    as collaborator in *Love's Martyr*
        58–62
    and Dorothy Halsall 42, 62
Salusbury, Ursula 7
Satires (Marston) 91
scholasticism *See* Aristotelianism
Sedgwick, Eve 33 n. 7, 64, 105 n. 14
Sejanus (Jonson) 86
shade 69–72, 86, 93, 95–6, 123
Shadow of Night, The (Chapman) 90
Shakespeare, William
    All's Well that Ends Well 129
    collaborative activity 1, 24
    Cymbeline 110–11
    as editor 2, 3, 9, 24, 37, 66
    Essex rebellion 8–9, 66
    King Lear 125
    Midsummer Night's Dream 125
    queer reading of 38–45
    Ramism 106 n. 15
    Rape of Lucrece 5, 9, 38, 51, 140
    Richard II 8
    Romeo and Juliet 50–53
    Tempest, The 110
    Troilus and Cressida 69, 125
    Twelfth Night 125
    Venus and Adonis 5, 9, 38, 40, 51,
        75 n. 14, 140
    see also 'Phoenix and Turtle';
        Sonnets
Shakespearean singularity 39–40, 44–5
Shapiro, James 76
Sinetes Passions (Parry) 7
Sonnets (Shakespeare)
    compared to *Love's Martyr* 54, 62–3

Dark Lady and the Phoenix 64
homosexuality in 38–9
themes in *Love's Martyr* 41–2
So, Richard Jean 14
Southampton, Earl of 9, 66
Southwell, Robert 7
Stockton, Will 12–13
stylistic deviation 15, 23
    in dendrogram of *Love's Martyr* 19
stylo 45, 136, 137
stylometry 3, 11–12, 11 n. 26, 136
    analysis of *Love's Martyr* 45–55,
        64–5
    authorial interactivity 33–8, 64
    intimacy 19
    methods 10, 73, 83 n. 45
    queer readings 12
support vector machines (SVM) 73 n. 8,
    83, 137–38

taxonomy 33–4
text processing methods 45, 135–38
textual deviance, analysis of 15
textual irruptions as encoded language
    42–4
they (singular pronoun) 39
'Threnos' *See under* 'Phoenix and Turtle'
trans *See* non-binary
Traub, Valerie 12–13, 165 n. 27
Tuve, Rosemond 106, 106 n. 15

Underwood, Ted 16

Vatum Chorus 73, 80–92
Vickers, Brian 23, 49–50
virility, literary 77

Walpole, Henry 7
war of the theaters *See* poets' war
Wells, Stanley 1
What You Will (Marston) 73, 81–2

Plates 7 to 10 in this paperback version of *Shakespeare's Queer Analytics* are best understood in full colour. Please see the digital or hardback version of this book to view them in their original format.

LOVES MARTYR:
OR,
ROSALINS COMPLAINT.

Allegorically shadowing the truth of Loue,
in the constant Fate of the Phœnix
and Turtle.

A Poeme enterlaced with much varietie and raritie;
now first translated out of the venerable Italian Torquato
Cæliano, *by* ROBERT CHESTER.

With the true legend of famous King *Arthur*, the last of the nine
Worthies, being the first *Essay* of a new *Brytish* Poet: collected
out of diuerse Authenticall Records.

To these are added some new compositions, of seuerall moderne Writers
whose names are subscribed to their seuerall workes, vpon the
first Subiect: viz. the Phœnix *and*
Turtle.

Mar: ─── *Mutare dominum non potest liber notus.*

LONDON
Imprinted for E. B.
1601.

Plate 1 Title page of *Love's Martyr*. Folger Shakespeare Library

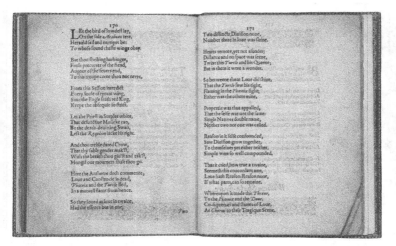

Plate 2 'The Phoenix and Turtle'. Folger Shakespeare Library

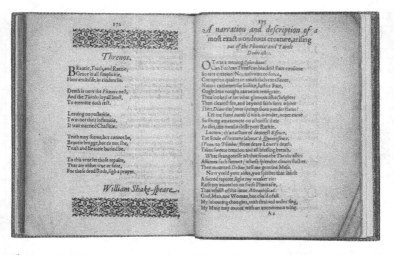

Plate 3 'The Phoenix and Turtle' and John Marston's response to 'Phoenix'. Folger Shakespeare Library

Plate 4 Portrait of Sir John Salusbury reproduced in Thomas Pennant's *A Tour of Wales*, 1778. Llyfrgell Genedlaethol Cymru (The National Library of Wales)

Plate 5 *A phoenix sat atop a tree.* Engraving after Raphael (Raffaello Sanzio or Santi), 1530–60. Metropolitan Museum of Art

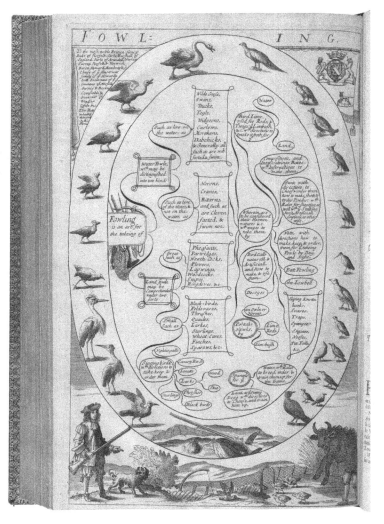

Plate 6 Ramist diagram of 'Fowling' from *The Gentlemans Recreation* by Richard Blome (1686). Folger Shakespeare Library

Segment #	Contents	Word Count	Chester Pagination
LM 01	Prefatory matter, dedications	507	A1-A6
LM 02	Blazon of the Phoenix begins	1208	1-6
LM 03	Blazon ends	1189	6-12
LM 04	Prayers	683	12-16
LM 05	"A Dialogue" between Nature and the Phoenix begins	1057	16-20
LM 06	"A Dialogue" between Nature and the Phoenix continues	1089	20-25
LM 07	Dialogue turns to historical detail; annotations begin to populate the margins	765	26-29
LM 08	Dialogue turns to monologue; Nature instructs the Phoenix on world history	988	29-34
LM 09	The "Birth, Life, and Death of Honourable Arthur King of Brittaine" begins	944	34-38
LM 10	"Arthur" continues	1013	38-43
LM 11	"Arthur" continues	937	43-47
LM 12	"Arthur" continues	946	48-52
LM 13	"Arthur" continues	938	53-57
LM 14	"Arthur" continues	969	57-62
LM 15	"Arthur" continues	976	62-67
LM 16	"Arthur" continues	1022	67-72
LM 17	"Arthur" ends	1006	72-77
LM 18	"A Dialogue" between Nature and Phoenix begins; flowers, herbs discussed	999	77-82
LM 19	"A Dialogue" continues; herbs, "balmes," vegetables considered	981	82-87
LM 20	"A Dialogue" continues; herbs, "balmes," vegetables considered continues	1008	87-91
LM 21	"A Dialogue" continues: plants, "rootes," trees, fruit	1021	92-97
LM 22	"A Dialogue" continues: fish, gemstones, ores, spices	1027	97-102
LM 23	"A Dialogue" continues: fish, gemstones, ores, spices continues	981	102-107
LM 24	"A Dialogue" continues: mammals, monsters, mythical beasts	997	107-112
LM 25	"A Dialogue" continues: insects, reptiles, birds	1004	112-117
LM 26	"A Dialogue" continues: insects, reptiles, birds continues	991	117-121
LM 27	Nature departs; Phoenix meets Turtle; their "Dialogue" begins	990	121-126
LM 28	"Dialogue" continues; the sacrifice is done	1047	126-131
LM 29	"Pellican" and Chester lament	673	131-134
LM 30	"Cantos, Alphabet-wise" begin and end	1380	134-140
LM 31	"Cantos Verbally written" begin	1006	141-145
LM 32	"Cantos Verbally written" continue	985	145-149
LM 33	"Cantos Verbally written" continue	967	149-153
LM 34	"Cantos Verbally written" continue	1036	153-157
LM 35	"Cantos Verbally written" continue	1183	157-162
LM 36	"Cantos Verbally written" end; Chester signs off	1133	162-167
LM 37	"Poetical Essays" begin	63	169
LM 38	Unattributed poems signed Vatum Chorus	297	171-172
LM 39	Unattributed poems signed Ignoto	120	173
LM 40	William Shakespeare's poem	358	174-176
LM 41	John Marston's poems	566	177-180
LM 42	George Chapman's poem	226	180
LM 43	Ben Jonson's poems	1177	181-187

Plate 7 Ribbon diagram of *Love's Martyr*

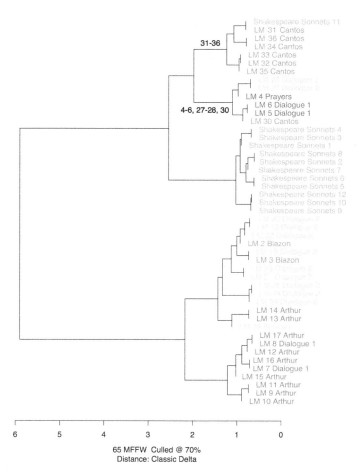

Plate 8 Dendrogram of *Love's Martyr* with Shakespeare's Sonnets

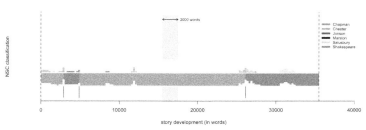

Plate 9 Rolling attribution graph of *Love's Martyr*

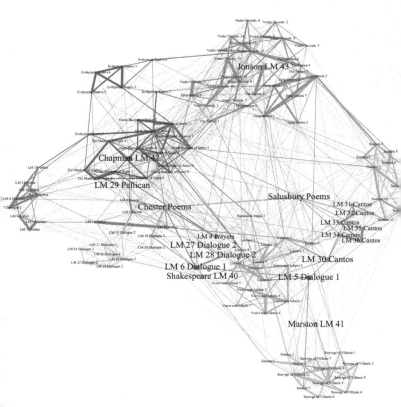

Plate 10 Network analysis of *Love's Martyr's* poets and their works. Stylistically texts, visualized as dense clusters of nodes with various degrees of distance an thickness, indicate a consensus of authorial signal. The denser clusters of nodes with linkages indicate high similarity. Nodes at the center (here represented as Chest Salusbury's poetry) have the most connections to the other clusters. Segments 4–6, and 30–36 of *Love's Martyr* consistently group with known Shakespearean material.

Printed in the USA
CPSIA information can be obtained
at www.ICGtesting.com
LVHW020737041223
765477LV00003B/102